TREATING SECONDARY VICTIMS

Intervention With the Nonoffending Mother in the Incest Family

VIRGINIA C. STRAND

Sage Publications, Inc.
International Educational and Professional Publisher
Thousand Oaks ▪ London ▪ New Delhi

For information:

Sage Publications, Inc.
2455 Teller Road
Thousand Oaks, California 91320
E-mail: order@sagepub.com

Sage Publications Ltd.
6 Bonhill Street
London EC2A 4PU
United Kingdom

Sage Publications India Pvt. Ltd.
M-32 Market
Greater Kailash I
New Delhi 110 048 India

Printed in the United States of America

Library of Congress Cataloging-in-Publication Data

Strand, Virginia C.
  Treating secondary victims: Intervention with the non-offending mother in the incest family / by Virginia C. Strand.
      p. cm.
  Includes bibliographical references and index.
    ISBN 0-8039-5286-4 (cloth: acid-free paper)
    ISBN 0-8039-5287-2 (pbk.: acid-free paper)
    1. Sexually abused children—United States—Family relationships—Case studies. 2. Incest victims—United States—Family relationships—Case studies. 3. Mothers—United States—Attitudes—Case studies. I. Title.

  HV6570.7 .S77 2000
  362.74′3′0973—dc21

                                    00-009216

This book is printed on acid-free paper.

00   01   02   03   04   05   06   7   6   5   4   3   2   1

Acquiring Editor:	Nancy Hale
Production Editors:	Elly Korn and Sanford Robinson
Editorial Assistant:	Candice Crosetti
Typesetter:	Barbara Burkholder
Indexer:	Teri Greenberg
Cover Designer:	Ravi Balasuriya

CONTENTS

Acknowledgments   ix

1. **Understanding the Impact**
   of Incest on the Nonoffending Mother   1

   Developments in the Field of Child Sexual
       Abuse Relevant to the Nonoffending Mother   4

   Theoretical Developments Affecting
       Conceptualization of Intervention and Treatment   10

2. **Gender and Countertransference**   19

   The Social Construction of Motherhood   20

   Ambivalent View of Women   25

   Effects of Professional Training   28

   Widespread Tendency to Blame Mother for a
       Child's Problem   32

   Victimization in the History of the Therapist   33

3. Contextual Considerations
   in the Engagement of the Mother   39

   Race and Ethnicity   39

   Class   45

   Work History   48

   Individual and Family History   49

4. Evaluating the Mother
   and Planning for Treatment   63

   Introduction to a Treatment Approach   63

   Phase 1: Engagement and Assessment   66

   Assessment of Social Roles   86

   Sexual History   90

5. Individual Treatment   93

   Phase 2: Early Intervention Around
            Traumatic Effects   93

   Phase 3: Strengthening Coping Capacities   100

   Phase 4: Surfacing Traumatic Effects
            of the Incest Behavior   107

   Phase 5: Identifying Relational Consequences   115

   Phase 6: Working Through and Resolution   124

6. Group Treatment   127

   Beginnings   129

   The Treatment Approach in Group Therapy   139

7. Family Treatment   155

   Beginning Treatment   158

   Middle Phases of Family Treatment   167

8. Case Coordination   179

Investigation 182

Litigation 188

Supervision 197

9. **Working With Mothers Involved
   in Custody and Visitation Disputes** 203

10. **Future Directions** 219

References 227

Index 239

About the Author 253

This book is dedicated to the hundreds of mothers of sexually abused children who have shared their lives with me and from whom I have learned most of what I know about the experiences of the nonoffending mothers of sexually abused children.

ACKNOWLEDGMENTS

I want to thank a number of people without whose support this book would not have been possible. First, I thank Mary Ann Quanta, dean of the Graduate School of Social Service at Fordham University, for her trust in the process and her practical assistance in granting me course reduction to help the development of the book along. I also want to express my great appreciation to my friends and colleagues who read all or part of the manuscript and provided invaluable feedback and encouragement. They are (in alphabetical order) the following: Barbara Bernstein, Steve Forrester, Valerie Homan, Kenneth Lau, and Pat Lemp. Finally, special gratitude is due to Melinda Schneider, without whose tireless patience in tracking down references and typing endless revisions, this effort would not have come to fruition. Again, thanks to you all.

Understanding the Impact of Incest on the Nonoffending Mother

What is special about doing psychotherapy with the nonoffending mother in the incest family, and why might a book devoted to this topic be important? When I first began to work with children who had been sexually abused and their family members, there was little to guide my understanding of the mother's unique dilemma. Yet it became apparent to me early on that to truly help children who were molested by parental figures, not only were more effective treatment strategies needed for the children but for the nonoffending mothers and offenders as well. Whether the offender was the father, stepfather, or even the mother's boyfriend, the necessity for intervention and treatment with the mother and her partner, if she was going to reunite with him, became evident. In most cases that I was treating early on, the children continued to live with the mother following disclosure, and the offender was out of the home. The nature of the mother's relationship with her children affected treatment outcomes for the children. The children's success in treatment appeared to be mediated by how supportive the mother could be, how effective her parenting skills were, and how much she endorsed the importance of therapy for her children.

Removing children to protect them from sexual abuse at home is sometimes necessary, but it is not a sufficient response to the problem of family sexual abuse. Even when a child is placed in out-of-home care, there is usually an obligation on the part of the public child welfare system to put in place services to help remedy the problem that brought a child into care in the first place. (With the passage of the *Adoption and Safe Families Act* in 1997, there may be some exceptions to this if sexual abuse is severe enough to be defined by a state as an "aggravating circumstance" that would excuse the public child welfare agency from its obligation.) Thus, intervention with the nonoffending mother is almost always a significant step in any intervention with sexually abused children. However, one tenet of this book is that intervention with the nonoffending mother for the purpose of helping her parent her child is a necessary but not sufficient goal for intervention. The mother may need to be approached as a secondary victim to trauma and her needs understood in regard to the resolution of that trauma, as well as in regard to her development of self and her functioning in the social roles of wife or sexual partner, companion, worker, and so on and not just her role as the mother of a sexually abused child.

Social workers and other mental health professionals traditionally have focused on interventions with individuals and families to resolve difficulties such as family sexual abuse. This indeed will be the emphasis in this book. It is important to note, however, that a body of opinion (Pelton, 1985) believes that clinicians have contributed to the "medicalization" of the problem of child abuse through the therapeutic focus on individual and family pathology and, consequently, "treatment" as the remedy. This focus on the individual, it is claimed, minimizes the role that male domination and institutional oppression of women and children has in the etiology of the problem (Fausto-Sterling, 1985; Van Den Bergh, 1995.

The purpose of this book is to provide a conceptual framework for the intervention and treatment of the nonoffending mother in the incest family. An effort will be made to explore the interaction of gender, race, and class with individual family experiences to avoid the pitfall of "decontextualizing" the woman and pathologizing a response that may or may not be a maladaptive coping response to her life situation. A specific treatment approach is outlined, and, where practical, suggestions for specific strategies are incorporated. I rely on case examples throughout to help the reader understand how the interventions I describe might be carried out. Although women with a common experience (the sexual molestation of their children by a sexual partner) are the focus of the book, it cannot be stressed enough that this group of women is extraordinarily heterogeneous in that each woman's life experience (due to factors such as social class, race, age, religion, immigration status—the list is endless) is unique. Contextual factors must be an important consideration for any generalizations about intervention to be operationalized in a meaningful way.

A limitation of the proposed framework for intervention is that it is not empirically based. It has, as its foundation, my work with hundreds of mothers in evaluation and treatment over two decades in both agency and private practice settings. Importantly, although agency clients were public clients in general, public agency clients also have been a focus of my private practice. This has given me experience over the years with mothers from many different racial, ethnic, and socioeconomic groups.

One of my goals in publishing this book is to stimulate discussion and critical thinking about our current interventions with nonoffending mothers. This interest stems from my observation that the nonoffending mother has not received as much attention in the literature as the child and adult victim and the adolescent and adult offender. It is hoped that this book will highlight the need for additional research with the nonoffending mother, particularly research that tests interventions and evaluates outcomes.

Definitions

In this book, the term *incest* will be used interchangeably with *family sexual abuse*. *Family sexual abuse* is defined as sexual contact between a child and father or other male in that role. Sexual contact is defined to include fondling, oral-genital interaction, attempted intercourse, and intercourse. The focus is on the nonoffending mother whose child or children have been sexually abused by her partner—be that her husband or "significant other." This is to emphasize the particular issues for the mother whose child is molested within the context of the family unit. Although the accent is primarily on the mother who is parenting her children at the time of a disclosure of sexual abuse, I will also address the consequences for the mother whose child, for one reason or another, may not be with her at the time of disclosure.

Many of the dynamics and strategies discussed will be applicable to mothers of adult children. Although some dynamics also will apply to the mother whose children are molested by other than the mother's partner, there are enough differences, I believe, to warrant a separate focus in this book on the nonoffending parent in family sexual abuse cases. The central distinction, it seems to me, is the significance of the mother's emotional, sexual, and financial ties to the offender in instances of family sexual abuse.

Developments in the Field of Child Sexual Abuse Relevant to the Nonoffending Mother

The lack of attention to the nonoffending mother in the literature on child sexual abuse is readily documented. The early literature on the mother in the incest family appears to reflect the influence of psychodynamic theory alone. The major book at that time, Weinberg's (1955) *Incest Behavior*, labeled the mother as unprotective and collusive. Kaufman, Peck, and Taguiri (1954), for example, viewed the mother's behavior as nonprotective and, in some cases, as contributing to the incest. They suggested that this behavior stemmed from the mother's own psychopathology, which was rooted in experiences of deprivation in her own family of origin. The anger and resentment felt toward her own mother was projected onto the daughter, who was then given special treatment and adult responsibilities, including the responsibility for a sexual relationship with the mother's husband or partner.

In the late 1960s and 1970s, the nonoffending mother in the incest family often was blamed for the abuse, in some instances more so than the offending parent. What literature existed tended to identify the mother as inadequate and conspiratorial. Meiselman (1978), for example, suggested that the mother's behavior was a result of her own individual psychopathology. Prominent features of this were passivity, dependency, and masochism on the part of the mother, as well as her inability to function adequately sexually. Others described the mother as often aware of the incest but failing to act protectively by reporting it to authorities (Anderson & Shafer, 1979; Machotka, Pittman, & Flomenhaft, 1967). A number of authors maintained that incestuous relationships between fathers and daughters were exacerbated, if not caused, by the mother forsaking her role as wife by refusing sexual intercourse (Gutheil & Avery, 1977; Meiselman, 1978) and failing in her maternal duties (Eist & Mandel, 1968). Justice and Justice (1979) were very explicit about the mother's contribution, stating that nonoffending mothers were "colluding and indirectly involved when her husband carries on sexual activity with her daughter. In either case, she cannot escape sharing responsibility for the problem" (pp. 96-97).

In the 1980s, although practitioners and researchers interested in the phenomenon of family sexual abuse paid some attention to the mothers in incest families, by and large the victim and the perpetrator received far more attention. Russell (1984) gave us groundbreaking prevalence data in her landmark study. She identified 38% of adult women with a history of incestuous or extrafamilial child sexual abuse prior to age 18. The characteristics of child and adolescent incest victims (Adams-Tucker, 1980; Briere, 1987; Briere & Runtz, 1986; Finkelhor, 1989; Goodwin, 1988; Johnson, 1989; Kolko, Moser, & Weldy, 1988; Lipovsky, Saunders, & Murphy, 1989; Vander Mey & Neff, 1988), short- and long-term effects of victimization (Briere, 1987; Conte & Schuerman, 1987; Lindberg & Distad, 1985; McLeer, Deblinger, Atkins, Foa, & Ralphe, 1988; Wyatt & Mickey, 1987; Wyatt & Powell, 1988), the plight of adult "survivors," and a variety of treatment approaches for working with sexual abuse victims (Berliner & Wheeler, 1987; Blake-White & Kline, 1985; Briere, 1989; Conte, 1984; Conte & Berliner, 1981; Courtois, 1988; Faller, 1988a, 1988b; Gelinas, 1983; Giarretto, 1992; James, 1989; MacFarlane, 1986; Walker, 1988) were elaborated over the 1980s. Likewise, continuing attempts to develop a topology of offenders (Abel, Becker, Murphy, & Flanagan, 1981; Abel, Mittelman, Becker, & Djenderedjian, 1978; Abel et al., 1989; Knight, 1989; Knight, Carter, & Prentky, 1989; Summit & Kryso, 1978), present theoretical explanations for the motivation to sexually abuse (Carnes, 1984; Groth, 1979; Johnson, 1988), and describe treatment approaches for the sexual offender (Abel et al., 1984; Faller, 1988a, 1988b; Giarretto, 1992; Knopp, 1984; Lang, Pugh, & Langevin, 1988; Marshall & Barbarbee, 1988; Mayer, 1988; Smith & Wolfe, 1988; Steen & Monnette, 1989), including the incest offender, began to dominate the literature in the field.

When the nonoffending mother received attention, until recently, it has been to paint a portrait largely based on an understanding of individual psychopathology (Zuelzer & Reposa, 1983) rooted in drive theory or to provide descriptive information of interpersonal, interactional dynamics characteristic of the mother-child, mother-husband or mother-partner, or family relationships. Clark, O'Neil, and Laws (1981) specified that "incest usually requires the passive cooperation of the wife" (p. 19). Sgroi (1984) looked at interactional styles of the mothers in her sample and described two categories of mothers: those who are wives of dependent men and those who are wives of dominant men. Not surprisingly, the former tend to be characterized as cold and domineering and the latter as passive and unassertive, all rather negative attributes. Other attributes that characterize the mother were identified as the inability to trust, "psychological absence" or the lack of psychological investment in relationships with both their children and partners, impaired self-image, denial, unrealistic expectations of husbands and children, impaired communication, impaired socialization, and a lack of assertiveness (Sgroi, 1984).

Although Myer noted as early as 1984 (based on her study of 43 mothers) that the mothers in incest families should not be considered a monolithic group but in fact reflect as much diversity as any other population, her results and subsequent research by others have only been slowly integrated into clinical practice. Myer (1985), for example, discovered that mothers fell into at least three groups in terms of their responses to a disclosure of incestuous behavior by their spouse or partner. Almost one half responded protectively, about one quarter was immobilized although not disbelieving, and about one quarter rejected their daughters. Important new understandings about the role of denial in the mother's response following disclosure have been elaborated with a research focus on the mother. Myer suggested that denial on the part of the mother may reflect the first part of a grief reaction, followed by "guilt, depression, anger and finally acceptance" (p. 55).

Notably, Salter (1988), although writing about the treatment of sex offenders and victims, contributed a useful framework for treatment with the nonoffending parent as well, perhaps because of her understanding of the dynamics in sexual offending. She maintained that for treatment to be effective with the offender, he needed to take emotional responsibility for the abuse and stop minimizing, externalizing, and projecting blame onto others. She described the goals of treatment as follows: "Each parent must take responsibility for his or her own behavior and not the other's. *Spouses are responsible for abuse only if they are involved in sexual abuse.* They are responsible for denying and minimizing if they do so" (Salter, 1988, p. 67).

The undertaking of empirical research with the mother in the incest family has begun to provide information that challenges the notion of the collusive and nonprotective mother. Sirles and Franke (1989), in their study of the reactions to disclosure in a group of 193 mothers from a treatment program, found that the overwhelming majority of mothers believed their children's reports of abuse. They conclude that there are "a variety of factors involved in a mother's decision to believe or disbelieve her child's report of intrafamily sexual abuse. Generalities about mothers in these families are unwarranted" (p. 136). The proportion of "believing" mothers in their sample was consistent with that found by Pierce and Pierce (1985), whose sample was drawn from the files of a social service agency, and DeJong (1988). In DeJong's study, mothers who had bought their children for a routine medical follow-up were studied. Results indicated that 71% were supportive, meaning that they believed their children.

Studies then began to refine our understanding of the relationship between support at disclosure and other variables in the mother's background. Everson, Hunter, Runyon, Edelsohn, and Coulter (1989) explored the degree of the nonoffending mother's support of the sexually abused child following disclosure. They found an inverse relationship between maternal support and recency of relationship with the perpetrator. Faller (1988a, 1988b) found a similar relationship in her study of three groups of mothers: those living with a biological father, those living with a stepfather, and those in which the perpetrator was the noncustodial father. Mothers no longer married to or living with the perpetrator were significantly more supportive than other mothers. Importantly, however, she noted that none of the mothers could be labeled *collusive*; in the group not living with the perpetrator, they were significantly more supportive.

In the 1990s, the literature continued to emphasize work with the victim and offender and, if anything, was extended. Increasingly, researchers and clinicians have explored and described attributes of different populations of child, adolescent, and adult victims (Berliner, 1992; Berliner & Conte, 1990; Boney-McCoy & Finkelhor, 1996; Gomes-Schwartz, 1990; Kendall-Tackett, William, & Finkelhor, 1993; Leitenberg, Greenwald, & Cado, 1992; McLeer, Deblinger, Henry, & Orvaschel, 1992; Saunders, Arata, & Kilpatrick, 1990) and introduced insightful and carefully described clinical and treatment accounts (Briere, 1992; Ciottone & Madonna, 1996; Cohen & Mannarino, 1998; Freidrich, 1990, 1991; Gil, 1991, 1996; Gil & Johnson, 1993; Herman, 1992). Work with offenders also has increased (Becker, 1990; Elliott & Briere, 1992; Freeman-Longo, Bird, Stevenson, & Fiske, 1995; Horton, Johnson, Roundy, & Williams, 1990; Marshall & Anderson, 1996; Prentky & Burgess, 1990; Schwartz & Cellini, 1995, 1997). The emergence of repressed memories as a major clinical feature spawned a major controversy (Alpert, 1995; Courtois, 1992; Fredrickson, 1992; Ofshe, 1994), with many implications for clinicians.

By 1990, a number of descriptions of treatment interventions with mothers began to appear in the literature (DelPo & Koontz, 1991; Hagood, 1991; Strand, 1990, 1991). They were few and far between when compared to the expanding volume of work on victims and offenders. A focus on the mothers that was again tinged with a negative connotation was the concern that mothers in divorce and custody battles were manufacturing false allegations of child sexual abuse (Gardner, 1987). In fact, research (Faller, Corwin, & Olafson, 1993; Thoennes & Tjaden, 1990) indicates that it is incorrect to assert that such a trend exists. The study by Thoennes and Tjaden (1990), the only one to involve a large, national sample, resulted in the finding that (a) only a minority of cases involving divorce results in custody or visitation disputes, and (b) of that group of contested cases, only a tiny minority involves allegations of suspected child sexual abuse. Furthermore, in most cases of suspected abuse, the allegations were substantiated.

Gomes-Schwartz (1990) evaluated reactions on disclosure and personality characteristics of 158 nonoffending mothers of sexually abused children. She found that 82% of the mothers acted to protect their children either consistently or some of the time and that 70% did not punish the children on disclosure. In addition, 90% displayed moderate to strong concern for the child. This finding is consistent with that of Pellegrin and Wagner (1990). In their study of the decision-making process of Child Protective Services (CPS) caseworkers' decisions to remove the child in cases of child sexual abuse, they discovered that caseworkers rated 65% of the mothers as totally believing their children and only 7% as totally disbelieving.

Gomes-Schwartz (1990) also concluded that most mothers "did not have serious emotional problems that would immediately identify them as candidates for psychiatric treatment. In fact, only 18 percent had prior psychiatric care" (p. 121). Dadds, Smith, and Webber (1991), in their comparison of incest families with a matched control group, found that incest families were "not marked by frank psychopathology" (p. 582). They also found no difference between the clinic and control group in relationship to marital satisfaction. Elbow and Mayfield (1991), in their study of 24 mothers in cases of father-daughter incest, found that most mothers (83%) believed their children.

Humphreys (1992), in a study of mothers at disclosure, posited a "continuum of belief" along which mothers fall. She found, for example, that at disclosure, most mothers *acted* in a manner consistent with belief but vacillated between degrees of cognitive belief and emotional acceptance of the reality of the abuse. Leifer, Shapiro, and Kassem (1993) contributed to the understanding of factors that might affect the mother's ability to be supportive at disclosure. In her study of the impact of maternal history on foster placement and adjustment of sexually abused girls, she reported that mothers who abused substances and had little social support were less likely to be supportive of their children following disclosure.

A recent study by Deblinger, Hathaway, Lippmann, and Steer (1993) more emphatically challenged the negative assumptions regarding the mothers. The study explored the differences between "incest" mothers and others. A group of 36 such mothers was compared to a group of mothers whose children were also molested by relatives, but not by partners, as well as to a group of mothers of children molested by nonrelatives. She found that (a) the incest mothers were not significantly different from nonincest mothers when psychosocial backgrounds were compared, (b) they were not more likely to be absent from the home (due to employment, illness, etc.) than nonincest mothers, and (c) they were just as likely as nonincest mothers to believe their children's allegations. In fact, the only distinguishing characteristic of "incest" mothers was that they were more likely to have been victims of domestic violence.

An interesting study by Morrison and Clavenna-Valleroy (1998) explored maternal support from the victim's perception. In their sample of 50 adolescents and their mothers from an inpatient trauma unit in an urban medical center, they found that at intake, 60% of the adolescents perceived their mothers as supportive. At discharge, 74% of the adolescents perceived their mothers as supportive. Of particular importance were the significant differences found at discharge and follow-up 3 months later between those with supportive versus unsupportive mothers. Those with supportive mothers demonstrated an increase in self-concept and a decrease in depressive symptoms, but those with unsupportive mothers had no change in self-concept and an increase in depressive symptoms.

Massat and Lundy (1998) have added to our understanding of the factors affecting the nonoffending mother's reactions at disclosure. They explored the reasons for the mother's differential reactions, hypothesizing that it may be due to the mother's perceived loss. They conceptualized four potential losses: relational (which included not only the loss of an intimate partner but also disruptions in relationships with friends and family), financial, vocational, and residential. Findings revealed that more than 50% experienced the loss of intimacy with the perpetrator, a change of residence, loss of income, and family dissatisfaction. Significant "costs," therefore, to nonoffending mothers may in some cases influence the mother's degree of supportiveness following disclosure.

The empirical research undertaken over the past 15 years has begun to add to our understanding of the nonoffending mother, suggesting that most mothers do believe their children, act protectively, and, to the extent they do not, appear to be influenced by both relational and other factors. The research on the psychological characteristics of mothers is less clear. Tamraz (1996), reporting on her review of nine studies from 1980 to 1995 that investigated the presence of psychological problems, found the results to be inconclusive. Thus, although much is beginning to be known and better understood, there is still much to learn. An intervention framework that takes these findings into consideration can help set the stage for testing a new appreciation of the nonoffending mother in the incest family.

Theoretical Developments Affecting Conceptualization of Intervention and Treatment

As noted earlier, until the 1980s, much of the literature on the nonoffending mother appeared to be rooted in psychodynamic theories, informing an understanding of the psychology of the individual and influencing treatment strategies. Two major developments in our understanding of how individuals advance psychologically seem important to consider in establishing intervention guidelines for the nonoffending mother. The first stems from the work of feminist theorists and researchers—specifically, the advances in our understanding of the ways in which women's psychological development is different from men's. The second is the developing body of knowledge about the effects of trauma on the developing psyche.

Feminist Contributions

In contrast to many of the earlier authors, whose approach to the nonoffending mother reflected a psychoanalytic perspective, the authors grounded in a feminist perspective put forward quite a different causal explanation for incest. One of the hallmarks of a feminist perspective is the emphasis on external or environmental factors in the etiology of pathology. Mothers, seen from a feminist perspective, exist in various conditions of impaired functioning, due to the power exerted by the father or father figure. Incest, therefore, is viewed as rooted deep within the patriarchal arrangements of family life and of the relationships between women and men. Herman (1981), for example, suggested that basic social inequality between the sexes contributes to the implicit sanction of the father turning to his daughter for sexual gratification. Much has been made of the wife's sexual unavailability. This not only places an unfair burden for the man's actions on the mother but also ignores the reality that the responsibility for sexual abuse must be placed squarely on the offender (Salter, 1988). As Herman (1981) stated, "No father is driven to incest for lack of sexual access to his spouse" (p. 43). She was among the first to develop a newer conceptualization of the mother in cases of child sexual abuse, attributing what is perceived as collusion to the mother's relative low-power position. Cammaert (1988) took a similar position, noting that some nonoffending mothers hold traditional views of marriage in which they have limited power. Birns and Meyer (1993) likewise emphasized that mothers of sexually abused children must be viewed through the lens of a feminist perspective on traditional male dominance.

Despite this, the mother traditionally has been seen as the one who must bear responsibility for the other parent's behavior (Taubman, 1984). As noted by Wattenberg (1985), "The father rapes, abuses, brutalizes and assaults children and the mother, but somehow it is the mother's or child's fault" (p. 206). She argues that incestuous assaults enforce male dominance and contests the theory that views the mother as the collaborator in father-daughter incest through her sexual rejection of her mate and her promotion of her daughter as a wife substitute. Wattenberg, like Herman, feels that this theory is based on fragmented observations and skewed clinical samples.

A fascinating fact is that this blaming of the mother goes on not only by the professional community but also by victims and mothers. This reflects a deep-seated cultural view of mothers that extends beyond the mother in the incest family and is connected to a fundamental attitude toward women. This attitude reflects the social arrangements of men and women, where women are undervalued and exploited socially, emotionally, and economically. This social organization that supports the patriarchal society need not be belabored here, as volumes have addressed this aspect of the social lives of women.

Importantly, the models for understanding women's development have been limited by a patriarchal lens, and thus theories of personality development are constricted in terms of their applicability to women. The 1970s and 1980s witnessed an important growth in the application of a feminist lens to theories of personality. Chodorow (1978) and Dinnerstein (1977) were among the first theorists to challenge the assumption that a woman's path to development was the same as a man's. Their work suggested a new emphasis on the primacy of women's mothering in identity formation. As Benjamin (1984) noted, "The focus on women's mothering suggested that . . . the early interplay of gender identity formation, self-formation, and the persistence of issues related to these processes in adult life could now be investigated in a new way" (p. 38).

Gilligan (1982) deepened this appreciation of differences with her contribution on the path of moral development for women. Both she and Chodorow have "made clear that women, in retaining their capacity for nurturance and empathy, embody the valuable side of human potential which may have been renounced and devalued" (Brody, 1984, p. 42).

Essentially, the new formulations suggest that the Eriksonian model of stage development that describes a progression from the beginning of a striving for autonomy at age 2 to identity formation in adolescence and the capacity for intimacy in young adulthood may be the sequence for *men* but not for women. This is inextricably connected to the fact that women are the primary caretakers for both boys and girls. For the boy, the repudiation of the mother is essential for the formation of autonomy and achievement.

For the pre-Oedipal boy, the beginning of an autonomous sense of self, as other, is logically tied to the differentiation of himself from the female mother. For the girl, however, the beginning sense of an autonomous self is more clearly related to seeing herself as one with and as connected to the mother who, like her, is female. Therefore, the need to separate psychologically and move away is not as great. She does not need to repudiate those aspects of femininity associated with the mother: nurturance, mutuality, dependency, and connectedness.

What Chodorow, Gilligan, and others postulate is that the developmental track for the girl is one in which identity is connected early on, in the pre-Oedipal stage, to the person-in-relationship and does not necessitate as strong a separate, autonomous stage before adolescent identity formation. This different developmental track explains quite well the fact that the well-adjusted female appears to arrive in early adulthood with the capacity for intimate relationships, with highly developed nurturing capacities. These are the foundation of women's identity and represent strengths for her, given that she has been guided to adulthood in a society with the particular social arrangements for men and women that stress her relational, nurturing, and caretaking roles.

Jordan, Kaplan, Miller, Stiver, and Surrey (1991), working and writing at the Stone Center at Wellesley College, have developed an alternative theory of women's psychological development known as the "self-in-relation" theory. This places an emphasis on the relational and interdependent nature of the individual, particularly the individual's need for connection and emotional joining. They postulate that relational capacities exist from birth and develop over time, more so for women than men because of socially reinforced gender differences. Men, it is maintained, arrive in early adulthood with a strong striving for independent actions and with a less well-developed capacity for intimacy and nurturance. Again and again in relationships between men and women in early adulthood, the same drama is reenacted. A woman wants the same emotional commitment from a man that she is ready to provide, but a man wants to keep his distance emotionally as he struggles to solidify his accomplishments in the larger world. She cannot understand why he cannot make this commitment, and he cannot understand why she is so dependent and clinging. A logical extension of this dynamic is that if our guiding theories regarding personality formation stress that normal development should proceed according to the male model, women are clearly more likely to be labeled as disordered and disturbed.

Recent writings from the Stone Center (Jordan, 1996) have attempted to make their theories more sensitive to race, ethnicity, and culture. They highlight the manner in which diverse backgrounds may affect some of their earlier notions, especially in regard to the development of empathy and the striving for relational connection. It is noted that when the prevailing culture marginalizes or oppresses women, they "may need to suppress feelings or inhibit reactions to others. . . . They may also have internalized racism, sexism or homophobia, thereby doubting the truth of their own perceptions or feeling responsible for relational breaches" (Jordan, 1996, p. 35). It is also pointed out that women in the dominant culture are vulnerable to "the insidious ways that unconscious, culturally embedded assumptions about others distort one's ability to see others as they would like to be seen" (Jordan, 1996, p. 35).

What does all this have to do with the mother in the incest family? If one accepts some of the newer concepts, because of the emphasis on relationship and the formation of identity within the context of intimate relationships (with mothers, sisters, grandmothers, aunts, girlfriends), a woman who is well adjusted will have strong relationships and feel the need for them in her life. If she is a mother who learns that her husband or partner has molested her child, she may be extremely torn because she will feel the pull of allegiance between her spouse and her child. She will weigh the "costs" of believing and protecting her child, and her decisions may be affected by race, culture, and ethnicity as well as her financial status. As will be discussed more fully later, this ambivalence about which connection to emphasize—that with her partner or that with her child—may in fact represent a healthier posture in terms of readiness for treatment than the mother who can readily desert either her spouse or child.

Concomitantly, evidence suggests that the degree of maternal support at the time of a disclosure of child sexual abuse affects the child's adjustment. Wyatt and Mickey (1987) found that maternal support had a positive mediating effect on subsequent traumatic effects. Lack of support at the time of disclosure has been associated with greater psychopathology on the part of the victim as well as with higher rates of out-of-home placement (Everson et al., 1989).

The feminist perspective on the etiology of incest, the newer formulations of women's psychological development, and the budding volume of empirical research suggest that an alternative understanding of the mother is warranted. It may be that the tendency to blame the mother has occurred largely because the mother has been judged against unrealistic standards. The traditional standard of the mother as nurturer and protector reflects an idealization of women. The subsequent, inevitable devaluation of mothers who do not live up to the idealized image may partially explain the blame attributed to the mother. This traditional standard fails to take into consideration the social context of women's lives and how the women's role in society is manifest in both subordinate relationships within the family and in the internalization of psychologically damaging self-images in personality development.

Theories of Trauma and Its Impact

Most of the theories relating to the impact of trauma are gender neutral, and consequently one must be cautious in applying them in their entirety to the treatment of women. However, the contributions are significant and should not be dismissed (Briere, 1996; Van der Kolk et al., 1996). Current theories of posttrauma reactions fall generally into three categories (McCann & Pearlman, 1990), which include the psychoanalytic schools of thought, the cognitive theories, and the biological and behavioral models.

Psychoanalytic schools of thought tend to view the reactions to traumatic life events as one in which affects (emotions) associated with memories of the event are blocked (defended against) so as not to overwhelm the ego. This can result in emotional blocking, cognitive constrictions, and impaired behavioral reactions. Self psychologists (Kohut, 1977; Palombo, 1983), as differentiated from drive theorists, have focused on the effects of traumatic childhood. However, they suggest that self-fragmentation and self-pathology can emerge as a result of extreme trauma in adult life (Brende, 1983; Brende & McCann, 1984; Brende & Parson, 1985; Briere, 1997b; Krystal, 1978; Parson, 1988).

Cognitive theorists focus on the impairment in thinking and distorted cognitive schemas that follow trauma. One of the most notable theorists is Horowitz (1975), who believed that traumatic events disrupt cognitive schemas. The effects of this disruption then have to be controlled (through the defense mechanisms) to regulate the ongoing processing of information. However, until the traumatic events can be integrated into existing cognitive schemas, the effects would continue to be disruptive, in the form of flashbacks, dreams, waves of intense uncomfortable feelings, and other intrusive traumatic reminders.

Janoff-Bulman (1986, 1992), another cognitive-behaviorist, suggested that trauma disrupts the major assumptions about the self and the world by upsetting individuals' fundamental beliefs. These include the belief in invulnerability, the perception of the world as benevolent and meaningful, and the perception of self as worthy. Behaviorists have tended to link the reactions to trauma and subsequent avoidant behavior. As one variation of this, the highly publicized notion of learned helplessness explains the reactions of withdrawal and passivity seen in victims of interpersonal violence.

Recent work has explored the manner in which the experience of child sexual abuse contributes to traumatic responses in adults. Both Herman (1992) and Briere (1992, 1997a) have emphasized the manner in which posttraumatic effects can be manifest in adulthood for childhood sexual abuse survivors, as well as describing helpful therapeutic interventions. Van de Kolk and Fishler (1994) detail the biopsychosocial implications of traumatic relationships in childhood, and Armsworth and Holaday (1993) have elaborated some specific traumatic effects of child abuse and neglect. An important concept in designing an approach to the treatment of the mother is that of trauma encapsulation (Burgess, 1987). This is a notion premised on Horowitz's (1975, 1976, 1979) information-processing model, which emphasizes the impact of trauma on cognitive schemas and the role of defenses in regulating the processing of information. In this model, which assumes past and current memory capacities, memories of traumatic experiences and the strong affects associated with them are stored in current memory unless the experiences have been processed and moved to past memory. The use of the defense of denial is often prominent in this process, and clinically this is one of the often-observed defenses of mothers in incest families as they are engaged in treatment.

Briere (1997b) presents a treatment approach that integrates elements of cognitive-behavioral theory with self psychology. She suggests that identity formation, the development of interpersonal boundaries, and affect regulation are involved in the person's response to aversive events. With children who are sexually abused, what starts out as a normal reaction to a traumatic event cannot be resolved due to the secrecy surrounding the incest, and dysfunctional coping patterns emerge. Feelings are warded off and defended against, resulting in emotional and behavioral symptoms. For the mother, the *disclosure* of the incest may be a traumatic event, and the emotional upset will be mediated by the self capacities of the individual. The likelihood of a heightened traumatic response is increased if the mother is also a victim of childhood sexual abuse and has not received therapy.

Two of the most profound reactions to trauma, widely found in adult survivors of sexual abuse, are conversion phenomena and dissociation. As Bloch (1991) points out, dissociation is a very effective defense and, in addition to the encapsulation and containment functions mentioned earlier, leads to the "development of specific adaptive competencies that otherwise would be inhibited by traumatic experiences" (Bloch, 1991, p. 13). Again, because the prevalence of past sexual abuse among mothers in incest families is high, this defensive reaction may also be quite common.

In keeping with the alternative view of the mother as a secondary victim to her child's sexual abuse, it is important to review the evidence that this may be the case. There is a growing recognition that intrafamilial sexual abuse, particularly *disclosure*, may have a traumatic impact on the mother as well as the child. Newberger, Gremy, Waternaux, and Newberger (1993) found that mothers interviewed shortly after disclosure scored significantly higher on a global symptomatology index than the mean for a normal population. A significant decline in symptom scores over a 12-month period led Newberger et al. to conclude that the distress was a reaction to the disclosure of abuse, rather than reflecting preexisting disorders in the mothers. Timmons-Mitchell, Chandler-Holtz, and Semple (1996) found that their sample of mothers whose children had recently disclosed sexual abuse scored significantly higher on two different measures for posttraumatic stress than did women in the normative sample for these measures. Green, Coupe, Fernandez, and Stevens (1995), in their work with four mothers whose children had recently disclosed sexual abuse, found that these mothers responded to the disclosure of sexual abuse with a number of symptoms associated with posttraumatic stress disorder, including the flooding of intrusive memories, the reexperiencing of painful affects, hyperarousal, and psychic numbing.

Carter (1993) found high levels of shock, guilt, anger, shame, and traumatic symptoms in a sample of mothers of sexually abused children and noted that the trauma was more severe in cases in which the mother's husband was the perpetrator. Another factor that appears to exacerbate mothers' distress is a personal history of sexual victimization (Brickman, 1993); this is particularly noteworthy in light of research findings that 40% to 50% of mothers of sexually abused children have been victimized or knew of a sibling being abused (Faller, 1989; Gomes-Schwartz, 1990). Deblinger, Stauffer, and Landsberg (1994) found that nonoffending mothers with a history of child sexual victimization tended to exhibit more symptom distress than mothers without such a history. Significantly, however, the mothers with a history of childhood victimization did not differ in their maternal responses to the allegations of abuse regarding their own children. One important implication is that although the mother may experience more symptoms of posttraumatic distress if she has a history of childhood victimization, this does not appear to predict her response to her own child's sexual abuse.

A useful framework for understanding the specific traumatic effects of child sexual abuse is provided by Finkelhor and Browne (1985), which seems to combine a psychodynamic framework with cognitive-behavioral theory. According to this conceptual framework, four traumagenic dynamics are *manifest in the victims of sexual trauma.* These are (a) traumatic sexualization, (b) stigmatization, (c) betrayal, and (d) powerlessness.

Traumatic sexualization refers to the impairment of healthy sexual functioning of the individual due to the sexual nature of the trauma. *Stigmatization* refers to the tendency for the victims to blame themselves for the abuse and to feel shame, guilt, and self-hate. The *betrayal* dynamic refers to the betrayal of trust experienced by the victim of sexual abuse. The fourth characteristic, *powerlessness,* relates to the sense of helplessness and vulnerability engendered in the child victim of sexual abuse.

Although originally developed as an aid in work with sexual abuse victims or survivors, it is possible to apply this model to mothers in incest families as well (Strand, 1990, 1991). The applicability of this model is relevant for a number of reasons, tied fundamentally to the concept of the mother as a secondary victim. Many of the mothers from incest families are sexual abuse victims themselves who have never worked through their own experiences as victims (Brickman, 1993; Deblinger et al., 1994; Faller, 1989; Gomes-Schwartz, 1990; Mrazek & Mrazek, 1981; Wells, 1981). Thus, they already may be suffering the from the long-term effects of *sexual trauma.* Even if they have not been sexually victimized, the reactions of the mother parallel those of the victim in many respects. A mother typically experiences her partner's sexual abuse of her child as an assault on her own sexuality. She may exhibit many of the same responses as the victim—negative association to sexual arousal, sexual dysfunction, and confusion about sexual identity.

The mother also feels *stigmatized* and shares many of the victim's feelings of shame and guilt. She often isolates herself from extended family and friends and may even want to move out of the community where she is known to avoid "exposure." This can deprive her of support and comfort at a time of crisis and exacerbate posttraumatic stress symptoms. *Most mothers experience betrayal,* and although this feeling may vary in intensity because of the nature and duration of the relationship with the offender, it may leave the woman not only with a mistrust of others, especially men, but also of herself. In cases in which the mother has a history of betrayal by her own parents or caretakers, feelings of betrayal may be heightened. Feelings of *powerlessness* are among the most salient ones immediately following disclosure, especially when the initial disclosure has resulted in either the parent or child leaving the home.

It is important to note that this is a conceptual framework and will benefit from empirical exploration and testing. It may not be equally applicable to all mothers in incest families. However, it is suggested here as an aid in evaluation and assessment and as a guide for prioritizing treatment issues. It is offered not as a comprehensive theory but as one model that may help guide the clinician. This conceptual framework incorporates an understanding of the stress emanating from the social realities for most mothers as well as reframing the mother's experience to emphasize the impact of trauma and the mothers' strengths rather than deficits.

In writing this book, I have chosen to emphasize the newer formulations of women's psychological development that take into account the preeminence of the relational being (Jordan, 1996). Throughout the rest of the book, an attempt will be made through discussion and case examples to incorporate both the feminist contributions to practice and the developing knowledge of the impact of trauma. In Chapter 2, potential countertransference issues are discussed, with a special emphasis on the role of gender. Chapter 3 explores the contextual considerations that come into play in the engagement of the mother in therapy, and Chapter 4 highlights the application of the traumagenic dynamics model in assessment and treatment planning. Discussions of assessment and interventions will focus on strengthening the role of the mother in the family, employing the use of empathy, and encouraging clients to become active in their social environment toward the twin goals of self-empowerment and institutional change.

Chapters 5 through 7 deal explicitly with the three modalities of individual, group, and family treatment. Recognizing the interface between mental health intervention and the legal system in most cases of family sexual abuse, I outline critical issues in case coordination in Chapter 8. Chapter 9 addresses the special concerns when working with nonoffending mothers who are involved in custody or visitation disputes, and Chapter 10 suggests future directions for research and application of clinical understandings.

GENDER AND COUNTERTRANSFERENCE

One of the more difficult issues for most therapists working with the mother in an incest family is becoming aware of their own counter-transference reactions. This is an arduous undertaking because so many of the reactions are deeply embedded in cultural expectations of mothers and are difficult to untangle. In this chapter, I will explore the manner in which some of the issues noted earlier about gender expectations affect what the therapist brings to her or his work with the mother in the incest family.

In this discussion, induced countertransference will be distinguished from personal countertransference. The former is considered to be within the normal range of reactions by most people (i.e., most people would react with similar feelings to the event, situation, or behavior). Personal countertransference issues, on the other hand, incorporate individual therapists' reactions, attributions, and attitudes based on their particular experiences with their family of origin as well as in adult relationships.

The specific issues that will be taken up in this chapter include the social construction of motherhood, the ambivalent view of women, the effects of professional training in a mental health discipline, the widespread tendency to blame mothers for a child's problem, and the therapist's own experience with victimization that shape her or his personal countertransference reactions. Each is discussed in more detail below.

The Social Construction of Motherhood

The social construction of a concept such as motherhood is defined by Phoenix and Woollett (1991) as the "ways in which ideas, and hence our experience of the world are dynamic, multiple, and highly complex. Furthermore, they are specific to the period of history and the society in which they are produced" (p. 14). Thus, the meaning of motherhood is influenced by the social needs, expectations, and demands on women in relation to their roles with children.

In the 1990s, the expectation that women will become mothers and that this is a normal and proper part of being an adult woman is alive and well (Phoenix & Woollett, 1991). However, many more women who mother children are involved in wage-earning employment outside the home than were even 30 years ago. If the mother is now in the public arena earning money, the children are being taken care of by substitute mothers, the female child caregivers in family day care or formal child care settings. In addition, raising children is still conceptualized as primarily a private matter. The social or political ramifications of this are that it becomes easier to lay family problems, family dysfunction, or children's problems at the doorstep of the individual family. The fact that society may fail to provide the social supports (income maintenance, quality child care opportunities, adequate affordable housing) is seen as irrelevant to the parenting job required of individual parents.

Society values some characteristics in mothers more than others do. For example, traits that are viewed as valuable if held by women include intuitiveness, gentleness, sensitivity, empathy, warmth, sweetness, softness, subjectivity, tenderness, and the ability to be generally loving and caring. These clearly grow out of women's traditional roles as nurturer and caretaker. Although these are highly prized in women, these same characteristics are devalued when compared with qualities commonly associated with adult males.

In her review of seven books or manuals published between 1976 and 1988, Marshall (1991) concludes that these characteristics generally work to construct motherhood as a wholly positive experience. The ambivalent or negative feelings a woman may have toward mothering are not emphasized, although as most women can articulate, mothering is often experienced as a demanding and sometimes unrewarding task.

In these books, however, the social context in which the woman is mothering is omitted. There is no discussion of the financial and social (i.e., single parenthood) constraints that might affect her ability to parent. An assumption is also made that the child will be healthy, and little consideration is given to the dynamics of the nuclear family, except that the inference is made that the family will be one in which there are two parents in a heterosexual partnership. The quality of that relationship is not addressed, and issues such as battering, alcoholism, and drug abuse and or sexual abuse are not mentioned in terms of the impact that these might have not only on the quality of the relationship but also on both parents' ability to be nurturing.

Being a mother is viewed as a valuable attribute for a woman, despite the constraints that having children may impose on one's lifestyle and the low status of women's domestic roles. Research into why women have children points to the value that the status and identity of the mother has for adult women. As Woollett (1991) stated, "Motherhood bestows positive identity on a woman. Motherhood is highly valued symbolically as the key to adulthood: having a child makes a woman a mother and an adult" (p. 53). By contrast, women who do not have children are often viewed negatively. The negative image of childless women is based on a number of assumptions, including "their psychological inadequacy, their ability to engage in close personal relationships, and their social position" (Woollett, 1991, p. 62). As Woollett summarized in her study of infertile women, "Women who do not become mothers are viewed negatively and have to account for their failure to achieve or their rejection of a social position to which, it is assumed, all heterosexual women in stable relationships aspire" (p. 62).

Because mothers carry the primary responsibility for child rearing, it follows that mothers bear the responsibility for ensuring that the child turns out "right." As therapists living in the United States in the late 1990s, it is difficult to avoid bringing these deeply ingrained attitudes toward mothers to the therapeutic encounter. A case example may highlight some of the common difficulties that can emerge for the therapist, especially when the therapist is just beginning to work with women in this situation.

Miriam, an African American, never-married woman with five children, has recently had a new baby. Miriam has never worked and supported herself and her first three children through support from public assistance until she met James, the father of her fourth and fifth children. He moved in with the family 6 months before the disclosure, and despite the fact that he does not "get along" with her oldest daughter, Laurie (age 11), Miriam and James were planning to marry at the time of the report of suspected sexual abuse.

In discussing the relationship between James and Laurie, Miriam reported that she believed that Laurie's discomfort with James was due to jealousy of her mother's relationship with James and with the new baby. Miriam had become increasingly frustrated with Laurie over the past 2 years, as Laurie had been skipping school and was oppositional and generally very difficult. Miriam had difficulty understanding why Laurie complains about James because James had been very generous with Laurie, taking her places and often buying her things that she wanted that Miriam could not always afford.

When Laurie disclosed to her school counselor that James had sexually abused her, Miriam was horrified. Before Miriam even knew about the allegations, however, Laurie had been interviewed by Child Protective Services (CPS) and repeated the allegations to them. The details included the fact that James went into Laurie's bedroom at night and fondled her breasts and vagina. When Miriam confronted Laurie, asking her if this was really the truth, Laurie seemed to change her story.

Both Miriam and her daughter were referred for therapy as the investigation continued. On coming into treatment, Miriam projected an angry, defensive stance, questioning why Laurie would tell everyone but her about this if it were really true. Laurie was equivocal and did not recant but was no longer willing to explain or discuss the incidents. Miriam said James adamantly denied any sexual contact with Laurie. Because she and James were sexually active and planned to marry, Miriam could not believe James would do this to Laurie.

Miriam also drew on her own history to explain to the therapist why she believed that Laurie was lying. She disclosed, with much emotion, that she was sexually abused by a family member more than once when she was a teenager. She revealed that she never disclosed this to anyone and inferred that if Laurie's accusations were really true, Laurie would not have told anyone. A key issue for Miriam was that when she was abused, she "stopped talking" to the member of the family who abused her. In outraged indignation, she told the therapist that not only did Laurie continue to talk to James but she also sought favors from him. Miriam thought that James treated Laurie well and often gave her things she asked for. Miriam could not reconcile this type of interaction between James and Laurie with her own experience.

The therapist struggled with her emotional response to Miriam. Although her training taught her to respond in a nonjudgmental way to Miriam, she was aware that her initial reaction was one of anger. She could not understand how this mother could apparently be impervious to the needs of her 11-year-old, who the therapist saw as in great need of support and encouragement from Miriam. It was difficult for the therapist to accept Miriam's inability to relate in a nonjudgmental, nurturing, and protective way toward her daughter. The therapist found herself beginning to blame the mother for her daughter's condition. If she had been a better mother and less invested in her relationship with this abusive man, the therapist hypothesized, she would have been able to respond to her daughter's needs more fully.

The therapist fortunately recognized her reaction to the client and sought help from her supervisor. In this consultation, the therapist realized that her reaction was reflective of the "baggage" that many therapists carry regarding the socially prescribed role of mothers. It is often easier to identify with the child than the mother. As Alice Miller (1984) points out, the unconscious need to rescue the child reflects one's own reality of unfulfilled needs in childhood. The specifics of the case had triggered some feelings for the therapist regarding her own history. The therapist had grown up in an alcoholic family and felt that her mother had been emotionally depleted and subsequently preoccupied with her marriage to the detriment of her parenting responsibilities to her children. She identified with the "abandoned" child and tended to overidentify and want to rescue abused and/or neglected children. In addition, however, this case tapped into the culturally sanctioned view of motherhood, which it is difficult for any therapist to stand outside of at all times.

As she discussed the case, the therapist began to suspect that Miriam's reactions might be connected to her own unresolved experiences. Initially, Miriam was closed to any exploration of how her childhood experiences might affect her reaction to this current life situation. Miriam's energies were involved in taking care of her 3-week-old baby and her other three children, and she viewed Laurie as the one who could take care of herself. Both these factors did put Miriam at risk for not being able to react in a protective way, supporting the therapist's desire to press for a removal of Laurie.

Although the risk assessment was in many respects accurate, it was the therapist's duty not only to assess this but also to *engage* the mother in a therapeutic relationship. Having realized that she was reacting in a judgmental way to Miriam, the therapist was able to approach her subsequently more emphatically. Without abandoning her concern about the risk to Laurie if the allegations were true, she was able to relate to Miriam in a way that allowed Miriam to "tell her story" and vent her concerns. As Miriam's life story unfolded, the therapist came to understand how the social context of Miriam's life affected her response in the crisis of the disclosure of sexual abuse. It was not that Miriam did not care about her daughter, but she was weighing and balancing the needs of herself and all family members. She had felt powerless and inadequate much of her life and had never had an adequate means of supporting herself. The planned marriage carried great psychological and financial meaning for Miriam, in that it would confer status, ensure financial stability, and reflect the personal success that she desired.

As treatment progressed, it become evident that the relationship with James held great meaning for Miriam. It was the most stable relationship she had had with a man. James met many of her needs, including her need for financial security, and he has met many of her other needs. As Massat and Lundy (1998) had found in their study, there were relational and financial "costs" for Miriam. Yet her initial defensiveness gradually declined as she was not challenged or blamed in the initial engagement process by the therapist. Miriam was eventually able to hear her daughter and to accept the bitter disappointment that James had in fact molested Laurie.

Miriam initially engendered anger and resentment in the therapist because, by seemingly rejecting her daughter for James, she was acting in a manner that is contrary to what is accepted as appropriate for a mother. Mothers should always put their children first; the apparent discrepancy between what the therapist believed was a "given," and Miriam's attitude engendered a defensive reaction in the therapist. As with any client, the therapist needed to start where the client was. Miriam was in crisis when she first came into treatment. Like most people in crisis, she was in shock, and the implications of the disclosure, if true, were far-reaching, traumatic, and economically devastating. It was no wonder she feared losing the most stable family she had known. For her to accept that James had molested Laurie would undermine the life she had built over the past 2 years and destroy her future. By appreciating the importance to her of the relationship with James, the therapist made it possible to engage her in treatment.

Ambivalent View of Women

Not only is the role of the mother socially constructed and defined primarily as one in which qualities associated with nurturing and caretaking are highly prized, but it is also idealized. At the same time, women exist in a subordinate position to men and are consequently devalued in many respects. The reasons for this are complex. Jean Baker Miller (1983) argued that as a subordinate social group, women's caretaking activities are essential to the dominant group (men) and are therefore glorified but also considered activities carried out by "second-class citizens." Others, such as Dinnerstein (1977), suggested that the domination of child care by women results in a deep-seated fear of women by men (and women, too) and that their power is therefore experienced as irrational and engulfing. Along these lines, Stiver (1991) noted that

> there is a very powerful theme in the literature that separation-individualization is the major goal of mature development. The need for both male and female children to move out of the relationship with their mothers, who are said to be experienced as overwhelming and powerful, is emphasized repeatedly. (p. 112)

To cope with this, women may be either idealized or devalued.

This ambivalence toward women permeates the collective unconscious and is a factor to be considered for any therapist who is working with mothers. In interacting with women in the therapeutic situation, therapists need to be in touch with their own implicit expectations regarding women. The implications for working with the mother in the incest family are worthy of special attention—especially because the mother does not usually live up to those characteristics positively valued. Consider the following case.

Mrs. C, a divorced Hispanic mother of a 6-year-old boy, was referred for treatment. Her ex-husband had weekly overnight visitation with Jamie and in fact took care of him often at other times also. About 9 months before the disclosure of sexual abuse, his teacher, who observed highly sexualized behavior, began to ask Jamie specific questions. Jamie made some statements to her, indicating that his father had fondled him sexually. The teacher called CPS. During the course of the investigation, the father was allowed supervised contact with Jamie, and the weekend visits were curtailed.

During the investigation, information came out about Mrs. C that left questions about her own parenting. For example, there had been an earlier indicated CPS report for neglect, when she had left Jamie unattended while she supposedly went shopping. She was thought to be a drug addict who relied on Mr. C to provide child care on alternate weekends while she went to visit her boyfriend in another town. She also relied on friends in the neighborhood, who likewise tended to be addicted to crack, to care for Jamie.

Jamie had done poorly in the all-day kindergarten program, largely because of behavior problems. A major issue, from the school's point of view, was that Jamie "told stories" often to get attention and had difficulty attending and following directions. The school perceived Mrs. C as unresponsive to their concerns while viewing Mr. C as more invested and interested in Jamie.

On referral for treatment, Mrs. C presented as an "ineffectual, passive woman" who appeared depressed and unable to assert herself. She was ambivalent about the allegations of sexual abuse, accepting them at face value but minimizing their significance. Her attitude seemed to convey a stance of "he told and now it won't happen again." She was going along with the request by CPS for supervised visits at the agency but also complaining about the restraints this put on her own social life.

Mrs. C's presentation induced a negative reaction in the therapist. Mrs. C did not fit the image of a concerned, nurturing parent. Although she had gone through a drug rehabilitation program and was in recovery (hence the current referral for psychotherapy), her history and current attitude suggested that she placed her own concerns above that of her son. The therapist felt that she was not connected to the pain and difficulty her son must be experiencing.

Treatment would probably not have proceeded well if the therapist had not been able to separate her reactions sufficiently to attend to the mother's concerns. The therapist was able to do this by stepping back to consider the mother as an individual. She thought about the influence of the culturally defined expectations of mothers on herself as well as on Mrs. C. She reflected on the fact that "good" mothers were not supposed to make mistakes, especially of the nature of Mrs. C's drug abuse. She hypothesized that Mrs. C might be experiencing excruciating feelings of shame and self-blame, given that Mrs. C might be feeling that she had not lived up to society's expectation of mothers, particularly given her cultural background. Spanish households stress the importance of elevating the responsibilities of motherhood above all else. Mrs. C's passive, ineffectual presentation to the agency could reflect her desire not to become engaged less she be "exposed" as a bad mother and further shamed.

The therapist also reflected on the importance of Mrs. C in her son's life. Despite Mrs. C's struggles, which had clearly had a negative impact on Jamie, he was attached to his mother. An evaluation of Jamie had revealed him to be functioning at age-appropriate levels cognitively with some social delays and indications of posttraumatic stress. However, he did not emerge as a severely disturbed child. The therapist reasoned that to the extent that Mrs. C could be helped to effectively parent, the better off Jamie would be. This provided an empathic opening for the therapist to begin to relate in a less judgmental way to Mrs. C.

Again, as in the case with Miriam, the therapist's reaction, despite her professional education, was deeply influenced by her worldview of mothers. This is not to say that the personal history of either of these therapists along with other influences did not contribute to their reactions. Any response is of course multidetermined. The point is that the social side of the equation, which considers gender and cultural influences, is often downplayed if not ignored altogether. In the interaction of therapists with mothers in incest families, the failure to appreciate the role of women in society has led to an overly harsh and negative portrayal that is probably not warranted.

Effects of Professional Training

Although attention to the role of women and the impact of culture and race are undeniably growing in the mental health professions, some evidence suggests that this is not systematically integrated into the curriculum in graduate schools of social work, psychology, psychiatric nursing, or psychiatry. Attention to the kinds of theoretical issues noted earlier and their implications for treatment does occur in electives and some courses, as well as in continuing education (Campbell, Raja, & Grining, 1999), but the failure to attend to them across the board raises the question of how widespread the basic knowledge base of graduate-trained mental health professionals is in these areas.

The effects of professional training are significant in terms of the reinforcement of culturally held attitudes toward women. As early as 1978, the Report of the President's Commission on Mental Health pointed out that women are the primary users of health care in a system controlled and administered by men. One might add that today, women of color comprise a large percentage of users of the mental health system, particularly in urban areas, and yet the same holds true (Rhodes & Goering, 1998). As Brodsky and Hare-Mustin (1980) pointed out, despite

> the number of female consumers of psychotherapy, problems specific to women and the woman's point of view in the development of theory and practice of psychotherapy have suffered wide-ranging neglect. Such neglect is not a result of conscious discrimination, but a concomitant of prevailing attitudes toward women. (p. 385)

The neglect may be partially explained by negative attitudes toward women. Studies undertaken during the 1980s tend to support the supposition that professional women's negative attitudes toward women tend to become reactivated in women psychotherapists' counter-transference. Ruderman (1986), for example, attempted to study the countertransference of women therapists in their treatment of patients through an in-depth interview with 20 experienced psychotherapists. She concluded that

women cannot adequately free themselves from the constraints of traditional role stereotypes without first coming
to terms with negative attitudes toward women which they
have internalized during the earliest phases of their development. . . . Without proper attention to their unresolved
conflicts, women psychotherapists run the risk of counter-
therapeutic interventions with women patients as a result
of unconscious mirroring of sociocultural attitudes. (p.
122)

Trained in psychoanalysis, Ruderman (1986) is nonetheless stressing the impact of negative social attitudes toward women.

This raises the question of whether treatment approaches have been developed that enable the therapist to respond differentially based on gender.
How does treatment reflect the fact that a particular event may have more of
an impact on women than men because of women's socialization to be dependent on others, particularly men? In the context of our focus here, one
might ask, to what extent has the particular crisis of being a mother in an incest family been conceptualized as requiring special services, with the particular needs and dynamics of nonoffending mothers identified and addressed?
    A case example may help to illustrate some of the dynamics present for
women in these family situations.

Mrs. N was a White, 37-year-old married woman when the day care
provider for her oldest child, Tami (age 4½), made a report of suspected sexual abuse, alleging that Mr. N had abused Tami. At the time,
Mrs. N was living with her husband of 15 years and her younger son,
William (age 3). The report indicated that Tami's behavior was highly
sexualized and that she had made statements about her father playing
with her private parts.
    Mrs. N worked outside the home as a retail clerk, and her husband
was an electrician who had a very good job. The family had bought a
modest single-family home just prior to Tami's birth. At the time of the
report to CPS, Mr. N adamantly denied the allegations. Tami would not
talk to her mother, and Mrs. N told the CPS worker that she did not
know whom to believe.

The reaction of CPS was to advise Mrs. N that they would have to remove Tami if she did not separate from her husband. Mr. N was unwilling to move out, so Mrs. N moved to her mother's house with the children, where she was living at the time of the referral to therapy.

In her initial presentation, Mrs. N appeared nervous and agitated. Her speech was tangential, and she seemed determined to paint a picture of herself as a hopeless victim of her husband's and daughter's stubbornness. She complained that her daughter would not talk to her and that she did not know what had happened. She also complained that her daughter was very difficult to manage, much more difficult than her son, detailing a litany of behavioral problems.

Mrs. N appeared needy and demanding, often calling the therapist in between appointments and attempting to have the therapist influence CPS in the manner she wanted. Mrs. N would become enraged easily with CPS, the therapist, her attorney, or others whom she perceived as not meeting her needs or understanding her position. When gently confronted by the therapist, she would assume a martyr posture, saying that she was ready to give up and that she could not handle everything.

Mrs. N was an only child whose parents had separated and subsequently divorced when she was 10. Mrs. N had been raised by her mother, with whom she spent a great deal of her time even before she moved in with her following the report to CPS. She described her mother as generally not supportive of her in any sphere of her life: child rearing, work, or in her relationship with her husband.

In the presentation of her case to the team for disposition, the therapist's assessment included elements reflective of ego psychology, object relations theory, and self psychology. Mrs. N was described as a woman whose ambivalence surrounding her daughter's disclosure to others of possible sexual abuse by the father suggested emotional immaturity and a dependent personality. The therapist described Mrs. N as having elements of a borderline personality and described her as being in a hostile and dependent relationship with her mother, with whom she was furious.

The therapist speculated that developmentally, Mrs. N had not successfully mastered stages of identity formation or the ability to be intimate. Thus, in the phase of life when one would hope to see energy devoted to nurturing her children (generativity), she was instead still involved with earlier, unfulfilled tasks. Preliminary diagnosis was of a borderline or narcissistic personality disorder. Dynamically, it was postulated that the internalization of a "bad object" in childhood and the suppressed rage and inexpressible anger associated with that interfered with her ability to connect in a meaningful way, thus inhibiting her object relations. She consequently presented as very needy and dependent and was viewed as incapable of acting protectively. The evaluation determined that she would need the structure of the legal system to keep her from returning to her husband.

This psychological analysis left out the social and cultural context of her life. It disregarded, for example, the degree to which women are socialized to be dependent on men and the manner in which the nature of the crisis of disclosure could stimulate an exaggerated psychological response. For example, using Surrey's (1991) "self-in-relation" theory of women's personality development, one might arrive at a different assessment. Unlike theories that emphasize the importance of separation from the mother in early childhood, from the family in adolescence, and from teachers and mentors in adulthood, Surrey would emphasize the centrality of the self as it develops in a relational context. Relationship is seen as the goal of development, not separateness.

Surrey (1991) defined *relationship* as the "experience of emotional and cognitive intersubjectivity: the ongoing, intrinsic inner awareness and responsiveness to the continuous existence of the other or others and the expectation of mutuality in this regard" (p. 61). She emphasized that her model stresses "a process of growth within relationship, where both or all people involved are encouraged and challenged to maintain connections and to foster, adapt to, and change with the growth of the other" (p. 60).

One might assess the relationship between Mrs. N and her mother, using this paradigm, as one in which Mrs. N's mother was not able to accommodate psychologically to her daughter's growth and expansion in her life, which included new relationships with husband, children, and work. Also, one might hypothesize that the disruption in the relationship with her husband and child, following the disclosure of possible sexual abuse, was enormous for Mrs. N. It could very well lead to a renewed attempt to connect with her mother, leading to frustration and further self-doubt because of the mother's inability to embrace her daughter's decisions about her life.

For Mrs. N to change, she will need to build on her primary sense of herself in connection with others. In her case, one such relationship could be with the therapist and, eventually, if she had the opportunity to connect with other mothers in a mothers group, to growth-enhancing peer relationships with other women. In fact, Mrs. N left treatment with the first agency and eventually found her way to a therapist who specialized in working with incest families. Progress unfolded much along the lines described earlier. This therapist was able to engage Mrs. N as someone in crisis, whose disruption in a major relationship had led her to fall back temporarily on an "outmoded" relational experience (with her mother). This, in turn, had only heightened her sense of isolation and disconnection, causing her to present in a disorganized, "immature," and "needy" fashion. When this presentation was reframed to highlight the relational needs of Mrs. N, which were then supplied in the form of the therapist and other mothers in a treatment group, Mrs. N was able to use these relationships to help her shift both her inner and outer relationships with significant others in her life.

This example illustrates how significant a therapist's professional orientation can be in work with women. Rich as the contribution of drive theorists, ego psychologists, object relations theorists, and self psychology proponents have been, a failure to understand that women's psychological development is different from men's (and will be as long as women are the primary caregivers for both boys and girls) has led to a failure to understand and articulate the psychological position of the mother in the incest family. Reliance on a psychodynamic formulation that does not take women's differential needs into consideration may mean that the therapist is not sufficiently prepared to help a client such as Mrs. N.

Widespread Tendency to Blame Mother for a Child's Problem

A fourth issue has to do with the widespread tendency to blame the mother for all of the child's problems. As noted earlier, this is the dark side of the attribution of irrational power to mothers, which is reflected in the idealization of motherhood. Importantly, this occurs not only in the lay public's reaction to mothers but also in the mental health profession. As Caplan and Hall-McCorquodale (1985) so vividly portrayed in their analysis of professional journal articles, mother blaming insidiously invades our theories of personality, our diagnostic schemas, and our thinking about therapeutic interventions.

The tendency to blame the mother is overdetermined, in many respects. Some researchers have begun to document this inclination on the part of both professionals and the client's own social network. For example, Carter (1993) found that mothers of sexually abused children suffered punitive and negative treatment by intervening professionals as well as family and friends. Mothers are blamed, she concluded, because the "deeply rooted practices of a gender-based intervention system, based on mainstream values about family life and the role of mothers in North America societies contribute to mother's feelings of blame for the victimization of their children" (pp. 88-89).

A current variation on this theme is the belief that if sexual abuse allegations arise in the context of a custody or divorce proceeding, coaching by the custodial parent (usually the mother) is suspected. The fact that a mother may be apparently hostile, vengeful, and even "inappropriate" in relationship to her husband or ex-husband appears to negate any consideration that there also might exist an incestuous relationship between the father and child.

In these cases, the mother is often unduly scrutinized, particularly if she has acted in a way that does not fit with an erroneous but still widely held view of the mother in the incest family: one who is passive, dependent, and unwilling to act to protect her child. A mother who is outraged and outrageous in her behavior—confronting systems that react slowly or not at all by appealing to local representatives, the press, or other "aggressive" acts—is often viewed as irrational and held highly suspect. Despite the fact that a current review of the literature on false allegations (Faller et al., 1993) illustrates that there is little empirical basis to the assumption that mothers use false allegations for leverage in custody or visitation disputes (Thoennes & Tjaden, 1990), the presumption is still widely held by the lay public and even the legal system.

Other family sexual abuse situations (those not specifically involving custody disputes) also engender reactions of mother blaming. In the cases of both Miriam and Mrs. C, described earlier, initial reactions to these mothers was to blame them for being "bad" mothers and, indirectly, for the sexual abuse. What is often overlooked in these situations is the active role and responsibility of the perpetrator, both in the commission of the acts and in the intentional efforts to mislead the mother about the nature of his relationship with the child.

Victimization in the History of the Therapist

Generally speaking, no woman—or man, for the matter—is without some experience of being a victim. These experiences can range from "nuisance" instances of being bullied in childhood, having someone cut in front in line, being robbed or having one's house burglarized, or being sexually assaulted. Based on empirical research to date, it appears that a female will be more likely to have experienced some form of unwanted sexual contact before age 18 (Russell, 1984) than will a man (Finkelhor, 1979).

For the therapist who has been sexually victimized in childhood, there may be the tendency to become overidentified with the victim. Unconscious needs to rescue children and unresolved anger at mothers for real or perceived failures to protect are often the derivatives in adulthood. The prevalence of these reactions is one important reason for the therapist to have had therapy in which these issues were specifically explored. Likewise, ongoing supervision and consultation are clearly indicated when the therapist works with clients whose issues may so closely mirror his or her own. Even if the therapist is not a victim of sexual abuse, disappointments generally associated with childhood (as Miller, 1984, has so eloquently described) make transference of feelings of anger to the mother likely.

The following case illustrates the potential for the clinician to become overidentified with the child and misinterpret the motivation driving the mother. This is especially likely to happen when the therapist is working primarily with the child, as, for example, when the child is separated from the mother. This can be due to the child's placement in care or the mother's institutionalization due to mental illness or incarceration. In the following case, the child had been placed in a residential treatment center.

CASE STUDY

Josephine, an African American child (age 11), is currently in a congregate residential care facility. She is a slight, olive-skinned child with an appealing manner and a wide smile that reveals large and crooked teeth. She has been in placement for about 1 year, following a finding of neglect and abuse. Josephine had been living with her mother and mother's boyfriend for 2 years prior to this. She had missed many days of school, and, more seriously, she had been sexually abused by her mother's boyfriend. Ms. D, her mother, did not believe the allegations at the time of Josephine's disclosure to a baby-sitter (who reported the case), and Mr. W, the mother's boyfriend, denied the allegations and has not followed through on family court orders to seek treatment with an offender specialist.

This is the second placement for Josephine. She lived with her mother from birth to age 5, at which time she was placed in family foster care because of Ms. D's inability to care for her. Josephine's birth ther has never claimed paternity and has never supported her. At the time of the first placement, Ms. D was drug addicted, reportedly prostituting herself for money, and left Josephine unsupervised on many occasions.

At age 7, Josephine was returned to her mother. Ms. D, age 24 at that time, had completed an extensive drug rehabilitation program and obtained her general equivalency diploma (GED). She was living with Mr. W, who supported the family while Ms. D continued training to become a home health aide. When Josephine was 10, the caseworker assigned to monitor the case noted decreased attendance in the job training program and had suspicions about increased substance use by Ms. D. Mr. W was believed to be an active substance abuser as well. Ms. D committed herself again to a residential substance abuse treatment program, and Josephine was placed again in foster care. It was during the 2-year period that Josephine lived with her mother and Mr. W that the molestation reportedly started.

Over the year that Josephine has been in care, Ms. D has been erratic in visiting Josephine and has not willingly participated in family therapy, despite the fact that sessions have been located in the agency's community-based office nearer to Ms. D's home. Ms. D did separate from Mr. W 6 months ago and is supporting herself through her work as a home health aide in a one-bedroom apartment. Within the past 3 months, she also has begun to attend therapy with a program specializing in helping incest families. Her therapist there sees Ms. D as motivated regarding individual therapy.

Mrs. G, the clinical social worker assigned as Josephine's therapist, is frustrated with Ms. D and perceives her as unmotivated and uncaring. She is suspicious of Ms. D's continuing use of substances, despite Ms. D's statements that she is abstaining and participating in both Narcotics Anonymous (NA) and Alcoholics Anonymous (AA) meetings as well as going to her own therapy. Mrs. G sees Ms. D's recent commencement of psychotherapy as manipulative, motivated solely by the desire to "look good" to the court.

Mrs. G, a 29-year-old woman married for 2 years, does not have any children of her own. She received her M.S.W. when she was 27 and has worked at the agency since that time. She has had a year of personal counseling, some in individual treatment and some in joint sessions with her husband. In her family of origin, her mother was depressed and actively addicted to prescription drugs for a time in her early childhood. The youngest of four, Mrs. G describes her childhood as one in which she felt her mother was unavailable, and she turned often to an older sister, who only partially met her needs.

Mrs. G describes Josephine to fellow workers—in a half-joking manner—as a child she wishes she could take home. She has taken special interest in her progress in the program and, through the development of a positive relationship with Josephine, has been helpful in facilitating her growth and development. Mrs. G's goal is to discharge Josephine to someone other than her mother. She has reached out to extended family members, and the maternal grandmother has become active in Josephine's life, visiting frequently. Ms. D's mother blames her daughter for not protecting Josephine from the sexual abuse by Mr. W and is willing to have Josephine come to live with her. Mrs. G has become an advocate for this plan, despite the fact that Ms. D and her mother do not get along. Ms. D does not want this for Josephine. She tells Mrs. G that her mother will "ruin" Josephine, pointing out that she was not a good mother to her.

The clinician's reaction is illustrative of both individual and systemic failings. Mrs. G's negative attitude toward Ms. D is based partly on her intensive involvement with Josephine and her relative lack of contact with Ms. D. Coupled with supervision that did not help her deal with her overidentification with Josephine, Mrs. G has embarked on a case plan that is unsustainable given the legal mandate to reunify families if the mother is responding to the case plan and carrying through with her obligation to attend services that will remedy the problems that brought Josephine into care. Despite the fact that the residential center is located 50 miles from Ms. D's inner-city neighborhood, in a suburban environment that can only be reached by a 2-hour trip on public transportation, Mrs. G feels that Ms. D uses this as an excuse and could be more regular in visiting like other families "if she really wanted to." She also blames Ms. D for not being more regular in attending family sessions at the satellite clinic, seeming oblivious to the fact that her dislike of Ms. D might be affecting Ms. D's willingness to attend the family sessions, which Mrs. G runs. More attuned supervision might also have helped her with this issue.

In her analysis, she has overlooked the crisis faced by this 24-year-old woman when the allegations of child sexual abuse arose and has apparently underplayed Ms. D's strengths. Recently out of a rehabilitation program and relatively content with her relationship with Mr. W, she was shocked and dismayed by the report of suspected sexual abuse and wanted to believe her boyfriend. He was the first person to treat her "decently," in her mind, and his willingness and ability to provide financially for her, enabling her to continue her schooling, were of enormous importance to her. In addition, she was not in close contact with her own family of origin and was only just beginning to form new relationships with other adult women her age, as she was so recently back in the community and searching for new, drug-free friendships.

The therapist also did not take into consideration the shortcomings of the foster care system in her area, which, still working on a 19th-century model of placing children outside the city in institutions far from their communities, placed obstacles to more extensive and perhaps effective involvement with the family of the child. This arrangement contributed to the focus on the child as opposed to the child *in* the social context of the family and community.

In addition, Mrs. G's own upbringing made her vulnerable to becoming overidentified with a child such as Josephine. Emotional deprivation in early childhood was mediated by a middle-class upbringing, enabling her to be successful academically with social skills seemingly sufficient to develop sustaining friendships and an intimate relationship. However, the residue from childhood of unmet dependency needs, coupled with the family history of substance abuse, contributed to the unconscious need to rescue Josephine.

Thus, even though Mrs. G was not a victim of childhood sexual abuse herself, her experiences in her own childhood contributed to a tendency to overidentify with a child such as Josephine. Apparently not fully processed in her own therapy and not adequately addressed in supervision, she was at risk for setting in motion a plan, as she did in this case, that was inappropriate because it undervalued the mother's strengths and Ms. D's commitment to parent Josephine. In real life, at the time of the foster care review, Ms. D's lawyer made a successful case for reunifying Josephine with her mother and not having custody go to the grandmother. Ms. D continued in individual therapy, kept her job, and, with the exception of one relapse that was handled through outpatient substance abuse intervention, remained free from substances. Josephine went home on a trial discharge at age 12.

Positive Aspects of Countertransference

In this chapter, I have treated both the "induced" and "personal" countertransference reactions as potential barriers to effective therapy. The manner in which societal influences on women, especially in their roles as mothers, have raised exaggerated expectations about their performance has been discussed. Therapists are encouraged to examine their own relationships and experiences with an eye toward raising their consciousness about the attitudes and attributions they bring to their work with women, especially to their treatment of a woman whose partner has sexually abused her child.

However, as Ruderman (1986) and others (e.g., Casement, 1986) have suggested, there are reparative effects of countertransferential reactions as well. Ruderman suggested that

> women psychotherapists and their patients have a special resonance with one another based, in part, on shared parallel issues and traits, some of which are located in female development and some of which occur by common exposure to sociocultural influences affecting women. (p. 54)

She also suggested that the shared experiences of women therapists and women clients provide the potential for a special empathic bond that can benefit the healing process for both client and therapist. This suggests that therapists need to be sensitive to their reactions not only to assess the potential for negative interactions with the client but also to ensure that beneficial aspects are not overlooked.

Contextual Considerations
in the Engagement of the Mother

In beginning to plan for treatment of the mother in the incest family, the therapist must take into consideration her social context. Although gender is a primary organizing factor and brings with it the array of counter-transference issues discussed earlier, race, ethnicity, class, and her specific family history are important aspects of the woman's social situation.

Race and Ethnicity

The introduction of these factors early on in the discussion of assessment and treatment is meant to underscore their importance. The tendency to decontextualize clients, to speak of "the sexually abused child" and the "nonoffending parent" without reference to the clients' racial, ethnic, class, and cultural heritage, often has the impact of marginalizing these factors in the treatment. These are actually quite complex concepts: As in the case with gender, mental health professionals tend to reflect the dominant values of the larger society. To be culturally competent they need to free themselves from the conditioning of their professional training and accept alternate worldviews (Sue & Sue, 1999). As a starting point therapists need to identify biases in themselves.

It is imperative that the therapist use exploration and assessment skills in developing an understanding of the centrality of race, class, and culture for a given woman, not only in terms of the impact on her but also in terms of the centrality of these factors in how she constructs her reality. As Kliman (1994) has argued, people of color are more oppressed on the basis of race than of gender. She believes that women of color put the oppression by men second to the oppression by Whites of people of color, concurring with Boyd-Franklin (1989) that for Blacks, it is more important for Black women to support their brothers, fathers, and husbands than it is to fight gender-based domination. Until I understood this, it was difficult for me, for example, to understand the position articulated by one of my students. An African American woman coming into social work with the background of an activist, she talked in a women's issues class about how her group of Black feminist friends had been in a dilemma about whom to support in the Anita Hill–Clarence Thomas struggle. She said that the group had decided to support Clarence Thomas, believing that he represented a victory in the battle against White suppression. Implicitly, this reflected their belief that this battle was more significant than the struggle against the oppression of women.

African American, Hispanic, Asian, and other minority group members are overrepresented in the reports of child abuse and neglect (Pelton, 1985) but underrepresented in the community of professionally trained psychotherapists (Vargas & Willis, 1994). This means that women of color are often in the position of turning to or being referred to White, usually middle-class women for help when a partner has sexually abused one of their children. The literature points to a difficulty in engaging clients of color in the mental health system, dominated primarily by White professionals (Vargas & Willis, 1994). In addition, women of color have unique needs, burdened as they are by both sexism and racism, being members of two subordinate groups in American society (Gutierrez, 1990).

Just as women as a group are in a subordinate position to men as a group, so are women of color to White women. As Miller (1983) has eloquently elaborated, one of the characteristics of any subordinate group is that members tend to know the dominant group much better than the dominant group knows or understands them. Women therapists can usually relate to this concept as it applies to their relationships with men: They know more about men than men tend to know about women. However, it is important to recognize that women of color know more about the dominant White culture and therefore more about White therapists than White therapists know about the lives of their clients of color. Women of color may bring a transference reaction that is normative based on their life experiences in mainstream American culture, which is dominated by norms and values affiliated with being Caucasian. As Boyd-Franklin (1989) pointed out in regard to African American women, "In order to survive, black women have become masters in the art of being bicultural . . . learning to comply publicly with white standards has not been as much a choice as a dictate necessary for survival" (p. 29). It would not be unusual for clients of color to bring feelings of anger, mistrust, passivity, or dependence to the treatment situation, based on their subordinate group experience in the culture. It is the job of the clinician to be careful not to misconstrue these as abnormal and mislabel as pathological what may be a very multidetermined and adaptive response in a racist society (Jones, 1979).

Some elaboration may be helpful. For example, for women of Hispanic, particularly Puerto Rican, background, the double standard for men and women may be stronger than it is in mainstream American culture (Comas-Diaz, 1994). The family is held in great esteem, and the role of men and women is culturally proscribed. For example, a "good" woman is patient, forbearing, and loyal. She should put her home and children before anything else. Men are the economic providers, and men prove their virility through the domination of women. Women are supposed to show respect to men, and there is an emphasis on what is good for the family rather than what is good for the individual. Children are taught to respect their elders and to show deference in all social situations. Family members hesitate to take problems outside the family, and informal solutions are often preferred over the interface with formal organizations (Comas-Diaz, 1989; Harper & Lantz, 1996; McKinley, 1987). Consequently, one can see how a woman who learns of suspected incest on the part of her spouse or partner would be particularly vulnerable to a sense of shame. Disclosure outside the family threatens the entire family. It takes family matters public and places the child in the position of challenging an elder's authority.

The Asian woman's position in the family and society is similar. As in the Hispanic culture, the Asian woman is viewed as the nurturer and caretaker and assumes primary responsibility for the children (Chin, 1983, Lee, 1997). The man is seen as the head of the family, and his authority is paramount. As opposed to Western societies, the emphasis is on the community and family as the organizing principle of society. This accentuates the sense of obligation to the family. This is manifest in the desire to maintain family harmony (Bradshaw, 1994). Saving face is an important part of the Asian culture (Sato, 1980), and seeking mental health services may be avoided out of a desire not to shame the family (Sue & McKinney, 1975; Tsui, 1985). The motivation to save face would mitigate against revealing a secret as shameful as sexual abuse, especially if it was the woman's sexual partner who had molested her child. In addition, reticence to seek outside help may be influenced by the belief that distress is caused by a failure of will (Sue & McKinney, 1975) as well as by adherence to the cultural mandate to suffer in silence (Lee, 1997; Kleinman & Lin, 1981; Sue & Morishima, 1982).

African American mothers, with the particular history of African Americans in the culture, bring their own vulnerabilities that may make it difficult for them to trust mental health providers. As Boyd-Franklin (1989) noted, White therapists may have to earn the trust of their African American clients. Unlike other groups, attribution of trust and respect for an authority figure is not as common, due to the specific history of oppression and racism for the African Americans. There is some evidence that African American clients already use mental health systems less than Whites when referred specifically for the treatment of child sexual abuse (Haskett, Nowlan, Hutchinson, & Whitworth, 1991). African Americans are also more likely to use informal helping networks for personal problems, rather than turning to professionals (Chatters, Taylor, & Neighbors, 1989; Neighbors & Jackson, 1984). Taylor (1999) suggests that the "heritage of racism and sexism found within traditional psychological concepts severely limits the effects of therapy"(p. 170). He suggests the use of an Afrocentrist-feminist perspective with African American women. The therapist who is sensitive to this position is better prepared to successfully engage the client.

A return to the case of Miriam and Laurie described earlier may help clarify this. As the reader will recall, Miriam, an African American, was the mother of five who initially had great difficulty believing that her fiancé had sexually molested her 11-year-old daughter.

Miriam's own history included growing up in a two-parent family, but her mother died when Miriam was a teenager. Shortly after her mother's death, an uncle had raped Miriam. She chose not to confide this to anyone, including her father. She suffered in silence, partly out of her unwillingness to burden her grieving father with her experience. She felt that the rape was less traumatic than the death of her mother and that she should be able to handle it by herself. When it happened again, she believed that because she had said nothing the first time, she could not do so now.

Miriam had her five children out of wedlock, and the father of the youngest two, James S (who molested her oldest daughter), was the first to have made a commitment to marriage. Her creation of a family as a single parent could lead to the conclusion that she did not value marriage, but this was not the case. Like many Black teenagers who become mothers out of wedlock (Farber, 1989), Miriam had always had aspirations of marrying and raising a family. And like many other young African American women, her failure to do this had not so much to do with her attitude as the lack of economically stable Black males in her network (Nichols-Casebolt, 1988). Her first child, Laurie, was a product of the sexual molestation by her uncle. Her second and third children were the products of a liaison with an African American man her own age. He lost his low-paying factory job when the company moved out of the inner city where they lived, and, unemployed and depressed, he became involved in drugs and eventually drifted out of Miriam's life.

As Hines (1989) eloquently delineated, for the poor, Black family, the life cycle is often truncated. "Family members leave home, mate, have children and become grandparents at far earlier ages than their middle-class counterparts" (p. 518). Teenagers who become single parents in adolescence often have less time to resolve developmental tasks and are required to assume roles and responsibilities before they are ready.

While she was raising her three children alone, Miriam lived with her father. He had retired on disability and helped her support the children. She also received Aid for Families With Dependent Children (AFDC). James, her fiancé, had stable if low-skilled employment, had made a commitment to marriage, and seemed to Miriam to offer her the lifestyle she had aspired to and valued. Her father, living with her, liked and admired her fiancé and did not believe his granddaughter,

feeling that she had elaborated or embellished certain incidents out of
her jealousy of her mother's relationship.

Miriam's anger and resistance at the time of the initial contact with the therapist need to be understood in the context of her life as an African American
woman. She had never been in therapy before, and her contact with the "helping professionals" had primarily been through her interaction with social service and income maintenance personnel. This staff, overworked and under-
trained, had often treated Miriam in a way that felt impersonal and uncaring,
contributing to her mistrust of formal helping systems.

In addition, her family and friends were skeptical of the report by the
White school counselor and the investigation being undertaken by the White
caseworker. The referral to the White therapist was likely to work only if the
therapist could communicate an appreciation of the social context within
which she lived and had been raised, in addition to an appreciation of the gender influences noted earlier. As described in Chapter 2, the therapist did
struggle initially with a negative countertransference reaction but, with help
from her supervisor, overcame that and was able to engage and work with
Miriam.

Another variable to take into consideration when working with women
of color is their immigration status (Austin, 2000; van der Veer, 1998, and
Sparks & Park, 2000). Their status may contribute not only to a fear of connection to formal systems, especially if they are undocumented persons, but
also to the degree to which they are acculturated. Because many Asian, Latin
American, and Caribbean cultures hold to a more traditional, male-domi-
nant sex role orientation than does mainstream American culture (Comas-
Diaz & Greene, 1994; Jones, 1979; Lorenzo & Adler, 1984), a newer immigrant may hold more patriarchal views of the role of men and women than a
more acculturated person. For the mother in the incest family, this status
may affect the degree to which she feels that she can accept a challenge to her
husband or partner, as well as the degree to which she feels comfortable being
engaged with the formal helping system. Immigration is a major factor in a
woman's psychological difficulties, not the least of which is that the woman
has often moved from being a member of a "majority" group in her country
of origin to being a member of a "minority" group in the United States. Strategies in working with immigrant women need to take into consideration
their social, political, and economic condition.

Whatever the cultural or ethnic background of the client, it is helpful if
the therapist gathers a detailed history, paying particular attention to pat-

terns of immigration with attendant separation and loss that are part of the individual and communal life stories of many women of color. When women of color are constantly dealing with oppressive institutions and racist individuals, it is not unusual for them to be guarded and lack openness to the therapeutic encounter with a representative of the dominant culture. Assessing this stance as "pathological" without exploration may lead to difficulties in engaging the client.

The other caveat is to be equally sensitive to the fact that Black women are not a monolithic group, nor are Hispanics, Asians, or any other group. Consultation with therapists of similar ethnic or racial roots may help the therapist raise her consciousness about some of the communal characteristics; each client's story must be explored in detail individually.

Class

Just as race and ethnicity affect a woman's experience with family sexual abuse, so does class (Minuchin, 1998). The dynamic interaction of gender, race, ethnicity, class origins, and an individual's personal and family history profoundly shapes a woman's reaction to the sexual abuse of her child. Class, therefore, cannot be ignored. Of particular interest to the therapist is the mother's knowledge and attitudes about sexuality in general and about deviancy in particular. Also of concern are attitudes toward therapy and the specific economic and financial constraints of a woman's living situation.

Class has been found to mediate all three variables: attitude toward sexuality (Farber, 1989), attitude toward therapy, and attitude toward the ability to master one's environment, although the interaction of race and class is not always easy to sort out (Moore, Simms, & Betsey, 1986). From what has been studied, it appears that attitudes toward therapy vary with class. In a comparative study of attitudes toward seeking professional help for personal problems, Kulka, Veroff, and Douvan (1979) found that "readiness for self-referral" increased from 1957 to 1976 in the general population. However, social class differences persisted in determining whether a person defined a problem as relevant for professional help, with those from the lower socioeconomic levels less likely to seek professional help for a problem. More recent studies illustrate that class differences continue to exist.

Helper, Quesda, and Chalfant (1983), in a study of perception of deviant behavior, found that social class strongly predicted whether deviant behavior would be defined as a mental health problem. Menicucci and Wermuth (1989) criticized the lack of attention to class and gender in the family treatment of drug-abusing individuals, highlighting the importance of social class in effective therapy. Bowen and Richman (1991) identified three clusters of variables from the literature that contributed to whether husbands and wives sought counseling for a marital or family problem. Results of their study indicated that, among other things, years of formal education were a significant predictor of the potential use of counseling services. In posttreatment studies, Collings and King (1994) found that social class was a significant predictor of favorable outcomes.

There is some indication that lower-class women, for example, are much more likely to relate to therapists as the experts and to expect guidance and advice from them, much as they do from medical doctors. In fact, medical doctors may be the model most lower-class women draw on in their initial attempt to understand the role of therapists. In engaging such a woman, it may be important to provide guidance and direction because this will fit with the expectations the woman often brings to the therapist. Help with concrete assistance during the engagement phase may also be crucial to making a connection. In addition, women with limited or no experience with therapy may need education about what therapy is: what the therapist expects and what the client can expect. The need for these strategies for women from lower socioeconomic classes cannot be overemphasized. They can be understood as a way of meeting the client "halfway" and may prove invaluable in engaging women in treatment.

Financial constraints are an extremely important variable. The mother who is living on Temporary Assistance for Needy Families (TANF) or whose husband has ceased supporting the family because of the allegations often has extreme financial pressures. Mothers in this category are either temporarily or permanently single mothers, and, as we know, economic stress is the single biggest burden for single parents. This reality cannot be minimized. One must be careful not to interpret missed appointments or the inability to obtain child care as "resistance." It is crucial to examine the social and financial supports in her life that may interfere with her ability to keep office-based appointments. The case of Doris may help to illustrate some of the issues presented by a lower-class woman who is referred for treatment following a disclosure of sexual abuse.

CASE STUDY

Doris, an Irish American woman from a lower working-class background, was in her second marriage when her 14-year-old daughter, Marissa, disclosed that her stepfather was sexually abusing her and had been for 5 years. The second oldest of two girls, Marissa alleged that the abuse had started prior to the marriage 6 years earlier and had involved her 15-year-old sister, Suzanne, as well. Suzanne denied the allegations, as did Louis, her husband. Doris did not believe Marissa. As a result, both girls were removed and placed in foster care. The case was prosecuted in both family and criminal court, and Doris was mandated to treatment by the family court. She came for the initial appointment 3 months after the report to Child Protective Services (CPS), saying that she was only there because she "had to be."

Doris had grown up in an alcoholic family, where her father was violent and physically abusive to her mother when he had been drinking. He had left the family when Doris was 11. Of significance was that Doris had no memories of her childhood up to age 11. She became pregnant when she was 13, and Suzanne was born when she was 14. The father of both Suzanne and Marissa was an unemployed substance abuser who was physically abusive. Louis, who "used to be an alcoholic," was not drinking or abusing substances during their marriage, nor was he violent. He had worked steadily as a mailman during the course of their marriage and always managed to support the family.

Doris had never been in therapy. She had received AFDC for much of her adult life but had managed to take advantage of training opportunities to become certified as a homemaker. She was working as a homemaker when she was referred for treatment. Her family's attitude toward mental health echoed her own, which was that going for therapy meant you were "crazy." She had resisted coming to therapy and voiced at the intake that she did not see how coming for treatment was going to help her get her girls home, which was her major concern.

In the first session, Doris appeared frightened and guarded. She wore her long dark hair so that it covered her face. Depressed affect was evident, as well as a sense of helplessness and hopelessness. Doris thought that the therapist, a clinical social worker, was just her new "worker." The role of the therapist, her background, and the purpose of therapy had to be explained to Doris. For example, when the therapist explained that it was her job to help Doris with her concerns and to be there for her, Doris said that it was the first time in the investigation process that she felt she was not being blamed.

Months into treatment, Doris began to feel free to share her thinking about her sexual relationship with Louis and revealed much about her attitudes toward sexuality. Like many women of her class

> background, she defined oral and anal sex as "immoral." Doris resisted Louis's requests for sexual interaction in this fashion, and she had later blamed herself for the sexual abuse of Marissa because she felt that her attitude toward sex had "turned Louis off."

Like many women of her class background, Doris had no experience with therapy, and both her attitude and the attitudes of family and friends in her social network were negative, based largely on ignorance and myth. This created a potential barrier to treatment. Likewise, her attitudes toward sexuality had deepened her own sense of responsibility for the abuse, increasing guilt and self-blame. These feelings were strongly defended against during the initial investigative process. Her defenses, primarily of denial, contributed to her being viewed as a resistant and unprotective client by the investigation staff. Doris was still in crisis and somewhat immobilized at the time of her initial contact with the therapist. By assuming a nonjudgmental stance and taking into consideration her limited knowledge of the therapeutic process and her likely attribution of self-blame for the incest, the therapist was able to engage Doris in a healing process.

Work History

In our moneyed economy, working and generating income are not only necessary for most adults during most of their adulthood but are also a source of self-esteem and self-worth. For the mother in the incest family, her employment history and market economy competitiveness in terms of employability often become crucial. Her ability to be competitive in the workforce is tied not only to her need to generate income because of the single-parent status noted earlier but also because lack of job skills or meaningful employment may increase low self-esteem. Issues around job training and child care may thus gain increased salience. Inability to resolve these satisfactorily often contributes to ongoing depression and lack of motivation accompanied by the concomitant difficulties in getting herself or her children to therapy appointments. The case of Teresa, a Hispanic single parent, may help illustrate how financial issues affect both self-esteem and the stress of managing daily tasks.

> Teresa was attending a community college when she was referred for treatment due to the sexual abuse of her 4-year-old daughter by her

live-in boyfriend. Teresa had separated from him at the time of the disclosure and was able within a short period of time (approximately 6 weeks) to accept the fact of the abuse, as her daughter Elana made more specific disclosures.

Teresa was not working but enrolled in an associate degree program at the time of the referral for treatment, approximately 2 months after the disclosure. She was highly motivated to complete her education but was feeling overwhelmed and unsure if she could manage work, school, and family responsibilities.

No longer receiving financial support from her ex-boyfriend, she was struggling with how to generate an income. She needed to work, but if she gave up her full-time status in the college program, she would not be eligible for the inexpensive and high-quality child care the college provided. If she went to school only part-time, it meant making new child care arrangements. Still reeling from the recent disclosure, she was ambivalent about placing her daughter in a new, unknown child care setting where, as she said, "I don't know whom to trust now, and I'm scared of leaving her with strangers."

Teresa was very erratic in her initial attendance in treatment, missing and canceling appointments for herself often and not always getting her daughter to her therapy appointments. The mother's therapist, attuned to the stresses caused by the family's new financial situation, arranged to have her daughter's appointment and her own at the same time, eliminating the need for Teresa to make trips twice a week. The therapist also assisted Teresa with finding a new day care setting. This help was not only concrete—by providing her with the name of a local registry of day care providers—but also helped Teresa explore her fears about a new setting and provided a forum for her to evaluate her choices.

The clue to the therapist's effective engagement was her ability to focus on the real-life concerns of Teresa in the initial phase of treatment. A less-experienced therapist might have felt the need to push for exploration of Teresa's feelings about the sexual abuse, her separation from her boyfriend, and her ability to be empathic to her daughter. By framing the initial sessions around Teresa's concerns, she was nonetheless able to weave in her own agenda (and the agenda of the referral source) without disrupting the fragile new alliance with Teresa.

Individual and Family History

History of Sexual Abuse

Of particular importance is the mother's own family of origin, especially when the mother has a history of incest in her own family. Given the high prevalence of family sexual abuse among the normal population (Russell, 1986), the low level of disclosure, and the scarce therapeutic resources for adult survivors who cannot access the private practice marketplace, it is not unusual for a mother who is a survivor not to have had any treatment that would have helped her resolve some of her own issues. Recent research suggests that although a history of childhood sexual abuse does not predict a less supportive or protective attitude for the child (Deblinger et al., 1994), it does suggest that therapy can address crucial issues. In their study of 183 nonoffending mothers, with 83 reporting a history of childhood sexual abuse and 100 reporting no such history, the mothers did not differ on the following factors: previously having sought therapy, substance abuse, medical difficulties, adult sexual assault, domestic violence, believing their children's allegations, acting as advocates for the children, and their perceptions of people's responses as helpful. The two groups of mothers did differ significantly with regard to the extent to which they felt they were facing the crisis alone and with regard to their level of symptom distress as measured by the 90-item Symptom Checklist Revised (SCL-90-R) (Derogatis, 1983). The mothers with a history of childhood sexual abuse felt more alone and were more symptomatic, but they still believed their children and acted protectively as often as mothers without a history of sexual abuse. These results supported those of Gomes-Schwartz (1990), who found in her study of 156 nonoffending mothers that mothers with a history of child sexual abuse did not respond differently to the disclosure by their children than mothers without such a history.

Timmons-Mitchell et al.'s (1996) more recent study supports and explicates the finding of Deblinger et al. (1994) in regard to the mother's experience of the disclosure as traumatic. Although this was a small sample (28 mothers), which affects the generalizability of the findings, results indicate that mothers of sexually abused children who were abused themselves as children manifest a greater degree of symptom distress than nonoffending mothers without such a history. All 28 mothers experienced high levels of posttraumatic stress when measured on the Purdue Posttraumatic Stress Disorder—Revised (PPTSD—R) Scale (Lauterbach & Vrana, 1996). However, findings on an additional measure, the Crime-Related Posttraumatic Stress

Disorder (PTSD) Scale, derived from the SCL-90-R (Derogatis, 1983), clearly indicate that mothers with a history of child sexual abuse are more affected by the sexual abuse of their own children, as manifested by greater levels of posttraumatic distress symptoms, than mothers without childhood sexual victimization in their history.

The following case example illustrates the interaction of the dynamic of a history of childhood sexual abuse at the time that a daughter disclosed that her mother's live-in boyfriend had molested her.

> Miriam, as noted earlier, had been repeatedly raped as a teenager by an uncle. The molestation of Miriam had occurred with the use of physical force and verbal threats, resulting in bruises and tears in her genital area. Miriam was enraged with this person as a result, and one of her reactions was to avoid talking to her uncle when he was at family gatherings. At the time of the allegations by her daughter, while asking her partner (James) to leave the home in response to an ultimatum set forth by CPS, she was ambivalent about whether to believe her daughter. Part of her difficulty was that her daughter's behavior toward the perpetrator did not fit her paradigm for how one who has been sexually abused responds. Miriam's daughter, Laurie, did not act "hateful" toward her fiancé, the alleged perpetrator. Laurie not only talked to James but would also "play up" to him. There were also no medical findings, and Laurie had never complained of any pain or discomfort.
>
> On intake, Miriam presented with anxiety, as manifested by loss of concentration, insomnia, intrusive thoughts, and heightened mistrust. Miriam had never disclosed her own abuse prior to her daughter's disclosure and had not received any treatment. Although acting protectively, her difficulty in believing her daughter was partially a result of her inability in resolving her own traumatic experiences. This set the stage for her ambivalent reaction, in which she switched back and forth between cognitive acceptance of the abuse and emotional disbelief.

In addition to the history of childhood sexual victimization that colored her perceptions, she also was affected by her relationship with the perpetrator in predictable ways. As discussed in Chapter 1, recent research has indicated that women who are involved in more satisfactory short-term relationships with a partner may have more trouble believing that the abuse occurred. Gomes-Schwartz (1990) undertook one of the largest-scale studies to date, examining the personality characteristics and reactions to disclosure of sexual abuse in a sample of 156 mothers of sexually abused children. She found that the mothers

CASE STUDY

were "least protective and the most angry when the abuser was not the natural father but a step-father or boyfriend" (Gomes-Schwartz, 1990, p. 117).

This echoed the findings of Everson et al. (1989), who in their exploration of maternal support following disclosure discovered that a strong relationship existed between level of support and relationship with the perpetrator. The more recent and intense a relationship with the offender—typically in the case of a boyfriend or live-in partner, rather than the long-term relationship more characteristic of marriage—the less likely for maternal support to exist following the disclosure of child sexual abuse. They hypothesized that "the child's disclosure may represent a threat to the potential for increased emotional and financial support that a new relationship offers compared to the problems and uncertainties of single parenthood" (Everson et al., 1989, p. 205).

Miriam clearly fit the profile outlined in these two studies, as well as being consistent with that of a mother with a history of child sexual abuse. She had a relatively recent relationship with James, and the intensity was illustrated by the fact that he had moved in just 6 months previously. In her case, the treatment needed to focus on crisis intervention, help relieve the posttraumatic stress symptoms, and then move on to ego-supportive therapy. In the course of treatment, she would need help with the aftereffects of her own abuse, but even in the initial stages, she was helped to reduce some of the cognitive distortions she held about the "typical" reaction of a sexual abuse victim.

Intimate Partner Violence

Another dynamic commonly associated with incestuous families is intimate partner violence. Although not causative, there is an association between battering and sexual abuse (Finkelhor, Gelles, Hotaling, & Straus, 1983). We know now that the scope of the problem of wife abuse is quite large, totaling at least 2 million women being battered by a spouse or intimate partner every year. In 1993, intimate partners perpetrated 22% of violent acts against women (Jasinski & Williams, 1998). For a fuller understanding of the dynamics and issues involved in working with battered women, the reader is referred to the work of Davies (1994), hooks (1989), Jasinski and Williams (1998), Kirkwood (1993), and Williams and Becker (1994).

We also know more about the psychological consequences of battering. We know that among women who are abused, physical acts of violence may be infrequent or episodic. Nonetheless, they often live in a climate of control and coercion in which they are subject to the use of threats, intimidation, emotional abuse, isolation, having children used against them, and economic abuse (preventing or keeping a woman from getting a job, making her ask for money, taking her money, etc.). We also know of a correlation between sexual assault and intimate partner violence (Finkelhor & Yllö, 1985; Russell, 1990). The impact of the trauma of physical or sexual assault is also better understood, manifesting what has been called the "damaged self" (Herman, 1992). As a result of the trauma, the secure sense of connection with caring people is disrupted, and the autonomy of the person at the level of basic bodily integrity is violated. This can result in feelings of guilt and mistaken beliefs that one could have done better or might have avoided the situation. These beliefs may be sustained by the individual because they are more tolerable than the reality of utter helplessness (Janoff-Bulman, 1992).

The dialectic of the trauma, the back and forth that goes on between the symptoms of intrusion (flashbacks, dreams, phobias, and other anxiety symptoms) and constriction (the numbing of affect), may cause the woman both to withdraw from relationships and to seek them desperately. The disruption in basic trust and the feelings of shame, guilt, and inferiority foster withdrawal from close relationships. The terror of the traumatic events intensifies the need for protective attachments, resulting in the oscillation between isolation and anxious clinging.

Having an abusive partner may deepen the crisis of disclosure for the woman (Walker, 1985). She may realistically fear physical harm if she separates or fails to believe him if he denies the sexual abuse allegations. If she does separate, she may need to live in a protected environment such as a shelter or else live with the daily fear of attack, even if she has obtained an order of protection. In these circumstances, when a basic sense of personal safety cannot be achieved, the woman may not be able to mobilize her emotional resources to attend therapy on a regular basis. Sometimes her preoccupation with the actions of the batterer and the oscillation noted earlier can be mistaken for resistance to engaging in treatment around the sexual abuse issues. They may even be interpreted as an inability to protect her children, as the following case illustrates.

Gina, age 26, was married to a 46-year-old man, John, whom she had met when she was 16. He was divorced from his first wife, with whom he had had a son, now 23, and a daughter, now 20. Married at 18, Gina had a 7-year-old daughter with John at the time of the report of suspected sexual abuse. She reported a history of battering for much of

CASE STUDY

her married life. She said that the physical assaults were infrequent but had increased lately. She described verbal harassment, including repeated, demeaning name-calling and swearing at her in front of her children. She also described how her husband had tried to control many aspects of her life, including keeping control of all their finances and limiting her access to family and friends. Two incidents of battering had been especially severe. On one occasion, John had broken her nose, and on another, he had slashed her upper arm with a knife.

Gina separated from John following the report by her daughter, Cathy, that John had been fondling her genitals and asking Cathy to perform oral sex. He was initially compliant with the CPS investigation, denying the allegations but voluntarily agreeing to leave the house. About a week later, he broke into the house at night and threatened to kill her if she did not let him have custody of Cathy. Gina, fearing that her life was threatened, allowed him to take Gina. For 5 days, she took no action.

CPS made a home visit at the end of that time and, on finding that Cathy was with her father, took steps that resulted in the county taking custody of Cathy and placing her in foster care. They also moved to name Gina as a respondent in a family court action, declaring that she was neglectful because she had failed to act to protect Gina from her father.

This action by the county increased Gina's sense that she could not trust authority figures. She was enraged at the county's action and agreed to seek treatment only because she thought it would appease CPS. Her anger at the county was transferred to the therapist, whom she viewed as an extension of the county and thus insensitive to her position.

The therapist was aware that the county's action had made the engagement process more difficult. Gina's ability to trust was severely challenged because Gina did not believe that the therapist could understand the impact of John's threats on her or could truly care about her position. In addition, she was truly terrified of what John might do next. A woman who was used to a middle-income lifestyle, Gina was unwilling to seek respite in a battered women's shelter, rightly or wrongly seeing this as a place for "poor" women. She moved in briefly with her mother, attending sessions regularly, and then dropped out of sight.

Within 3 weeks, the therapist heard from Gina. Gina told her that she had become even more afraid of John, as criminal charges of assault against him were pending, and she therefore had left the state. She did not plan to return until the day of the trial. This occurred approximately 6 weeks later, at which time John's case was successfully prosecuted, resulting in his being incarcerated for 6 months to a year. During those 9 weeks, Gina did not see her children, nor was she able to be in consistent telephone contact. The county viewed this as an additional indication of inadequate parenting, believing that there were alternatives she could have chosen to leaving the state. The family court matter against her proceeded.

Mills (1996) argued that a dogmatic approach to battered women that stresses that a woman must leave the relationship is not the most useful. She notes that the economic and social reality for poor women (and many women of color fall into this category) mitigates against their leaving. She also highlights the norms, such as family honor and other cultural barriers that decrease the woman's sense of legitimacy about abandoning a spouse or partner. She argues that social workers need to develop interventions that take into account the importance of relationships to women, even if they include violence. The actions of county agencies in Gina's case reflect the kind of perspective that can undermine a woman's trust in authority. She had many strengths, but the terror of the abuse and potential for harm to herself were overwhelming.

Gina returned to therapy after her husband's conviction and used the initial 6 months of treatment to gain support for the family court hearing and to deal with her grief over being separated from her children. The focus on the sexual abuse, although intertwined with these issues (especially in regard to feelings of powerlessness and betrayal), needed to wait explicit focus until her life with her children had become more stabilized. This case illustrates the significance of a life-threatening condition, such as living with a man who is physically abusive, and highlights the need to address this in therapy before expecting the woman to be able to focus on the incest and its meaning for herself and her child.

The relevance for the clinician of working with a mother in a family sexual abuse situation in which the woman has had the experience of intimate partner violence is that the traumagenic dynamics of powerlessness (particularly the feelings of helplessness), stigmatization, and possibly betrayal will be heightened. Using an approach that deals with her immediate social needs as well as one that addresses the psychological impact of the trauma will probably be the most successful.

Children With Special Needs

A factor that may make a child vulnerable to abuse and also make a mother more emotionally depleted is the presence of special needs—whether psychological, intellectual, medical, or a combination of these—in her child. It is now well documented that children with intellectual, physical, or emotional deficits appear to be more vulnerable to sexual molestation (Sgroi, 1988). Not only are they at greater risk, but their mothers are also more likely to be highly stressed, due to the increase in demands of caring for a disabled child. When the mother is also functioning as a single parent, as is often the case following the disclosure of sexual abuse, interventions need to take into account the special structure of the single-parent family and of the special demands, including the role strain that may make it difficult to perform all the necessary family functions.

A single parent will, even without the difficulties of a special needs child, experience demands that will vary with the age of the child. Women with preschool-age children face taxing demands for attention and time. A child who is disabled can drain the mother's strength, and if there are other children, she may be less available to them. Women who become single parents as the result of separation or divorce, especially if they hold traditional sex role orientations, often experience particular difficulty as they take on additional functions.

The case of Elaine, with a 10-year-old daughter, Karen, may serve to illustrate some of these issues.

CASE STUDY

Elaine, an African American woman (age 30), was referred for treatment following a disclosure by Karen that Elaine's live-in boyfriend (whom she planned to marry) had molested her. Karen, who could only get around on crutches due to her condition of cerebral palsy, had reported that James, her mother's boyfriend, had begun by fondling her thighs, telling Karen that he was helping her do "therapy" for her legs. This had progressed to fondling her genitals and inserting a finger into her vagina.

James had moved out following the disclosure. Because Elaine claimed that she had broken off the relationship, the county took the position that it could not proceed with a family court action against

James because he was no longer part of the household. The district attorney's office was unwilling to prosecute criminally, feeling that it did not have a good witness. In fact, Elaine was ambivalent about taking this action against James and was very reluctant to have Karen go through the process of a criminal trial.

In treatment, Elaine complained about the burden of being a single parent again, with all the responsibilities of supporting herself and Karen and getting Karen to the special programs she needed. These included Karen's special schooling, physical therapy, and weekly speech therapy appointments. She confided that James had admitted to her that he had touched Karen and had apologized and was very remorseful. Although enraged at James, Elaine was still considering continuing the relationship with him after "things died down."

In her case, participation in a mothers group was crucial to her ability to be engaged around the incest issues. She was a bright, verbal client who had had therapy previously and was well equipped to move quickly into a group. In fact, she welcomed the opportunity. This experience of sharing with other women in the same situation and of gaining additional support strengthened the part of her that was outraged at James's behavior. She moved to a position of considering that she would reunite only if James sought treatment. Fortunately, he was willing to do so.

This case might have turned out very differently. The therapist was able early on to communicate a sense of trust, enabling Elaine to confide her thoughts about reuniting with James. Had the therapist not been able to see that Elaine was "sitting on the fence," with the chance of going in either direction due to the environmental pressures she faced, she might not have moved so quickly to mobilize the strengths Elaine had. Elaine's outrage at James was a healthy sign. Through the intervention of the group, the therapist was able to provide sufficient support so that Elaine could more realistically evaluate her involvement in the relationship with James, including what she wanted to demand of him.

This support included sensitivity to her needs as a parent of a disabled child, in addition to a great deal of appreciation and praise for the job she was doing in raising Karen. The positive steps she had taken all along Karen's development were often acknowledged and underscored by group members, raising Elaine's self-esteem when she badly needed it, and enabled her to get on with her decision-making process.

Substance Abuse

A final issue that must be taken into consideration is the mother's history of drug or alcohol abuse. Again this must be heard and evaluated within the matrix of gender, class, race, and cultural considerations and norms of the mother. First and foremost, it is important for the clinician to be aware of gender differences in substance abusers. When alcohol is the major substance, women generally start to drink later than men do, and their alcohol-related difficulties emerge later than for men. Women's lives are more disrupted, and spontaneous remission occurs less frequently. For women, drinking is more likely to be associated with the use of mood altering, and the majority of alcoholic women exhibit symptoms of depression or anxiety and report more problems with regulation of self-esteem than men do. Leifer et al. (1993), who conducted a study of mothers of sexually abused girls, found that substance abuse (and dissatisfaction with social support) was significantly correlated with lack of maternal support to the child and more abuse incidents. The more abuse incidents, the greater the degree of symptomology and the greater the likelihood that a child enters the foster care system. In addition, maternal history of abuse or poor childhood attachment relationships was positively associated with current maternal substance abuse. These findings are supported by Fullilove et al. (1993), whose study of women drug users found an association between intimate partner violence, trauma, and posttraumatic disorder among maternal substance abusers. Thus, maternal substance abuse can have severe consequences for the child.

There are three ways in which the history of substance abuse becomes critical in the treatment of mothers of sexually abused children. First, the mother may have a history of substance abuse that has gone unrecognized. In many cases, the disclosure of family sexual abuse and the intervention by outside agencies have precipitated the referral for therapy that might otherwise not have taken place. Thus, it is often the first time that a woman has sought professional help. Even if the mother has been in therapy before, this is no guarantee that the therapist has recognized the substance abuse. Due to the denial that is a hallmark of substance abuse, there are, of course, other reasons that the mother's condition has gone untreated—she may have never sought treatment in the first place, for example. Thus, the first task is to carefully assess for substance abuse. Specific strategies and techniques for doing this are beyond the scope of this book, but if the reader needs information, he or she is encouraged to turn to the quite substantial body of literature now available as well as to consult with local experts in his or her agency or area.

The second issue arises when the client has recognized the problem of substance abuse and is in recovery. The crisis of the disclosure of sexual abuse may stimulate a relapse. The therapist should anticipate this with clients if there is a history and focus on reinforcing cognitive-behavioral strategies that the clients can use to help themselves avoid this as well as urging closer contact with an Alcoholics Anonymous (AA) or Narcotics Anonymous (NA) sponsor or group meetings. This referral can be confounded by the mother's unwillingness to divulge the fact of the sexual abuse to other potentially supportive figures due to the sense of stigmatization. In that instance, the therapist may need to consider the benefit (and her ability) to offer more sessions to the mother during this time of crisis. If the client does have a relapse, it is important to help the client reenter a substance abuse program. Psychotherapy aimed at dealing with the incest issues will need to be adjusted to the woman's phase of readiness to address the substance abuse issues.

It is increasingly important that mental health professionals become knowledgeable about the harm reduction approach to substance abuse treatment. As dissatisfaction with dropout rates in abstinence-oriented chemical dependency programs has grown (Porochaska, Declementa, & Norcross, 1992), an approach acknowledging that people are at different points in their motivation to change has gained recognition. The harm reduction model acknowledges that people need to go through stages of recognizing that they have a problem and consider how they are going to address this. Because people are at different stages, interventions must be tailored to their individual needs. Feedback from a substance abuse provider about the woman's readiness to address her substance abuse issues is key to any treatment plan for the mother in terms of the sexual abuse issues.

The third possibility is that a history of drug or alcohol abuse may have been a significant part of the client's past history and affected the mother-child relationship in a way that becomes particularly important at the time of the disclosure. One common situation is that of mothers who have lost custody of their children, often early in the child's life, if not at infancy. For the past two decades, in major urban areas particularly, the rate of infants born with a positive toxicology due to mothers' abuse of crack and cocaine has risen dramatically (Halfon, 1990). There is a population of mothers of sexually abused children whose relationship with their children has been disrupted because the children are currently in or have been in foster care because of neglect due to the mothers' drug abuse. In some of these instances, the child has made a disclosure after he or she has been in care; in other instances, the abuse occurs after the child has been reunited with the mother. In

this category of cases, the mother's substance abuse may not be an active issue, but because it was the reason for her separation from her child or children, it carries significant meaning. An example is the case of Mary.

Mary was a 29-year-old White unmarried woman with a 4½-year-old
daughter. She came from a working-class Italian background and was
supporting herself with public assistance while she tried to complete
her associate degree at a local community college. Her daughter was
sexually abused by her live-in boyfriend of 2 years. Mary had been in a
relationship with him at the time her daughter returned to live with
her.

Mary almost immediately believed her daughter and was supportive of treatment for herself and her daughter. She presented with severe self-blame and guilt in the initial sessions. In obtaining her history,
it emerged that she had twice been incarcerated as a result of drug-
related crimes. In fact, she had been separated from her daughter from
her daughter's birth to the time she was 2½ due to her use of drugs.
Since the reunification with her daughter, she had struggled with becoming the parent. This had involved coping with the fact that her
daughter did not view her, psychologically, as her mother at the time of
reunification and was only now beginning to accept this. It also meant
struggling with the concrete demands of parenting a preschool-age
child.

At the time of disclosure, Mary learned that the sexual abuse (fondling and oral-genital contact) had been going on for almost a year. She
was horrified that her daughter had not told her sooner and blamed
her separation from her, along with the fact that her daughter did not
trust her, for the lapse of time in reporting. She blamed herself for her
abuse of drugs and participation in the drug culture. Her degree of despair was so profound that although she did not relapse, she required
medication for depression and extra support to help her through the
time of crisis.

The instructive lesson in Mary's story is that one's self-blame and the "normal" emergence of a feeling of stigmatization can be exacerbated by a client's
beliefs about herself and the destructive role that substance abuse plays, not
only in her past but also in the derivative effects on her current functioning.

This chapter has attempted to highlight some of the contextual considerations in the evaluation of the mother in an incest family. It has stressed the

relevance of the impact of ethnic, racial, and class considerations on the meaning the mother attaches to the disclosure and on one's "readiness" for professional help. It also has underscored the need for the therapist to place these considerations in the foreground to adequately and accurately assess and engage the client. Beyond that, this chapter has considered the relevance of work history, and the special contributions of a woman's family of origin and current family status are discussed, noting the importance of a history of sexual abuse, battering, and substance abuse, as well as the unique challenges for a mother with a handicapped or developmentally disabled child. The next chapter looks more specifically at the techniques and processes that can be used in undertaking an assessment.

Evaluating the Mother and Planning for Treatment

Introduction to a Treatment Approach

In this chapter and the next three chapters, I will elaborate a treatment approach that is offered as a *conceptual road map* for the clinician. This chapter is not intended to be a prescription for treatment, and, in fact, as noted earlier, interventions would need to be more precisely specified and outcomes tested before one could assert that this approach rises to the level of a treatment model. That being said, the following outlines a process that encompasses a thorough assessment and a number of treatment phases. Although the notion of engagement was introduced in the previous chapter, it is elaborated here.

The six phases of the approach are (1) starting engagement and assessment, (2) beginning early intervention around traumatic effects, (3) strengthening coping capacities, (4) surfacing traumatic effects of the incest behavior, (5) identifying relationship consequences of the incest behavior, and (6) working through and resolution. The approach presupposes that the nature of the disclosure of an incestuous relationship between the woman's child and her partner is stressful and often rises to the level of a traumatic event. Applying the definition of a traumatic event used in the *Diagnostic and Statistical Manual,* fourth revision *(DSM-IV)* (American Psychiatric Association, 1994), both of the following characteristics of the disclosure event must be present: It *confronted* the woman with *a threat to the physical integrity of others,* and the woman's *response involved intense fear, helplessness, or horror.* When the woman (a) reacts to the disclosure with the persistent reexperiencing of the event (through distressing recollections, distressing dreams, or other symptoms), (b) persistently avoids stimuli associated with the disclosure, (c) experiences persistent symptoms of increased arousal, (d) the disturbance lasts more than 1 month, and (e) the disturbance causes clinically significant distress in social, occupational, or other areas of functioning, the woman's reaction meets the *DSM-IV* criteria for posttraumatic stress disorder.

Even if the symptom level does not meet the criteria for a *DSM-IV* diagnosis, traumatic effects are often present. It is appropriate to approach the mother as one would a secondary victim of a traumatic event. Secondary victims are defined as those whose distress results from either witnessing or being confronted with "an event or events that involved . . . a threat to the physical integrity of . . . others" (American Psychiatric Association, 1994, p. 209). Other examples of secondary victims would be partners of rape victims and children of domestic violence victims. Thus, before one delves into the process of reworking the affective responses and cognitive distortions that usually accompany the traumatic event and assist in the reduction of role conflict, it is important to stabilize the woman and strengthen ego functioning as much as possible.

Phases 3 through 6 may be revolving phases; that is, certain effects may be worked through before the need or capacity to address others can be faced. A woman may identify the impact of the betrayal (Phase 2) and decide to trust her instincts more (Phases 3 and 4). She may be ready to accept her child's reaction and work with it more directly (Phases 5 and 6), only to find that it raises new issues for herself in dealing with a new intimate partner. She may thus find herself back to Phase 3 and a new cycle of work.

Each phase is elaborated in more detail in this and subsequent chapters. This chapter will focus on Phase 1: engagement and assessment. The subsequent chapters describe how individual, group, and family treatment can be used in a treatment process that emphasizes early intervention around traumatic effects, strengthening coping capacities, surfacing traumatic effects, identifying the impact of traumatic effects on significant relationships, and working them through.

Treatment with incest family members is often most effective when it is *long term* (more than 6 months) and *intensive*. Although it may be possible for some specialized treatment programs to still offer such long-term care, this may not be universally possible. In an environment of managed care and short-term therapy, treatment may need to occur over time and in stages, broken by time away from therapy. This approach takes that into consideration. *Intensive* refers to the presence of multimodality treatment or the availability of individual, group, conjoint, and family therapy. It may be difficult for an individual program or therapist to provide this. To the extent possible, given the particulars of any given case, it is often important to arrange for other than individual treatment of family members.

In this chapter, I seek to answer the following question: What is different in undertaking an evaluation of a mother in an incest family from conducting a typical psychosocial assessment? What is suggested here is an elaboration of a basic biopsychosocial assessment, in which physical (medical), psychological, and social functioning are evaluated. Based on current research and practice experience, three aspects need to be emphasized in an assessment: (a) assessing for traumatic effects, (b) evaluating the competency of the woman in her social roles as mother and wife, and (c) developing a sexual history. The initial clinical assessment should answer a number of basic questions that focus primarily on the mother's reaction to the disclosure, her psychosocial functioning, and her strengths and tools for coping as well as tensions and conflicts that limit and complicate effective functioning.

The tendency on referral for treatment, particularly if the referral to a mental health professional comes from Child Protective Services (CPS) following a disclosure of sexual abuse, is to look for the problems and inadequacies that led to the mother being unable to protect her children or that contribute to her being less than fully believing or fully available to her children. The concern at the time of referral may be on a woman's role as a mother and not for her as an individual in crisis. The goal of the referral, in fact, is often to "fix" the mother so she functions better in her parenting role. Part of the reason for this emphasis in a referral may come from the misattribution of the cause of the sexual abuse.

It is important for the therapist to remember that although coordination with other intervening systems is critical in these cases and protective issues may be a concern, the therapist is functioning in his or her role as a clinician.

As such, the focus needs to be on what the woman's needs are, and they may be on stabilizing her own emotional reactions, some of which will relate to her role as a parent, but not all. The approach outlined assumes that until ruled out, a mother referred for treatment soon after the disclosure of child sexual abuse is in crisis and may be suffering from traumatic effects.

In general, two areas of inquiry need to be addressed initially: the impact of the trauma and the strengths and vulnerabilities she brings to coping with the crisis. Over time, a more in-depth assessment can be done, which will include an evaluation of preabuse functioning, individual history and social functioning, a sexual history, and an evaluation of psychosocial capacities.

Phase 1: Engagement and Assessment

To effectively evaluate a woman in the crisis of disclosure, the therapist must first engage the mother. It is not possible, in my estimation, to undertake a reliable assessment if the therapist cannot, from the beginning, establish a positive alliance with the mother. To do this, the therapist must convey empathy. This is often easier said than done because many barriers exist for the therapist in the shape of gender expectations of mothers, class and racial biases, and sometimes ignorance about the specific effects of a history of childhood sexual abuse, being a battered woman, or having any number of other debilitating life experiences, such as substance abuse.

In my role as a teacher, I often find it necessary to help my students identify their biases and prejudices toward mothers in incest families. I often have them do the following exercise. In a classroom situation, I ask the group to identify the first adjectives that come to mind about the mother of a sexually abused child.

In general, the list ends up looking somewhat like the following:

> passive
> dependent
> unprotective
> selfish
> jealous
> needy
> self-centered
> inadequate
> blaming the child
> neglectful
> cold

I then ask the students if they think that a mother might pick up on unspoken feelings that the therapist has about a client. Most think that the mother would, that it would be almost impossible for the therapist not to communicate his or her feelings in nonverbal gestures, tone of voice, and the kind of questions that were asked of the mother. I then discuss with the students how they think a mother would feel about working with a therapist who held these attitudes. In general, they see this as a potential barrier for the client and identify possible biases in an evaluation based on the therapist's work from this perspective. We then go through the list, and I ask the students to reframe each concept and come up with an adjective that conveys a more positive or empathic connection to the mother's plight.

For example, in discussing the term *passive*, the students are asked to describe what contributes to their understanding of the word. They often define this as a "lack of action" and move then to an elaborated definition: "the inability to take action on behalf of self or others." I then ask them to consider what might have contributed to the mother's inability. They often are quick to hypothesize that it might be because she does not know how to assert herself, is depressed, does not know how to get her own needs met (sometimes because they were not met for her as a child), is afraid of her partner, may be a battered wife, and so on. Often, students give specific examples of mothers they have worked with in making their suggestions. They are then usually able to come up with terms that convey a more empathic connection to the mother, so that the result is a reframing that looks like the following:

passive	beaten down
dependent	lacks options
unprotective	trapped
selfish	scared
jealous	confused
needy	uncertain
self-centered	self-protective
Inadequate	in crisis
blaming the child	uncomprehending
neglectful	lacks resources
cold	overwhelmed

When students look at this list, not only does a profile of a more sympathetic figure emerge, but they are often struck by the extent to which the social structure and socially induced role expectations are reflected in the presentation of the mothers. For example, in considering the qualities of passivity and dependency, they often comment on the fact that these are socially desirable traits in women. They recognize that despite recent changes, women are less often prepared for an adult role that emphasizes employability and marketplace productivity over that of wife and mother. Even when they are, the fact is that women still earn consistently less than men, and even in the most lucrative professions, there is a "glass ceiling."

Thus, it is not uncommon for women—who are being asked to separate precipitously from a spouse or partner, are unprepared financially to do so, and do not have the skills to support themselves and their children—to appear unprotective, inadequate, and neglectful. The dynamic of a mother's jealousy, on reflection, may become viewed as an extension of her own low self-esteem rather than a punitive and uncaring attitude toward the child. Likewise, when I ask students what makes them describe the mother as "cold," they often attribute to her qualities that are clinically associated with depression (lack of affect and emotional connection to the child) or with low self-esteem (angry and rejecting attitudes toward the child). With other clients, when the issue is not child sexual abuse, they are often able to more clearly identify these dynamics, suggesting that it is something in the countertransference that contributes to the negative and more pejorative views of the mother in the incest family.

Clearly, the lesson here is that to effectively engage and thus evaluate, the clinician must examine the reactions, including their own biases, that they bring to an individual case situation. What is your feeling, as a therapist, that a woman who you will meet in 15 minutes has "chosen her partner over her child" because she has stayed with the alleged perpetrator and allowed her child or children to be placed in foster care? Or the woman who has used and abused crack/cocaine for years, who was out using when her child was molested? Or the woman who, despite the fact that she has asked the alleged perpetrator to leave, reportedly has said that her daughter must have made a mistake? If one cannot identify one's own prejudices and be prepared to work to rectify them, one is likely to project them onto the client.

The section on engagement in the previous chapter dealt with the internal work that a therapist may need to do to be as open as possible to the woman's dilemmas. This section emphasizes strategies that the clinician may adopt in interaction with the woman. As with any other person who has suffered a trauma, the woman may have a strong need to talk about what happened in her family to find some meaning for herself. Tapping into that need, without being biased with presumptions about what the woman knew or how she appeared to react vis-à-vis her child at the time of disclosure is not only useful to the woman but is also an excellent engagement tool. The following approach to engagement emphasizes a strengths perspective and solution-focused interviewing. Attention is then devoted to three specific tasks of engagement: dealing with powerlessness, reframing ambivalence, and overcoming feelings of betrayal.

The Strengths Perspective

The "strengths perspective," as it has come to be called, is not a theory but a body of principles that emphasizes the universality of resilience or the individual's inherent tendency to heal, recover, or rebound from real problems and difficulties (Saleebey, 1997). Women's strengths lie in inner and outer resources that can be identified and mobilized. It is important to help women identify their strengths, identify how they have overcome obstacles and barriers in the past, and know how to use oral renditions of individual and family history as a stimulus for symbols, metaphors, and new paradigms for recovery and healing. Of particular relevance for the work with the subgroup of women who have a history of childhood victimization is the notion of "survivor's pride." This concept suggests that for trauma and abuse victims, underlying the shame, guilt, and pain accompanying the trauma is pride in the fact that one has survived. If the clinician can help tap into this despite the difficulties the woman may be facing, it can provide some of the foundation to rebuild and strengthen functioning (Saleebey, 1997).

The notion of resilience, the second concept central to this perspective, is that individuals have the capacity to be resourceful and active in problem solving. It incorporates the idea of innovation as well as rehabilitation and recovery. The resilient individual does not deny pain and struggle but proceeds despite it. The perspective challenges three basic notions that have dominated mental health professionals' thinking about personality and treatment. The first is that development occurs in fixed, critical, and universal stages. The second is that childhood trauma predicts adult psychopathology, and the third is that some interpersonal and social arrangements are so destructive that they inevitably lead to dysfunction (Saleebey, 1997).

Probably one of the best sources of support for the strengths perspective comes from the longitudinal study of children as they grew into adulthood, begun in 1955 by Werner and Smith (1992). They found that one of every three children who was reported in childhood to be at serious risk developed into confident and competent adolescents by age 18. In addition, by age 32, two out of three of the remaining two thirds had developed into persons who could be characterized as compassionate and productive adults. This landmark study contributed to the evolution of the notion of "self-righting" tendencies. It resonates with the earlier work of Hartmann (1958), White (1974), and even Erikson (1963, 1968), who stressed the conflict-free spheres of ego functioning. Hartmann introduced the idea of an effectance drive, and White expanded on this in his development of the concepts of coping and adaptation. Even Erikson (1968), despite his reliance on the theory of phase or stage development, introduced the principle of epigenisis. He believed

> that anything that grows has a ground plan, and that out of this ground plan the parts arise, each part having its time of special ascendancy, until all parts have arisen to form a functioning whole. . . . The maturing organism continues to unfold, not by developing new organs, but by means of a prescribed sequence of locomotor, sensory, and social capacities. (p. 93)

Thus, the principles that define the strengths perspective are rooted in a very real sense in the history of ego psychology and elaborate certain aspects of that tradition.

An important manifestation of the strengths perspective is solution-focused interviewing that rests on the assumption that it is critical to formulate treatment goals. DeJong and Miller (1995) believe that it is important for the clinician to help clients develop goals that are well formed, small, concrete, specific, and behavioral. They believe that the goals should articulate the presence rather than the absence of elements or activities. Thus, rather than inquiring about what problems the woman faced during the last week that contributed to depression, the clinician might ask about when the woman felt less depressed and what activity that the woman engaged in made her feel better about life, if only for a moment. They also advise that goals should be realistic, recognizing that achievement of them is a process, not an event, and that achievement represents hard work.

As the therapist undertakes the process of assessing for specific traumatic effects, it is critical to keep in mind the need to explore with the client the resources that she brings to this and past problems in living. This will provide the therapist with important clues to important client strengths.

Assessing for Traumatic Effects

There are both short- and long-term effects of trauma, the latter manifesting themselves in problematic adaptation and coping strategies. For example, the mother of two young children who were sexually abused by their father presented for treatment 14 months after the disclosure of the abuse. Threatened with criminal prosecution, the husband fled the state and had not returned. The mother, with the financial help of her parents who lived in a distant state, had not gone to work but stayed at home with the children. In the time since the disclosure, she had not left the children with anyone and has been continually at home. She had no friends, having moved to the vicinity 6 months before the disclosure, and had no social contact other than when her children were present. She had developed paranoid tendencies (e.g., she would give the therapist her telephone number but not her address and would pay for all sessions in cash) and mistrusted everyone.

Inquiry into preabuse functioning revealed that she was college educated and had worked for 5 years prior to the birth of her first child. She chose to stay at home to care for her child. The sexual abuse had occurred when she had left the children in the care of her husband to run errands, go shopping, and, in a few instances, to socialize with women friends. Her postabuse functioning illustrated a clear elaboration of traumatic reactions that, although interacting with preexisting coping strategies to some extent (the tendency to isolate, for example, had been present even before the abuse disclosure), also show the power of the trauma on learning of the incest behavior on the part of her husband. She suffered from sleep disturbance; found her concentration was poor due to intrusive, unwanted thoughts about the abuse; and alternatively sought out people when she felt a desperate need to talk, oscillating with a desire to withdraw and be alone. This had recently led to family members telling her she appeared to be "two people."

It is possible, using the concepts introduced earlier, to assess the impact of the trauma. There is one general pattern that corresponds roughly to the manifestation of posttraumatic stress disorder and a number of specific dynamics that are particularly useful. The general pattern is the one identified by Judith Herman (1992) in her book *Trauma and Recovery*. Writing on the dialectic of trauma, she eloquently explains the oscillation between constriction and intrusion and the plethora of symptoms associated with each. Constriction of affect results in the lack of affect and the feeling of being numb, and intrusive flashbacks, dreams, and thoughts induce tremendous feelings of anxiety, even panic. The former tend to interfere with seeking satisfying interpersonal relationships that provide both a sense of intimacy and of belonging. The latter often drives the individual to compulsive, repetitive behaviors or, in needy desperation, to relationships that, in the long term, may not be the most gratifying.

Therefore, one of the first areas of inquiry relates to assessing the presence or absence of this general pattern of oscillation of affective responses. To do that, the specific traumagenic dynamics outlined by Finkelhor and Browne (1985) (traumatic sexualization, betrayal, stigmatization, and powerlessness) are particularly useful from a clinical standpoint. These dynamics were evolved to aid in understanding the impact of sexual abuse on the victim, as explained in Chapter 1, but they are helpful in understanding the mother's reaction as well. However, if the mother is also an abuse victim, her reaction probably will be intensified, as appears to be the case in studies that have looked at the mother's response to the sexual victimization of a child.

Assessing the Degree of Betrayal

Assuming that a mother will have issues about trust as a result of the betrayal by her spouse or partner, an initial question is, "How and to what extent is this a salient issue for her?" One of the first things to look for is her attitude toward the therapist. Does she approach the therapist in a help-seeking manner? Is she overly compliant and easily directed? Or does she challenge and resist both questions and suggestions? In describing her situation, is she guarded or open? Are unconscious defense mechanisms evident? For example, in an initial session with a mother, I was interested in her own mother's reaction to the disclosure because she appeared to be a significant person in the woman's life. I had to ask the question directly three times before I got an answer. Not surprisingly, the answer was that the mother blamed her for the abuse—she had told her not to marry her husband—and had always been critical of her choice. The disclosure brought an "I told you so" reaction from the mother, and because the woman was currently living with her mother, she felt her criticism keenly. The introjection of her mother's attitude contributed to an exacerbated sense of shame and low self-esteem.

The degree to which the mother feels betrayed can also be established by asking the following types of questions: What was the nature and duration of her relationship with the alleged perpetrator? Was this a long-term marriage or a recent, more intense partnership? Was she living with the alleged perpetrator, married, or currently separated or divorced? How long did the sexual abuse go on? What was the nature of the abuse? Does the degree of intrusiveness carry particular significance for her? Also, was this a relationship in which she had strong, positive feelings for the man, or was it a relationship characterized by tensions, conflicts, or outright abuse? How does she feel about her role as a mother? How crucial to her identity was being a parent?

Did she value that over the role of wife or partner? What has been her husband or partner's reaction? Has he taken responsibility or denied the abuse? Has he blamed her or her daughter? What is the extent to which she feels she sacrificed her own needs for the relationship with her partner?

What might be some behavioral manifestations of the relevance of the feelings of betrayal? It is fair to say that the feeling of being betrayed leads to anger, if not rage. How does anger manifest itself? Usually, women have learned to deflect their anger and not express it directly. It may emerge in the form of displaced anger. The woman may not follow through with recommendations by CPS and in other ways fail to conform to expectations. She may miss or cancel appointments with the therapist. To avoid feeling the anger, she may become impulsive, and this may be reflected in increased substance abuse, financial irresponsibility, or in sexual promiscuity. All of this needs to be evaluated within the context of the crisis of the disclosure. Are these chronic patterns, patterns that are exacerbated by the current stress, or are they a new phenomenon?

The following case example may help illustrate how the dynamic of betrayal can play out in a woman's life.

Maureen came into therapy 4 months after the disclosure of sexual abuse of her two daughters by Maureen's husband and stepfather to the girls. Maureen's initial reaction to the report was to feel betrayed by her daughters.

Maureen was a 30-year-old woman of Irish-Catholic descent. She had grown up in a lower working-class family. The second oldest of four sisters, her father had abandoned the family when she was 10. He was a laborer who worked intermittently and was physically abusive to her mother as well as being an alcoholic. Her mother had supported the family through work as a domestic and, at times, had aid from public assistance. Maureen reported remembering little about her childhood before the age of 10. She described her relationship with her mother as distant and saw her favoring her older and youngest sister. She had the strongest connection to her grandmother, who lived with the family until she died, when Maureen was 21.

Maureen became pregnant at 14 and had her first child, Eileen, at 15 and her second, Josephine, at 16. She dropped out of school when she was 16, having finished only 10th grade. She lived at home. At 17, she married the father of these two children, a man 13 years older who was violent and an addict. He was killed a few years later in a drug-

CASE STUDY

related incident. Maureen subsequently married again at 20. This man was also physically abusive to her as well as being an alcoholic. She separated from him when she was 23, after an incident in which she came home and found him anally sodomizing Josephine, then 8 years old. She had one child, Steven, from this marriage.

Maureen moved back home and finished her general equivalency diploma (GED). She married a third time when she was 26. Her three children were then 11, 10, and 4. This man, John, held down a full-time job as a doorman. He did not drink excessively, and although he was verbally abusive to both her and the children, he was not physically abusive, unemployed, or alcoholic. John had met Maureen when the children were 9, 8, and 2. Unbeknownst to her, he had started molesting Eileen and Josephine shortly before they married. Josephine was most often the target. She had a more distant relationship with her mother than Eileen and had initially been drawn to John, who paid attention to her.

From Maureen's point of view, the period of time since she married John had been the best time of her life. She completed training and started working part-time as a homemaker. Though not well off, she experienced financial stability. She described her relationship with John as one that did not demand a great deal from her emotionally. She described him as a quiet person who did not talk much. Much of what the children did annoyed him, and he complained to Maureen that they were out of his control. Many of their battles were around his attempts to discipline the children, especially Josephine. As she grew older, Josephine started to skip school, get poor grades, and disrespect curfews. She finally disclosed the sexual abuse to a guidance counselor after an incident in which John had taken away a privilege.

Maureen had what she described as a satisfactory sexual relationship with John until 2 years prior to the disclosure. She said that he became uninterested in sex, which she attributed to the fact that she gained about 20 pounds. She also attributed his lack of interest to what she described as his "moods," when he became very withdrawn and apathetic.

She had few friends, socializing mostly with her sisters and their children. Her mother had died the year before the disclosure, and she found that she was drinking beer more than she "used to," usually in the company of her sisters.

At the time of the disclosure, she did not believe Josephine, who had also revealed that Eileen had been abused. Eileen denied this ini-

tially, then told her mother. However, both girls had already been removed and placed in a group home by CPS because Maureen had refused to ask John to leave the home. CPS found Maureen to be
uncooperative, suspected her of being an alcoholic, and deemed her
unable to protect the girls.

At the time that Eileen disclosed, John made a suicide attempt and
was psychiatrically hospitalized with a diagnosis of severe depression.
John was subsequently arrested and, on discharge, went to jail. He denied that he had abused the girls, and Maureen, not knowing whom to
believe, stuck by his side, visiting him in jail.

At the time of the initial family court hearing, Maureen was referred to therapy. However, she did not come until after the second
court hearing 4 months later. At intake, she presented as angry and
guarded. She stated that she was only there because she "had to be" if
she wanted the court to give her back her daughters. She said she did
not understand why the court would not let them come home because John was in jail and no longer any threat to them. She had never
been in therapy and believed that coming to a mental health clinic
meant that she was "crazy."

Issues of loss and betrayal were central in her life and had been ac-
tivated by the recent disclosure. Initially feeling betrayed by her daughters, she was beginning to experience a sense of betrayal by John. Her
history was one of emotional deprivation. Starting with her parents,
she had never been nurtured and did not have her needs for affection,
positive mirroring, and unconditional acceptance met. She had turned
to a seemingly more powerful and loving figure in the form of her first
husband, only to have him "turn on her" and then abandon her. Her
second husband had also betrayed her, in his abuse of her daughter, as
had now the third, if she were to believe the latest allegations.

Maureen had never had close friends outside her family, also reflecting a lack of trust and inability to negotiate gratifying relationships.
She had told no one except one of her sisters about the real reason
she and John were separated. She felt particularly betrayed by Eileen,
her eldest daughter, who she had viewed as the "good" daughter and
with whom she believed she had a good relationship. Her ability and
willingness to trust the clinician were very limited, as indicated by her
posture at intake.

The above illustrates how pivotal the disloyalty by her third husband was in
shaping her reaction. Fueled by earlier unresolved betrayals, her stance at the

time of the intervention by CPS led to her being perceived as hostile, uncooperative, and antisocial. This posture reflected the major psychological concern at the time of referral for treatment. This is not to say that she did not also have issues around powerlessness, stigmatization, and traumatic sexualization—she did. But for Maureen, the sexual abuse heightened her concern about being betrayed, and this was the most influential.

Assessing the Degree of Powerlessness

A second major dynamic that is helpful to appraise at intake is the degree to which a woman feels powerless. (Note that to the extent that this dynamic captures feelings of helplessness and desperation that engender anxiety, this dynamic can be viewed as an elaboration of Herman's [1981, 1992] description of the effect of intrusive symptoms.) What part of this response is reality based, and what part is due to the subjective experience of not having any control over her world? *Reality based* refers to the following questions: To what extent have external authorities—CPS, the family court, the police or district attorney, or the criminal court—exercised their power and influence over where a mother can live and with whom she can live? Has she been given an ultimatum of having her children removed from her care if she does not separate from the alleged abuser? Has her husband or partner threatened to beat her up if she leaves him? Has he threatened to fight her for custody of siblings of the victim?

In addition to some of these real influences that may encourage a woman to make drastic changes in her lifestyle, place of residence, household composition, and so on, what are her perceptions of her own power or lack of it? One of the crucial issues for many mothers is the feeling that the world is falling apart after they learn of the allegations. This is usually described in terms of a contrast to life before and after the disclosure. The allegations call into question all that women thought was true about themselves, their world, and their relationships—with both partners and children. The knowledge that what they believed was *not* the foundation of their world makes a woman distrust herself, her perceptions, and her ability to know what is true and what is not and leaves her feeling ineffective—and thus powerless.

To what degree has the woman in the therapist's office experienced this? Did she have forewarnings that make her somewhat less susceptible to this feeling? Is this betrayal one more in a string of personal betrayals that have left her feeling resigned more than anxious? Given that feelings of helplessness, fear, and vulnerability result in feelings of anxiety, what are the behavioral manifestations of this for this woman? Is she sleeping and eating properly? Does she have intrusive thoughts that affect her daily functioning? Is she irritable, bothered by excessive worry? Does she have muscle tension? Does she have the feeling of "walking around in a daze"? Does she have more direct symptoms of panic attacks or traumatic reactions (i.e., marked avoidance of stimuli that arouse recollections of the incest, recurring distressing dreams, etc.) that interfere with her functioning?

More important, to what extent are her fears grounded in reality? If she has been in a relationship with an abusive man, is her husband, ex-husband, or partner going to stalk or abuse her because she separates? If he is denying the abuse and she believes her children, does he have financial resources that will allow him to launch a prolonged court battle that she can ill afford? Will the court take her children or allow unsupervised visitation? If she does not believe her children, will the court believe the abuse and take action against her because she should have known and protected her children?

At other times, the fears may be simply a reaction to an overwhelming situation. For those of us who work with the "system" on a regular basis, it is easy to forget how complex and arbitrary it appears to a mother. A mother may wonder why she does not have the same worker who first interviewed her children. She may ask, "What do you mean, if family court finds him guilty, he won't go to jail? What is the difference between the county attorney and the district attorney—I thought they were the same. Don't you [the therapist] work for Child Protective Services?" All of these questions are normal, but answers may not be easily forthcoming, leaving the mother anxious about people and systems that control her life but that she cannot understand.

Symptoms of anxiety may rise to clinical levels, leading to specific diagnoses. For example, a woman may suffer from posttraumatic stress disorder, a panic disorder, phobias, or an acute stress disorder following the disclosure. These need to be evaluated and may need specific remedies—whether in the form of medication or psychotherapy—as part of the beginning phase of treatment.

The following case may help illustrate the points made earlier.

Lydia, a Hispanic woman of Puerto Rican descent, was 40 years old when her 17-year-old daughter Elisa told her that her father, Lydia's husband of 20 years, had been molesting her. Lydia had been born in Puerto Rico but moved with her parents to this country when she was 2. Raised in New York City, she had married at 20 to the son of a family who attended the same church. Lydia's father had been disabled as a result of an accident on his job, and since the age of 5, Lydia's family had moved frequently as her parents struggled to provide for the family on her father's disability check and what her mother could earn by sewing.

Lydia described her father as the "boss" of the house, despite his physical handicap, and her mother as passive and acquiescent. Both parents were very protective of her growing up—she was not allowed to date until she was almost out of high school and then only boys approved by the family. This is consistent with norms in Hispanic families. She had had no other sexual experiences outside of the relationship with her husband.

Lydia had chosen a man much like her father to marry. From what she described, he was a tyrant around the house. Buttressed by the Catholic religion and Hispanic tradition, he demanded that she acquiesce to his rules and desires. She had a son 3 years younger than her daughter. He did not want her to work outside of the home, insisting that her first responsibility was to her children and her family. She had not done so until the children were 14 and 11, starting about 3 years before the disclosure of sexual abuse.

Over the years, Lydia had suffered from anxiety and fears. When her children were little, she had what sounded like a phobia. She was afraid of heights and would not take escalators. She also was afraid to drive and for many years had not driven. It was only since she had started to work that she had begun to drive again. She described herself as someone who liked and needed routines and security. She was a "planner" and not one to act impulsively or quickly. One of the things she liked about her job was the predictability of the routine. Although some found the detailed work of the office "boring," she felt a sense of satisfaction in achieving what she had planned each day.

At intake, Lydia presented as a slim, drawn woman with short, dark hair. The disclosure by Elisa to her teacher had occurred about 2 weeks previously. José, Lydia's husband, had moved out and was living temporarily with his mother. Lydia complained of difficulty sleeping and being awoken at night with bad dreams. She had very little appetite and said that she had lost 5 pounds in the past 2 weeks. She found that she had difficulty concentrating at work—she worked as a secretary in the local county clerk's office—and had taken a leave of absence to deal with all the changes that were occurring as a result of the allegations. She found herself worried excessively and tended to focus on issues around money, particularly her husband's legal fees. She described herself as irritable with her children.

Her response to the allegations was to vacillate between believing her daughter and believing her husband. Her husband denied the allegations, but she tended to believe her daughter. She had always felt that her husband had an "unhealthy attitude toward sex." By this she meant that he had been more interested in masturbating to "adult" movies than in having sex with her. When they did have sex, she felt that he treated her like an object and was much more concerned with his own satisfaction than in gratifying her. At the same time, she thought that it was possible that her daughter was fabricating the story because she had been upset with her father's restrictions on her social life. Elisa had also disliked her father's strict rules at home and his tendency to yell and be verbally abusive to her.

Lydia described herself as a "private" woman and found the intervention of CPS, the police, and the district attorney to be very intrusive and disruptive. She said that the neighbors all wondered who the strangers were who came to the house, and she had been embarrassed by the police coming to the house and by the article carried by the local paper. An inquisitive acquaintance at work had asked pointed questions about what had happened to Elisa, infuriating and humiliating Lydia. She reported feeling that her "life was no longer under her control," that it was controlled by the agency and institutions that were intervening in her life.

Lydia's presentation at the time of intake illustrates another type of profile. Vulnerable historically to anxiety and fears and by nature a quiet, private person whose ethnic heritage emphasized solving problems within the family, she was overwhelmed by the events following the disclosure. "Choosing" her daughter over her husband engendered tension—her upbringing and ethnic background dictated that she should support her husband, particularly against "outsiders" and even her daughter. At the same time, the cultural emphasis on the importance of motherhood pointed to the correctness of supporting her daughter though this time. In her culture, it also went against the grain to be talking to strangers from formal institutions about such personal issues. Lydia did not know what the future would bring, and change was difficult and uncertainties threatening. She reached in ways that suggested that feelings of powerlessness were the most salient and thus needed to be the focus of early intervention.

Assessing the Degree of Stigmatization

Another dynamic that is very critical is that of stigmatization. This encompasses the shame and self-blame that the mother may experience. Why is this an issue for the mother? Thoughts about what the disclosure of sexual abuse means for her may be a concern as the reality of the situation sinks in. The woman may begin to reflect on what it says about her to have a husband or partner who has or may have sexually abused her child. To the extent that feelings of guilt and shame result in a turning inward and in preoccupation, it is not unusual to see this dynamic of stigmatization become manifest in depressive symptoms.

What happens for women in the early period following disclosure? Clinical experience suggests that women tend not to confide in family and friends, or, if they do, they do so in a selective manner. The response by many women seems to be one in which they begin almost immediately to question their adequacy as mothers and wives. Despite how they appear to the world—particularly the authorities, who may be coordinating the intervention in their lives—they often blame themselves for the abuse. They view themselves, at some level, as inadequate mothers. They ask, "Why didn't my child come to me?" If the child had told the mother or alluded to the abuse in some manner that becomes clearer to the mother after the abuse, she often asks herself, "Why didn't I believe her [or him]?"

If questioned about why they have not told significant others, their reactions may be the following: "She would not want to hear that," "He has heart problems and it might cause him to have a heart attack and I don't want to be responsible for that," "She would not understand," "I would be too embarrassed," "She couldn't keep her mouth shut and it would be all over the neighborhood," and "She would blame me because she has always said that he was no good." Behaviorally, there is a tendency to isolate themselves from these significant others—they feel that they cannot confide in them and therefore feel ambivalent and fearful about asking for emotional support.

Crisis theory teaches that the time of a crisis is one of both hazard and opportunity; individuals are most open to new information and ways of coping, which, if not accessed, may lead to rigidified and outmoded adaptation. In addition to the provision of information and concrete services, help in the form of social support is crucial. Yet, for the mother in an incest family, when she needs the help the most from significant others, she may not avail herself of it because of the sense of shame and stigma induced by the allegations of sexual abuse.

What are some of the emotional manifestations of feeling stigmatized? In addition to low self-worth and feelings of shame and guilt, the woman may become mildly to severely depressed. She may indulge in activities that reflect self-deprecation, such as self-mutilation or other self-abusive acts. Overeating, bingeing and purging, or relying on alcohol or other substances may indicate depression. Withdrawal from others or a diminished ability to think or concentrate, indecisiveness, fatigue, and insomnia may all be present. As with anxiety disturbances, depression may reach clinical levels and call for medication or other focused therapeutic intervention to reduce the anxiety.

The following case example highlights the situation for a mother in which this dynamic was the most profound.

Teresa, a Hispanic woman age 30 when her daughter, Nadia, disclosed her sexual abuse, was born in New York City to parents who had immigrated 6 years before her birth from Central America. Her family shared a two-bedroom apartment with another family, their cousins from the same hometown, while Teresa was growing up. Teresa had not finished high school when she became pregnant with Nadia, who was 11 at the time of the disclosure of sexual abuse.

Nadia's father never supported her and did not keep up a relationship with Teresa. Teresa had a second child, Eddie, by another man and a third child, Jeannette, by Juan, the man who was alleged to have molested Nadia. At the time of the disclosure, Eddie was 8 and Jeannette was 4. Teresa had been living with Juan for about 5 years; they had no plans to marry.

Teresa had dropped out of high school after ninth grade. She had never learned to read, which she was ashamed of, and had supported herself through public assistance after her children were born. She had never worked and had depended heavily on Juan for the past 5 years to help her out financially. They had moved into a two-bedroom apartment soon after Jeannette was born, and Juan's name was on the lease.

Nadia's relationship with Juan was conflicted and troubled. He was possessive, overbearing, and abusive. The local police had numerous domestic abuse calls from the home because Juan tended to become physically abusive when he had been drinking. At these times, Teresa would often take her children and go stay with her aunt or sister.

The disclosure had come about when Jeannette told her mother that she had seen her father lying on Nadia and that Nadia had been crying. When questioned, Nadia told her mother that Juan had been fondling her and had recently started lying on top of her and rubbing his penis against her. Teresa was horrified and, not knowing what to do, turned to her sister. Her sister called CPS, somewhat against Teresa's will. When CPS told her that Juan would have to leave or the children would be placed in foster care, Teresa did not know what to do. She was afraid of Juan and vacillated, forcing CPS to take the children into care.

The trauma of losing her children helped Teresa rally, and by the time of the court hearing, she had gotten an order of protection and gotten Juan out of the apartment. He denied the allegations and was hostile and verbally abusive to Teresa and her family, and the court ordered that he have supervised contact with his daughter and no contact with the other two children until CPS had completed their investigation.

At the time of referral for treatment, although Teresa was relieved that Juan was out of the home and felt safe for the first time in a long time, she was also depressed. Teresa was feeling exposed and shamed when she was referred for treatment. She sat in the therapist's office during the first few sessions, avoiding eye contact. Her speech seemed labored, and despite the fact that she had grown up in this country, she struggled to find words when expressing herself in English. She had not told any of her neighbors in the apartment building what had occurred. Already feeling ashamed of how Juan treated her and embarrassed by the number of times she had called the police, she was sure that the neighbors were relieved that Juan was no longer living there.

Deeply embarrassed by the sexual abuse allegations, she had told only her sister what had really happened. She was afraid to tell her aunt, who she believed would blame her for not taking better care of her children. This aunt had already been critical of Teresa for staying with Juan after he had beaten her. She had also never been in therapy and was fearful that coming to the clinic meant that she was "crazy." No one in her family or extended family had been in therapy except for an uncle who was often hospitalized with severe depressive episodes. He lived in a halfway house between hospitalizations, and Teresa initially believed that coming to the clinic meant that she was like her uncle, who was ostracized by the family.

Teresa complained of difficulty getting out of bed each morning, and she was not getting her two oldest children to school on time or even always getting them there. She did not feel like leaving her apartment, partly out of her fear that she might run into Juan and partly be-

cause she did not want to run into friends or acquaintances and have
to answer questions about Juan.

Teresa is a good example of a woman who was feeling particularly shamed in
response to the disclosure of the sexual abuse of her oldest daughter. Her class
and ethnic background stressed privacy about family matters and the avoidance of formal helping systems when dealing with a problem. Teresa had a
number of preexisting areas in her life that contributed to a sense of shame and
self-blame. She was not married to the father of any of her children and had
been in an abusive relationship with Juan, for which she blamed herself. In addition, her family, who was her primary social support, was critical of this relationship and of her parenting. In her culture, with the emphasis on being a
good mother, this latter criticism was experienced as particularly shameful.
She also was dissatisfied with her life outside the home. Ashamed that she did
not know how to read, she limited her social life lest strangers become aware
of this great "failing." She was in a cycle of trying to make the commitment to
return to school, failing, and then blaming herself even more. The disclosure
by her daughter of the sexual abuse heightened the feelings of guilt, resulting
in a depressive reaction and signaling that for her, the stigma of being a mother
whose partner had sexually abused her child was the most powerful of the
four dynamics.

Assessing the Degree of Traumatic Sexualization

This is perhaps the most difficult dynamic to understand and assess.
How is the revelation of the child's sexual victimization by the woman's
partner relevant to the woman's own sexual identity and functioning? As discussed in Chapter 1, if the woman is a former victim herself, this experience
of having her child abused may trigger issues that she needs to address in therapy. Even without that, however, the abuse of a child is usually experienced
at some level as an assault on the woman's sexuality, and in general the reaction is to internalize and blame oneself. Thus, rather than asking or in addition to asking what is wrong with him, the woman asks, "What is wrong
with me?" Sometimes, the woman already has distorted notions about her
sexual adequacy based on her relationship with the abuser.

I am reminded of a woman who said in treatment that she used to wonder if she satisfied her husband. He wanted to have sex much more often than
she did—"every 5 hours," as she reported in group—and she described how
she would be too tired or find him too intrusive so that she did not want to

have sex. She recalled that in all their 8 years of marriage, he had never kissed her when it was not a prelude to sex. Yet, when the sexual victimization of their 5-year-old daughter was uncovered, she asked herself if in fact the times that her husband was with her sexually was somehow the "pretend" time, the preparation for the sexual interaction with the daughter, which she thought was the relationship that was somehow more satisfying.

Another woman, in reflecting on her husband's 8-year involvement with her daughter and his stepdaughter, said that she thought at first that he must have turned to the child because she was unappealing physically. She talked about all the weight she had gained, particularly over the 2 years prior to the disclosure of the incest. She had concluded that her physical unattractiveness had turned him away and "forced" him to turn elsewhere.

Both these vignettes reflect the cognitive distortion that it is the woman's job to be physically attractive to the man and to satisfy him sexually. These women believed that they were responsible for the sexual relationship, for keeping him "interested," and that if their partners turned to another, even a child, it reflected on their sexual inadequacy. They did not, at one level, hold the men responsible for their sexual choices. They also did not view sexual relationships as reciprocal, meaning that it was the responsibility of both partners to negotiate a relationship that was mutually satisfying. Their own sexual satisfaction was rarely raised as an issue for discussion, much less having been contemplated as a reasonable request for them to ask of their partners.

Assessing for the degree to which the woman feels traumatized in this sphere of her life is difficult. Women are understandably often very guarded initially, and many of these issues can only be addressed later on in treatment. However, to the degree that the woman is open to discussion, questions can be asked about her sexual desire, repertoire, and level of satisfaction. What was the frequency of their sexual interaction? Who usually initiated it? Was this a satisfactory arrangement for her? Had there been any recent changes? What was her reaction to that? Were there sexual acts that her partner was interested in that disturbed or upset her? Had she ever refused to participate sexually? In what way was the sexual interaction that he allegedly engaged the child in reminiscent of his sexual desires? Had he engaged the child in sexual acts that she had withdrawn from? If the latter is the case, and I have often found this to be true, the woman may suffer from performance guilt and make a direct connection between her unavailability and the sexual victimization of her child.

The feeling of sexual inadequacy may be expressed directly, in overcompensation, or by withdrawal from sexual relationships. Many women are repulsed by the disclosure of their husbands' or partners' sexual relationships with their children and withdraw from relationships with them. In a number of instances, however, the woman may feel that she wants to continue the sexual relationship, sometimes out of the need to prove to herself that she can satisfy him sexually. If the woman has resumed a relationship with her partner after the disclosure, it is important for the therapist to discuss her motivation for this because it may be a clue to issues that need to be addressed in therapy.

Another common way women choose to handle their anxiety about their own sexuality is to withdraw completely from any sexual relationship. Even after a divorce, a woman may choose not to date or explore any relationship that may lead to sex. She may also become overly protective of female children, especially female child victims, out of a concern that she could be easily exploited. Sometimes, this reflects her own feeling that her daughter is "damaged goods" and will not be able to control herself because there will be no "purpose." In other instances, she may feel that any expression of sexuality on her daughter's part will put her at risk for further victimization.

What is critical to keep in mind is that the mother's reactions are not easily categorized. Other than to look for some expression of traumatic sexualization, the reactions are probably quite diverse and individual. The following case provides some clues to the depth of this feeling that were not to become fully evident until further into treatment.

Donna, age 32 at the time of referral for treatment, had been married for 8 years and had two children at the time of the report to CPS. Of German-English background, she had grown up in upstate New York and moved to the city after high school to look for work. She had developed good computer skills over the years and was employed full-time until she had her first child. She had married a man, Stuart, who ran his own business. They had waited 3 years before having children. Their oldest daughter was 5, and the younger daughter was 3 at the time of the disclosure of sexual abuse.

Donna described her relationship with Stuart as "OK." She reported that she had not been "in love" with him at the time of marriage but had been drawn to the financial security he offered. She described their sexual relationship as one in which her husband had been interested continually in having sex, and she had often been too tired. She

said that he would count the days between their having a sexual relationship and would "hound" her if it had been more than "36 hours."
She reported feeling inadequate and wondered if all women "ser-
viced" their husbands as much as her husband seemed to demand.

Donna talked in the initial sessions about her struggle to feel like a
"grown-up." She said that she had nursed her children to feel "wom-
anly." She was a slim woman, with small breasts and hips, and had also
felt that she did not appear sexual. She wondered if she satisfied her
husband because she did not have a fuller figure.

Donna's discussion early on in treatment suggested that she had harbored in-
securities about herself as a woman and about her adequacy as a sexual partner. These came out even in early sessions as preoccupations with her husband's sexual demands—always questioning whether there was something
wrong with her and rarely considering what might be wrong with him. Even
the sexual abuse was first conceptualized as his response to her inadequacy as a
wife, rather than viewing his behavior as deviant.

Once the manifestations of the four dynamics have been identified for a
given woman, the next step is to decide which are the most salient for her.
The premise is that all four dynamics will be present, to a greater or lesser degree; the challenge for the clinician is to determine which are the most debilitating at the point of intake and to prioritize treatment accordingly. As noted
repeatedly throughout, the mix will be different for every woman because
each person's situation is unique. However, given the commonality of a traumatic response, the task for the therapist is to discern in what way, for this
woman, the issues have emerged and need to be addressed.

Assessment of Social Roles

So far, this chapter has focused on an assessment of the degree to which the
mother has been traumatized by the disclosure of child sexual abuse, stressing
the need to evaluate the impact and the degree to which coping strategies
adopted by the woman are maladaptive or empowering. This section will focus on the evaluation of the mother's role competency as wife and mother and
the degree to which she has a network of social support. Although areas assessed in a more traditional psychosocial assessment are always important to
evaluate, it is crucial that social functioning becomes an important emphasis
in the assessment. Family history, including employment history, financial

history, peer group involvement, and social supports, are critical elements to evaluate.

There is growing evidence that mothers in incest families are not significantly different from other mothers presenting for clinical services, suggesting no basis for assuming that these mothers are more impaired than other mothers seeking treatment. In a small study of 21 mothers who were or had been in treatment, Wilson (1995) explored the question, "Are there levels of ego development which are common to mothers of sexually abused children?" Her findings suggested that the mothers clustered at the mid-level of ego development, as measured by a projective instrument developed by Loevinger and Wessler (1970). More important, there was not an association between the mother's level of ego development and either an active or passive role in stopping the abuse. In addition, the mothers in her study with a history of childhood sexual abuse functioned at a relatively integrated level of ego development.

Wagner (1991) found no difference between mothers of sexually abused children who brought children for a clinical evaluation and mothers who sought services for their nonabused children in regard to the mother's depression. About half the mothers in each group (59% and 50%, respectively) described themselves as being mildly to moderately depressed. Deblinger et al. (1993) found that mothers of incest victims did not differ significantly from mothers of children abused by other relatives and mothers of children abused by nonrelatives in three crucial areas: (a) background variables (age, race, education, religion, familial income, marital status, employment, substance abuse, and medical difficulties), (b) the response to the abuse (believing the allegations, feeling alone, acting protectively), or (c) the degree of symptom distress they experienced. This study raises serious questions about a premise that the preexisting psychopathology influences her choice of an abusive mate.

Results of another important study (Peterson, Basta, & Dykstra, 1993) appear to support the notion that the degree of symptom distress manifested by mothers in incest families may be a function of the effects of the knowledge of the victimization rather than a factor predisposing the woman to choose a partner who molests her child. The study compared mothers of children molested by teachers with mothers of children molested by family members with a group of mothers whose children had not been molested. Peterson et al. found no difference between mothers of teacher-molested children and mothers of family-molested children on measures (Clinical Analysis Questionnaire—CAQ) of personality characteristics. Significantly, however, the mothers of abused children, when grouped together and compared to the mothers of nonabused children, did differ on scales measuring clinical symptoms. Their heightened level of psychological distress suggests that this may be a reaction to the event rather than a factor contributing to the cause.

Recent literature on nonoffending mothers has pointed the way to particular aspects of the woman's performance in her roles. Role conflict experienced in the family, involving how the woman has coped with the tensions between being a wife and mother, is one such area. DeYoung (1994) studied role conflict in paternally incestuous families. She obtained a sample of 20 women who were the biological mothers of the children who were molested and in court-ordered treatment. She hypothesized four categories of coping abilities: (a) social role redefinition, (b) interpersonal role redefinition, (c) intrapersonal role redefinition, and (d) reactive role behavior. She described the first as a situation in which the woman was either "involved in political action to alter the social role description or social exploitation of the mother and/or wife role" (DeYoung, 1994) or had abandonedthe wife or mother role. None of the women in her sample fell into this category.

The second category is characterized by women who negotiate with other people in their lives—either partners or children—to obtain help in managing their roles. Strategies in this category include implementing active problem solving, seeking role support from the husband or daughter, eliminating role activities (i.e., reduce a set of behaviors), seeking role support from individuals outside the family, delegating role responsibilities, or integrating the roles. DeYoung (1994) defined this as the most effective category. Her findings revealed that only 20% of the mothers engaged in that type of coping strategy.

The third category, defined as intrapersonal role redefinition, occurs perceptually, without changes in behavior. The strategies include overlooking the demands of one or both of the roles, changing their attitude, rotating attention between the roles, developing interests outside the role, and ranking obligations. Forty-five percent of the mothers engaged in this strategy as a way of managing role conflict.

The fourth category was termed *reactive role behavior* and is described as the most defensive and accommodating strategy. Women who adopted this posture worked harder to meet all the demands; assumed a passive, even helpless, orientation; or increased their efficiency in role performance. Thirty-five percent of the mothers engaged in this type of behavior.

Cumulative results suggest that most women (80%) adopted either a partially defensive or totally defensive and accommodating pattern of coping with role conflict in their families before the disclosure of incest. This is an important finding for clinicians because it suggests areas of inquiry in the assessment phase of treatment as well as reinforcing the need for certain treatment strategies. For example, in the assessment, the therapist can explore how the mother handled the role conflict. Did she "overachieve," or did she "give up" and become passive, thus falling into the most defensive position? Did she try to develop outside interests, such as taking a job, or become socially active in an activity that excluded other family members? Did she start to ignore the demands of daughter or husband, failing to negotiate and handle stress by avoiding certain responsibilities? The particular manner in which the woman responded will provide clues that are useful in designing a treatment plan that fits an individual woman.

The other aspect of social functioning that is critical to assess is the degree of social support available to the mother. Support from partner and family appears to be the crucial variable that affects the degree to which the mother feels alone in the crisis and the development of depressive symptoms (Kinard, 1996). This points to the importance of a thorough discussion with the mother of the response of her partner and of her extended family members. Mothers whose partners confirm the abuse (i.e., admit to it) are more likely to be consistently supportive of their abused children, whereas mothers who have a strong allegiance to denying offenders are less likely to consistently believe their children (Everson et al., 1989). However, what is suggested here is that the degree of role tension and the lack of support create difficulties in functioning for the mother. The relationship to the perpetrator needs to be evaluated with that in mind.

For example, to what extent does the mother's siding with the perpetrator put her in conflict with her child? Or, conversely, to what extent does her siding with her child reduce the support from her partner? In addition, the question of family support is crucial. As discussed earlier, it is hypothesized that the greater the degree of stigma and shame felt by the woman, the less likely she may be to share the reality of the abuse with family, thereby eliminating a source of support. In addition, extended family members (sisters, mothers) who are significant support to the woman may react in a stigmatizing manner, thereby reducing the level of support generally available to the woman. These are important dynamics to evaluate at the time of initial referral.

Sexual History

In working with this population of women, it is important to become comfortable and skilled in obtaining a sexual history. Not only will this help the therapist understand the nature of the relationship between the woman and her partner and to identify issues that may need to be addressed in therapy, but it will also provide important clues as to why and how the disclosure of sexual victimization affects her sense of herself as a sexual person. This assessment is virtually an elaboration of that described earlier in regard to evaluating the degree to which the woman experiences the disclosure as sexually traumatizing. It is part of an ongoing evaluation and treatment planning process and is emphasized here to stress its importance.

One way to proceed is to think of the sexual history as a timeline. One can ask a woman to talk about her earliest memories of sex: how old she was when she remembered learning something about sex, what she remembers about her parents' sexual relationship (were they affectionate, did she ever witness them engaged in sexual intercourse?), what she remembers thinking about sex when she was school age, and so on. If she is a victim of childhood sexual abuse, this may be a difficult and painful process. Although it will be helpful eventually to have a full history, it is important to move at the woman's pace in telling her story. If the woman has never had treatment or, as is often the case, has not even talked to anyone before about the victimization experiences, this may be a focus of therapy for months or longer.

After discussing with the woman what her earliest memories are and what transpired for her in childhood, it is important to inquire specifically about what she thinks she learned about sexuality based on these experiences. One needs to have the same discussion about her adolescence and young adulthood because this is the age when many women become sexually active and begin to have children. It is important to obtain not only the chronology but also the meaning of different sexual experiences, with different sexual partners, if that applies. One asks the same type of questions about each phase of life, bringing the woman up to her current relationship.

One may discover tremendous deviation from the norm. For example, a woman who has a history of childhood incest herself may never have had a peer relationship. She may always have had relationships, even in adulthood, with partners 20 and more years older than herself. It is also critical to ask about the nature of sexual experiences—how often, if at all, she has engaged in sexual acts against her will or reluctantly. Has he been a willing partner in sadist or masochistic acts?

It is also critical to find out what role her racial or ethnic background has played in the development of sexual norms. For Hispanic women, the combination of a Catholic upbringing interacting with norms for Latino cultures seems to breed particularly harsh criticisms of self and other if the woman engages in premarital sex and in other than vaginal intercourse. For lower-income African Americans, who often follow a life cycle course different from mainstream White America, having children in adolescence and outside of marriage is not necessarily stigmatizing. All of this information will be helpful in understanding a woman's reaction to the discovery that her child has been sexually abused.

Summary

This chapter has introduced a six-phase treatment approach and described the first—engagement and assessment—in some detail. It has suggested that special attention be given to the traumatic effects of the disclosure, to the woman's management of role conflicts and availability of social support, and to undertaking a detailed sexual history. The next chapter explores treatment strategies in individual treatment that elaborate on this focus and expand on the treatment approach.

Individual Treatment

In this chapter, I focus on key dynamics in individual treatment—specifically, the work typically associated with Phases 2 through 6 of the treatment approach introduced earlier. To reiterate, Phase 2 involves early intervention around traumatic effects; Phase 3, strengthening ego capacities; Phase 4, surfacing the traumatic effects; Phase 5, identifying relational consequences; and Phase 6, working through and resolution.

Phase 2:   Early Intervention Around Traumatic Effects

In the previous chapter, the four traumagenic dynamics of powerlessness, betrayal, stigmatization, and sexual traumatization (Finkelhor & Browne, 1985) were introduced as key issues to assess and prioritize in the mother's treatment. In this chapter, these dynamics are used as a framework for organizing strategies that can be used to shape interventions.

Dealing With Powerlessness

A central issue following disclosure is a woman's feelings of powerlessness. As noted earlier, this is often true whether or not the child has been removed. In engaging mothers in treatment, it is important for the clinician to attend to ways in which the mother can be helped to feel more powerful. Feelings of helplessness and powerlessness are usually reduced if one feels he or she has no control over life or even over aspects of life. One way to help a mother feel more in control is to illustrate the areas where she can make decisions. There are many ways that the clinician can help the woman with choices. One of the most immediate is to provide choices about what is discussed in treatment. Women often come in and present details from the week that may or may not be important to discuss fully. The following describes the choice a woman made about how to use her time in a specific therapy session.

CASE STUDY

Mrs. W came into a session shortly after she began treatment. This mother believed her daughter's disclosure to her kindergarten teacher and had separated immediately from her husband, the alleged perpetrator. She was an intelligent, verbal woman who, by her own admission, was somewhat of a "bullshit artist." She began the session by talking about a pamphlet she had seen at her daughter's school about child abuse. She commented, in an outraged tone, that there was not one reference in it about the fact that the abuser could be a family member. She talked about wanting to contact the Parent-Teacher Association (PTA) and talk with them about getting out different kinds of literature. She launched into a discussion about how kids were not being taught to say something if a family member bothered them. She also asked for information about prevalence statistics, saying that she wanted to be able to back up her point when she went to talk to the PTA person.

It can be important to encourage this kind of activism as a means of helping Mrs. W feel more powerful. However, knowing Mrs. W, I suspected that the anger Mrs. W was conveying about this might be displaced from somewhere else. I said to her that there was written information that I would be happy to give her about prevalence data after group and wondered if there was something going on in her own life that might be fueling the anger.

This led her to say that she was really struggling with her angry feelings about her husband. At this point in the session, I asked again if she would prefer to talk about what she could do with the PTA or if she would rather talk in more depth about the struggle she was having with her husband. She ruefully acknowledged that she needed to talk about her feelings about her husband.

Choices can be made not only in the office but in daily problem solving as well. The following illustrates how this can occur:

One mother, Ms. M, a woman with three children ages 11, 9, and 4, had separated from her live-in boyfriend and father of her third child only after Child Protective Services (CPS) had removed her oldest daughter (the victim of the partner's sexual abuse). She had relied on her partner to help her with parenting, especially the discipline of her 9-year-old son. With him out of the household, she was facing a crisis in parenting—she felt that her son and even her daughters were increasingly out of control. A recent event had left her feeling particularly helpless. Her son had been suspended from the school bus for 3 days because of his disruptive behavior.

She came into a session the day after this had happened, describing how angry she was because her son was at home watching TV. She was very frustrated, complaining that she had no way to get him to school. She did not drive, and since she had asked her partner to move out, he was not around to help. She talked about how if her partner, Steven, had been there, her son would have gotten to school and would have been grounded effectively because he was afraid of Steven.

Part of the session was devoted to helping her come up with another strategy for getting him to school. There was in fact a city bus that he could take. This would mean him getting up and out about an hour earlier, and it would put more pressure on her because she would want to take him to the bus stop. She would need to take her youngest daughter with her because her oldest daughter would need to get on her own bus before Ms. M could get back from accompanying her son. Ms. M was placing all kinds of obstacles in her way about why she could not get her son to the city bus. It was winter, and she did not want to wake her youngest daughter up and "drag" her out in the weather. Furthermore, she was worried about her son riding the bus alone. We discussed her riding the bus with him, and she raised a concern about the cost of extra bus fare for herself and her daughter.

When the solutions to the problem were posed to Ms. M as a choice, it was easier for her to make a decision. The choices were whether she would prefer to have her son at home and in essence get a "break" from school, with all the accompanying frustration for her, or whether she would prefer to expend the extra energy and money to get him to school on the city bus. These choices were reached through asking questions about what she would like in her life over the next 3 days (the concept of "presence" rather than "absence") and what her life would be like if her son was in school. When framed in this fashion, she had less trouble making a decision and opted for the bus, now viewing this as the lesser of two evils.

In addition to helping her solve a real-life problem, the session was useful in providing her with a new paradigm for problem solving. She took a small step along the road of being able to remove herself from the emotional entanglements of the immediate situation and think through what would make her life more gratifying in a small time period.

Another strategy to deal with feelings of powerlessness is to help facilitate experiences that make a woman feel *successful* and *competent*. For a woman to feel competent in the world often involves her participating in a task or activity that involves other people. When mothers are encouraged to do this, another element that is advocated for strengthening the woman often can be fulfilled—that of membership and community. Many mothers whom I have worked with have not explored the ways in which their talents, skills, and interests can be developed. For some women, this may mean advancing their education. Ms. M, for example, had not received her general equivalency diploma (GED) at the time she began therapy. This was an important goal she set for herself, and as she took the steps to achieve it, she became involved in classes in which she met teachers who provided encouragement and fellow students who provided emotional and academic support, as well as concrete help in the form of assisting with child care or travel.

Other women may be motivated to become more involved in a religious organization. Still others may find that they can reactivate informal social networks that have been neglected due to their preoccupation with their family problems. For some mothers, the separation at disclosure does become an opportunity to focus more on what they want for themselves, and therapy is an ideal place to assist the woman with this.

For a certain percentage of women, often those with a history of childhood sexual abuse themselves, the posttraumatic stress symptoms of flashbacks, intrusive thoughts, and disturbing dreams or nightmares are particularly troublesome. A number of techniques can help a woman regain some control. These include teaching breathing and relaxation exercises and imagery work. These overlap with the section on strengthening coping capacities and will be dealt with in more detail there.

Dealing With Betrayal

Many mothers come to therapy with an expectation that they will be blamed. Some of this is projection of their own self-blame onto the clinician; some of this may be a result of shaming experiences with earlier intervention systems. Women often hear about specialized treatment services or therapy from someone in these systems and may understandably feel that the clinic is an extension of other social services, the court, or family and friends. The woman may or may not have had therapy before. Being sensitive to this and projecting a nonjudgmental attitude are crucial to engaging the mother.

It is critical that the therapist discusses the limits of confidentiality with the mother. This discussion should be more than the clinician simply informing the mother that her communication with the therapist is privileged and that the privilege can only be overridden in a limited number of circumstances (i.e., if the woman is a danger to herself or others, if the clinician learns of her in any way abusing or neglecting a child in her care, or if the court should so order). These circumstances need to be elaborated to ensure that the woman understands. For example, despite the *Tarasoff v. Regents of University of California* (1974) decision highlighting the therapist's duty to warn potential victims, only a limited number of states have laws that require clinicians to warn others if a client makes a threat of harm to another person. The clinician should be familiar with the statutes and case law in her or his state.

Many women, referred directly from CPS or the court, have been encouraged to sign releases as a condition of referral. Even if that is the case, it is important to discuss the ground rules with the woman. What will be the nature of the clinicians' communication with CPS—will it be verbal, in writing, or both? With what frequency does the clinician expect this to take place? Will the clinician be filing a report to the family or juvenile court? Is the clinician part of an agency team that will be filing such a report? If other clinicians are working with other family members, what will be the nature of the communication between those therapists? How much of what the mother reports will get back to the child's or partner's therapist? Will anything get back to the other family member?

The woman's concerns often center on having some control over the communication of information and details about their intimate thoughts and feelings to others. It is crucial for the therapist to discuss with the woman his or her plan for communicating information. Will the therapist inform her before there is a telephone or written communication with another staff member? Will the therapist let her review written material? Will the therapist allow for input into the substance of what gets communicated?

In my experience, all of these details are important to raise in initial sessions. This does a number of things. First, it communicates respect and consideration to the woman. Second, it says that the therapist takes his or her responsibility very seriously and is professional in his or her approach. Third, and perhaps most important for the purpose of establishing a strong working alliance, it gives the woman a sense that she will have some control over the treatment. If possible, I do think that it is important to take the time to discuss with the woman the issues that will be taken up in every communication with someone outside the agency. If the therapist works as part of a team within an institution or agency, I think it is important to let the woman know how often the therapist meets and the purpose of the meetings. I have found that clients are usually pleased to learn that their family is being given attention and consideration outside of the time spent directly with clinicians.

In terms of written reports, it has become my policy to share the written report with the client before it is submitted to the court or another agency. I find this helpful for two reasons. First, clients often pick up unintentional factual errors, sometimes related to a report of family or personal history, that the clinician has recorded incorrectly in his or her own material. Second, it provides an opportunity to open up issues or deal with subjects that may have been missed or need more attention.

The other major stance on the part of the therapist that assists with developing a trusting relationship is more general. It involves putting into operation two major principles. Simply stated, these are as follows: "Don't promise anything that you cannot carry through on, and if you promise something, do it." If there is some reason that the therapist cannot do this, he or she must notify the woman as soon as possible. If nothing else, the experience of being in therapy should be one in which the woman has the experience of working with someone who is trustworthy. There is no guarantee that the woman will come to trust the clinician; however, it is the therapist's responsibility to act in a trustworthy manner. Thus, it is especially important for the therapist to take care with the client and not to be glib or overly ambitious in what he or she thinks can be accomplished. Again, the range of issues in which this can be practiced ranges from the very large (e.g., unrealistic assurances about what treatment or the legal system will or will not do for an individual or her family) to the minute (e.g., reading resources that the clinician promises to locate or help locate). Each interaction needs to be guided by careful thought and follow-through if that is indicated.

A significant modality that is both appropriate and helpful in dealing with sensitivity to betrayal early on in the relationship is assistance with concrete services. This can range from facilitating entitlements to problem solving in regard to issues such as child care and transportation. Providing information about the systems she is involved in may be very helpful. For the mother, CPS and the court system are often confusing and overwhelming. Helping her negotiate them can be very helpful in developing the kind of relationship with the mother that will facilitate her ability to make use of therapy.

Reframing Ambivalence

As discussed earlier, many mothers come to treatment feeling very conflicted because of an allegiance to both their partners and their children. Many women believe their children but feel that they also need their husbands or partners. If a woman comes into treatment saying she does not believe her daughter, the therapist needs to accept her position. Even if the mother is in denial about the sexual abuse, the therapist needs to respect a woman's right to make choices about her life. This is the kind of situation in which the therapist's need to have the woman be a "good" mother, in the sense of putting the child's needs before her own, can interfere with the clinical task of engagement. If the therapist overidentifies with the child's understandable needs to have a more responsive parent and is not able to hear the mother's story, he or she may be on a collision course with the woman that will evolve into treatment dropout or an unsatisfactory or marginal allegiance with the woman.

Many women who have had their children placed in foster care are in this situation. In my experience, in these cases, there are usually many pressing issues for the woman to attend to in addition to sexual abuse. Substance abuse, serious domestic violence, poverty, and lack of job skills are endemic among women coming to the attention of the child welfare system. In cases in which a child has been removed, if a woman has come for therapy, it reflects a desire to continue to parent. Questions that are aimed at eliciting the woman's perspective on the situation—what does she think contributed to her child making the allegations, what is it about the background or family history that makes her think that the abuse could or could not have occurred—may be helpful.

For example, one mother, whose son was in foster care when the allegations of sexual abuse by the woman's common-law husband arose initially, stated that she believed that her son had been molested by her husband. However, in treatment it emerged that, in truth, she thought that her husband could not have done it because he was not "gay." In her way of thinking, only homosexual men molested boys. Although she had a number of concerns about the nature of her sexual relationship with her husband, the fact that he was heterosexual in his peer relationships convinced her that he could not have molested her son. This was an example of where education about offender dynamics was helpful in clarifying cognitive distortions.

Rather than viewing a woman's divided loyalty as a weakness, it can be seen as a strength. Respecting the meaning of her relationship with both her child and partner can help the woman develop a perspective by which to more realistically weigh the benefits—and costs—she reaps from both relationships. The therapist for the mother must recognize and accept that not all women will make the choice to parent over that of staying in an intimate relationship. Many who experience ambivalence will, however, and these are the cases in which an empathic connection to the mother will allow her to act protectively toward her child while working out the future of her relationship with the perpetrator. Part of the clinician's role may be to help her face difficult choices. The child protective and family court system may force choices for which she is not emotionally ready. Helping the woman identify consequences for her actions may be the most that the therapist can offer in these situations. The therapist can provide the safe forum for the woman to sort out her desire for an ongoing connection to the perpetrator while recognizing her desire to parent her child.

Phase 3:   Strengthening Coping Capacities

This third phase can be conceptualized as both crisis intervention and preparation to the work of surfacing traumatic material. It can be crisis intervention when it overlaps with the preceding stage as the therapist works with the mother to mobilize existing ego strengths to help her overcome a debilitating reaction to the crisis of disclosure. Success is defined as the woman's ability to reach a state of equilibrium, when acute symptoms are reduced and the woman can function on a day-to-day basis.

Strategies that I have chosen to emphasize include those that (a) deal with anxiety, (b) encourage ventilation of feelings, (c) reduce cognitive distortions, and (d) reduce depressive symptoms. The reader is referred to the work of Deblinger and Heflin (1996) for an expanded discussion of intervention with the nonoffending mother from a cognitive-behavioral perspective. Their emphasis on coping skills training and behavior management is especially useful in describing strategies that are helpful in this stage of work with mothers.

Overcoming Anxiety. A range of techniques have evolved in working with trauma victims to assist with the occurrence of flashbacks, nightmares, and night terrors and intrusive thoughts that can reflect overwhelming anxiety. These may be especially applicable when the mother has a history of child sexual victimization herself. These include the incorporation of breathing and relaxation techniques into the mother's repertoire for handling stress. These are relatively easy to teach and learn. They can be rehearsed in the therapist's office and practiced at home. Sometimes, it is helpful to have the client make an audiotape for herself or to purchase one that is already made.

Another category of techniques can assist specifically with dissociation symptoms. In general, these can be classified into strategies that help "ground" a woman physically. For example, women can be trained to identify the feelings and bodily sensations that characterize a dissociative state. They include visual, audio, and physical sensations. Typically, if the woman is dissociating, objects or persons close to her suddenly begin to seem far away. Voices or other noises become muffled, and the woman may have the physical sensation of becoming lighter or unable to move. I have had clients for whom wearing a rubber band around their wrist and snapping it to break the trance-like spell has been effective. Others learned to rub their arms against the arms of a chair, if sitting, or to stamp their feet.

In addition, the use of guided imagery can be helpful. With one woman, who tended to have disruptive and frightening dreams, it was helpful to use guided imagery in conjunction with relaxation techniques. The importance of such techniques, as in the case example that follows, is that they may help a woman regain control over sleeplessness or intrusive thoughts that have disrupted daily functioning.

This mother, Mrs. R, was an African American woman who had been severely molested in childhood. She had not remembered much about her own experience until the sexual victimization of her daughter. She began to experience extremely terrifying dreams, often reenactments of abusive experiences.

At the time she came into treatment, she was suffering from sleep deprivation. Afraid to fall asleep, lest the dreams occur, she was keeping herself awake at night. She had taken a leave of absence from her job and described herself as not functioning. We worked out a routine whereby she would put herself into a state of relaxation prior to falling asleep through a deep-breathing exercise. Then she would imagine having a dream in which her father was approaching her. She would put a powerful figure in between herself and the image of her father. In her case, she chose the figure of an aunt. This aunt, her mother's older sister, had often taken Mrs. R in for short periods of time when there was stress and turmoil in Mrs. R's family. At age 13, she had gone to live with her aunt permanently, and her father's abuse had stopped. In her visualization, Mrs. R would tell herself that if her father approached her in the dream, her aunt would step in to stop him. After a few nights of practice, this began to work. Sometimes, the dream would recur the same night, and the presleep routine would not hold. Eventually, however, the intrusive dreams dissipated.

For Mrs. R, visualizing the prelude to a victimization experience and then inserting the figure of her powerful aunt worked. For other clients, imaging the scene of an actual victimization was too frightening. In these cases, rehearsing through telling themselves that, if they had a dream, a powerful figure or barrier would block the assault was sufficient.

Along those lines is the use of the thought-stopping technique. A number of women would report that intrusive thoughts—or, in some cases, flashbacks—were being triggered as they went through their day. One client found it helpful to visualize a red stop sign in her mind when the thoughts began; another found that if she could physically stop what she was doing and tell herself to stop thinking now, then she could deal with this memory later. In both instances, it was important for them to be able to function at work, and the involuntary thoughts were distracting and irritating. They were motivated to gain greater control, and with these kinds of suggestions, they were able to follow through and help themselves.

There is no one technique that will work for everyone. The therapist can approach the task of finding effective ones for a particular client through a problem-solving approach. The client can be engaged in a discussion of the kind of thought, strategy, or relaxation technique that would work best for her. The therapist's task is to identify motivating factors and suggest strategies and alternatives that the woman can pick and choose from and revise as she sees fit.

Encourage Ventilation of Feelings. Strategies associated with ventilation of feelings are probably among the more familiar techniques for clinicians. One of the approaches I use in a session is to use time carefully. I often think in terms of three blocks of time in a session. The beginning of the session is used to reconnect and engage with the client and determine an appropriate direction. The middle section is the "work" phase. This is when one might help the client identify and express feelings. The last part of the session is for regrouping, summarizing, and preparing the woman for reentry into the world of tasks and responsibilities that she usually faces on leaving my office. The goal in the last phase is to promote closure and some cognitive understanding of a particular issue, if appropriate.

In addition to asking a client to articulate feelings as a means of helping her connect to her emotions, focusing on body language is an important tool. Careful attention should be given to shifts in body posture, facial expressions, and eye movements. Strong emotional reactions generally follow the disclosure. As illustrated earlier, some of these feelings, especially angry ones, may be displaced onto the intervention system. Others may be avoided because they are painful and are difficult to approach. Helping the woman develop the ability to process feelings about more immediate issues will prepare her to do this with underlying issues later on.

The process of ventilation also can help women identify strengths. "Hardiness" is one such strength. In a study of 255 women survivors of child sexual abuse, Feinauer, Mitchell, Harper, and Dane (1996) defined *hardiness* as a "learned transformational coping method that buffers stressful life events such as childhood sexual abuse and other external/internal variables that influence the event" (p. 207). They contend that their results support other studies that found a relationship between effective coping skills and general adjustment factors in women survivors of childhood sexual abuse. This is a particularly relevant finding for work with the nonoffending parent, many of whom are survivors, as noted earlier.

Deblinger and Heflin (1996) described the emotional expressive skills that can be taught, and the reader is referred to their work for a fuller description of a particular cognitive-behavioral strategy.

Reducing Cognitive Distortions. This is an additional area that may require attention. Cognitive distortions are introduced as "dysfunctional thoughts" by Deblinger and Heflin (1996) and are helpfully defined to include inaccurate thoughts and nonproductive thoughts (the latter including pessimistic or negative thinking). These authors identify areas where cognitive distortions typically contribute to emotional distress. These areas are responsibility or guilt, sadness, anger, and confusion. Stern and Azar (1998) provide a useful summary of the literature that focuses on the nature of cognitive problems for abusive parents. Although not explicitly comparable to this population, many of the problem areas—including distorted expectations and attributions, poor cognitive problem-solving capacities, and poor anger control and stress management skills—are found in nonoffending mothers. They suggest a range of interventions, including communications skills training, problem-solving training, and anger management skills training.

For the population of nonoffending parents, cognitive distortions can take many shapes and forms and involve misconceptions about CPS, the court system, therapy, the nature of incest, or their own role in it. The latter is the area that can be of particular value for the therapist to understand. What is it that the mother believes about her behavior that may represent a distortion and barrier to effective action currently? A case example may help illustrate this.

CASE STUDY

Mrs. B, a Hispanic woman of Puerto Rican heritage, had married a Dominican 6 years prior to the disclosure of alleged sexual abuse. Cassandra, age 5 at the time of the disclosure, had been spending time with her father on overnight visits from the time she was 3½. Mrs. B began to notice behaviors that concerned her when Cassandra was 4. When she was 4½, Cassandra told her mother that her father was touching her vagina. Mrs. B took Cassandra to a pediatrician, who found no physical evidence. Mrs. B refused to send Cassandra on overnight visits, and Mr. B sought help from the family court. The court threatened to give Mr. B custody if Mrs. B did not allow the visits to continue.

Mrs. B reluctantly allowed the visits to continue. When Cassandra was 5, she again began telling her mother that her father was fondling her vagina. After one visit, her genitals were irritated, and Mrs. B again took Cassandra to a physician, this time to a hospital with a pediatrician who specialized in child sexual abuse examinations. Cassandra told the physician about the latest incident of fondling by her father. Results of the medical examination revealed that Cassandra had contracted a sexually transmitted disease. A report was made to CPS, which resulted in the referral for treatment for both Cassandra and her mother.

In the early phases of treatment, Mrs. B was preoccupied with her own perceived failure to act protectively. She continually cried in sessions, articulating despair about her action to allow her daughter to start visiting her father again after she "knew in her heart" that he was hurting her daughter. Initially, she was impervious to efforts to have her look more realistically at what her options had been.

As she was helped to analyze what steps she could have realistically taken without risking the loss of custody to her ex-husband, her mood changed from one of depression to anger. She began to talk about how one of her brothers had "connections," intimating that she could, if she wanted, have her ex-husband killed. The focus of treatment then rotated to a focus on the consequences of this behavior. Initially, her response to probes was, "I don't care what happens to me—as long as I can get that b. . . ." With continuing attention on the elaboration of consequences (e.g., If you went to prison, what would happen to your daughter? Do you want your daughter to grow up thinking that this is how one resolves disputes?), she was able to redirect her anger in ways that were helpful, rather than hurtful, for her.

Assisting clients to manage affect more productively, especially in the early phases of treatment, helps not only with the substantive issues that the client is dealing with but also with setting the stage for the kind of work that can be done down the road.

Reducing Depressive Symptoms. As illustrated by the case example above, the reduction of depression may come about not only as a result of specific attention to this symptom but also in reaction to attention being paid to other distressing manifestations. However, for some women, a depressive reaction is so overwhelming that it needs particular attention. For some women, the classic presentations of a depressive clinical syndrome are present. For example, consider the following case.

> Mrs. W was a White 42-year-old woman of Irish-German ancestry. She had been married and divorced two times and had three children as a result of the first marriage. At the time that her youngest daughter, Chelsea, then 17, made disclosures of sexual abuse, she had been living with a man, David, for 3 years. Chelsea had reported a history of sexual victimization going back a year, including intercourse over the past few months. Mrs. W's initial reaction had been one of disbelief. Her parents, on whom she was emotionally dependent, spending most of her time with them when she was not working, did not believe their granddaughter. They liked David and said that they thought Chelsea was fabricating the allegations because she was upset about David's attempts to discipline her. In their view, Chelsea was out of her mother's control and reacting to the structure that David was attempting to establish. Mrs. W, very much influenced by their perspective, yet feeling that her daughter was telling the truth, went into a deep depression.
>
> She had stopped going to work, was not getting up in the morning, and was at risk of losing her job. She described herself as not being motivated to clean or cook, being tired but unable to sleep at night, and then sleeping in the mornings after her daughter went to school. Although physically she presented as neat and well groomed, she said that it took her hours to get ready to go out now, whereas she used to get ready quickly. Because many of the symptoms indicated a possible depressive reaction, a referral was made to the agency psychiatrist. This evaluation resulted in a prescription for an antidepressant that was effective and helped Mrs. W mobilize, return to work, and address some of the issues around the disclosure of the sexual abuse.

Although there is no indication that all mothers will have difficulty with depression, there is evidence that many mothers do. Recent evidence suggests that focused, short-term cognitive behavioral treatment may be specifically helpful with this population. Cohen and Mannarino (1998), in an outcome study of sexually abused children, found that children receiving a 12-session program in a cognitive-behavioral course of treatment manifested fewer depressive symptoms (as well as fewer behavioral problems) at the end of the sessions. Although the study focused on children, the complementary nature of the issues for the nonoffending mother suggests that such an approach may be helpful for them as well. Attending to depressive reactions and focusing on reducing anxiety, increasing appropriate expression of feelings, and correcting cognitive distortions early on in treatment will help prepare the mother for the more strenuous work of surfacing the traumatic elements of the incestuous behavior and working that through.

Phase 4: Surfacing Traumatic Effects of the Incest Behavior

In this section, I will emphasize strategies for surfacing traumatic and ego-threatening issues directly connected to the incestuous behavior. This is part of the work of mid-phase treatment and may not be reached in clinical interventions that need to be of short duration, given the realities of managed care and other factors. However, whether addressed as part of an ongoing process or as part of sequential treatment (perhaps even with different therapists), issues that are involved in surfacing the traumatic effects of the incest behavior will probably need to be dealt with to enhance effective functioning and healthy interpersonal relationships.

For purposes of management of material in this book, issues dealing with powerlessness and betrayal will be handled in this section focusing on individual treatment. Issues dealing with stigmatization and sexual traumatization, as they become significant effects that a mother needs to address, will be dealt with in the chapter on group therapy.

For many mothers, after the initial crisis has been resolved and their lives have stabilized, a central question becomes, "How could I have been so out of touch, or so unaware, that I chose a man who would do this to my child?" A corresponding question is often, "How could I have been so unaware, or so overwhelmed, that I did not see what was going on in my family?" These questions often reflect deep, underlying concern about women's ability to make choices and to control their lives. The foundation of their world, what they believed to be true about themselves and their family lives, has been shattered by the disclosure of the incest. "How can I ever trust myself again?" and "How can I trust my partner or another man?" become themes in their lives.

It is critical in therapy to revisit the intimate nature of the relationship with the perpetrator. How was the woman feeling about herself when she became involved with her partner? Who initiated the relationship, and how satisfied was she with different aspects of the relationship—sexual, division of child-caring responsibilities, financial, emotional, social, and so on? How did she resolve conflicts between the demands of being a wife and a mother? Was she able to negotiate successfully in certain arenas but not others? Did she abdicate or delegate responsibility to other family members? How integrated is her level of ego development?

In addition to revisiting the nature of her relationship with the perpetrator in its early development and as it evolved, it is also often important to discuss in detail the nature of the sexual victimization. The reasons for this are similar to the reasons for having a victim recount her memories of the sexual abuse. Therapy provides a forum in which there is a caring person to bear witness to the victim's pain. Second, the telling in detail can generate buried affect that may be important for the person to be in touch with and process. There are often distorted thoughts connected to the initial surfacing of these difficult feelings, and processing them provides an opportunity to correct this.

Deblinger and Heflin (1996) did a nice job of elaborating techniques for gradual exposure to the sexual abuse. They articulated an additional reason for discussion of the abuse, noting that it is an important step in helping the woman broach the topic with her child. Having done the individual work in her own therapy, the mother also will be in a better position to model how thoughts and discussion of the abuse can be tolerated.

Some case vignettes may help illustrate how these issues get played out in the lives of women.

CASE STUDY

Mrs. A was a White college-educated woman and mother of a 4-year-old girl at the time of disclosure. She had been married a number of years out of college. Raised in a well-to-do Irish family that valued sons over daughters, she had been both marginalized and parentified in her family of origin. She had been expected to take care of her brothers, despite the fact that she was the second oldest of five. Her way of obtaining any kind of recognition had been to comply and be a "good" girl. She had had little in the way of sexual relationships before meeting her husband, whom she married at age 29. She described herself as somewhat ambivalent about the marriage but had allowed the social pressure of turning 30 and not being married to sway her. Her husband was already successful in his career, and she was dazzled and impressed by his money and apparent sophistication.

Shortly after the marriage, she became more aware of how dependent he was. He refused to make any choices about the people they socialized with, leaving that entirely up to her. He began to work more out of the home, and after their daughter, Tiffany, was born, Mrs. A quit her job as an accountant.

As Mrs. A looked back on her life at the time she married, she described herself as "not sure of herself" and "searching for someone to look up to and rely on" in her choice of Mr. A. He had appeared to be all of these things when they were dating. She realized, in reviewing the course of her relationship, that she had denied some disturbing impressions evident even before the marriage. As she revisited the courtship period, she became more aware of how unassertive and easily intimidated she had been by any display of discomfort or irritation on his part.

During the time that she was living with her husband, she described him as becoming increasingly verbally and emotionally abusive. When she discussed some of the interactions she had observed between her husband and her daughter, she described feeling uneasy. She felt, for example, that her husband would relate to her daughter more like a peer than an adult. She also remembered being concerned about her daughter's behavior starting at age 3. She described how she would "hump" a large stuffed toy dog. When her daughter first began to reveal things to her, Mrs. A remembered feeling lightheaded and confused.

As she was asked to discuss in detail what she had learned from her daughter about the abuse, she experienced some of the same sensations. Her face became flushed, she reported feeling lightheaded, and she had difficulty articulating her thoughts. Over a period of weeks, she became more able to tolerate the anxiety associated with retelling the abuse. Details that she had absorbed about her daughter's behavior, in particular, poured out. She talked about how she had learned that her daughter was probably repeatedly fondled from the time she was 2. Consistent genital irritation and fearful responses to having her diaper changed now made sense. With the separation from Mr. A, Tiffany had increasingly verbalized what had occurred. The molestation seemed to have included Mr. A fondling Tiffany and many instances of Mr. A rubbing his penis against her unclothed body. It also appeared that he may have masturbated in front of her.

In discussing this, Mrs. A's affect ranged from anxiety to shame and then anger. Initially, it was difficult for her to verbalize her anger. She spoke softly, having grown up believing it was "unladylike" to raise one's voice. Gradually, while her face would still flush, her voice gathered strength, and she was clearer about her anger and more able to articulate it.

When answering questions such as, "What is it that you see in yourself now that was not there then?" she identified greater self-awareness and less dependence on the opinions of others to define herself. Some of this had been achieved through maturity and being in the world of work; some had come through her relationship with her husband. She recognized that she had placed her husband on a pedestal and expected him to meet all of her needs. Not unlike many young women in our society, she was searching for a sense of power and competence in the world and thought that by coupling with Mr. A, she had found this. When he had not helped her increase her sense of power and status in the world and had also been verbally and emotionally abusive, she had felt betrayed and demeaned.

In her case, the mistaken assumption that she could achieve power, status, and authority in the world by attaching herself to a powerful male figure had driven her to choose Mr. A as a partner. Unconsciously, she had been trying to overcome a sense of inferiority and powerlessness that had infused her development of growing up female in a family that preferred males. The disclosure of the incestuous molestation of her daughter triggered the feelings of helplessness and shame as well as rage. She reported feeling that her whole world had been turned upside down, that she had "lost her bearings," and that the incest confirmed her sense of herself as inadequate and adrift.

In treatment, the emphasis was on her strengths. She was helped to see that her college education and work experience were good tools to help her stabilize her family economically after the separation from her husband. She was encouraged to direct her rage productively into her work and into advocacy on behalf of her children. When she became frustrated with the first attorney she retained, she was motivated to replace him and felt powerful after making that choice.

After a year, during which time she obtained the divorce and stabilized herself and her daughter, she began to experiment with dating. At first, she was very cautious and reserved. As she became more involved with a man about her age who was also divorced, she began to see herself differently. She struggled with how to evaluate if he was trustworthy. Encouraged to take her time and discuss the relationship in therapy as it proceeded, she became increasingly confident about asserting her needs, confronting him, and raising difficult subjects. She became more outspoken about her wishes, including her sexual desires, and found that he was responsive. As this and other relationships progressed successfully, she achieved a sense of control over her life and enjoyed the feeling of connection and fellowship that being with others imparted.

The following case illustrates a slightly different dynamic, in which a divorce from a first husband had left a woman feeling inadequate and a failure in her relationships with men. This contributed to a poor choice in a second marriage, which resulted in feelings of devastation when the incest was revealed.

Mrs. L was a first-generation Puerto Rican, both parents having immigrated from there and settled in New York. She grew up in an intact family, as the youngest of four children. The family was Catholic, and although Mrs. L described them as not particularly a churchgoing family, religious values infused her upbringing. She was taught to believe that a man's desires came first, and she witnessed her mother obeying the wishes of her father. In her culture, family honor was important, and her family always chose to resolve disputes themselves. If an outside opinion was sought, it was from Mrs. L's paternal grandmother, who, through her age and gender, enjoyed a position of respect in the family.

Her father was disabled and at home from the time she was 5, and the mother helped with the financial support of the family by doing domestic work. Mrs. L was her father's favorite child, and she adored and looked up to him. At age 20, under the influence of her parents, she married a man 7 years older. Her husband was the first person with whom she had a sexual relationship. They had one son. When her son was 10, they were divorced. Mrs. L experienced this as a failure on her part—she had not wanted the divorce and was bitter and resentful when it occurred. She also felt that she had failed in her duty to the church by being divorced.

During the 2 years between the divorce and when she met Mr. L, she said that she did not date and was conflicted about becoming involved in another relationship. She described Mr. L as being very attentive and "charming" during the courtship. She said that she had not initially viewed him as someone with whom she would become involved but that he did things such as send her flowers and was very responsive to her needs. They were married, and she had a daughter, Rosa, who was 4 at the time of the disclosure of the sexual abuse.

In looking back, Mrs. L became aware that she had been very passive about asserting her own needs. Having ignored her need to be in an intimate relationship, she was vulnerable and somewhat inexperienced in relationships with men. This evolved in the marriage to difficulty asserting her own needs. When her husband "became a totally different person" after the marriage, began to ignore her, and started using cocaine, she felt helpless and trapped. Not wanting to go through another divorce and busy with her daughter, she became more and more withdrawn and depressed.

It was initially very difficult to get Mrs. L to examine exactly what had happened to her daughter. She presented with a stern exterior, stating that it was over, her daughter was in therapy, and she did not really want to know more—she "had heard enough." What she had learned from her daughter was that her father used to come into her bed at night. She said that her daughter had told the police more details, and she knew there was a full statement that had been forwarded to the district attorney's office, but she did not especially want to know what it contained.

While Mrs. L was in treatment, her daughter's behavior escalated. Rosa began to masturbate excessively and to verbalize to both family and friends that her "daddy" had touched her bottom. She became very aggressive with other children and destructive with her toys. She began to throw up her food and wet her bed. In coping with her daughter's behavior, Mrs. L was forced to accept the level of disturbance that had resulted from a severe history of sexual abuse. Mr. L had anally sodomized Rosa, in addition to forcing fellatio. When Mrs. L first verbalized this in therapy, her face crumbled, and she reported feeling "that her limbs were trembling." She was hyperventilating and crying at the same time.

Over time, as the particulars of the acts were discussed, Mrs. L reported recalling incidents when she had woken up and found that her husband was not in bed. She felt a tremendous amount of shame and guilt about the "kind of mother" she had been. She blamed herself for not reading the signs—why, for example, had she not picked up on what she had always thought was Rosa's unusual anger toward her father? When this particular issue was explored, it became clear that Mrs. L had believed that Rosa was devoted and attached to her father. Mrs. L had come to believe that the anger was sporadic and did not mean that much and that this was just her daughter's temperament. In addition, as the abuse had escalated, Rosa had become increasingly oppositional with her mother as well, also contributing to the conclusion that Rosa was just a "difficult" child.

In this case, with the disclosure of the incest, Mrs. L felt completely overwhelmed. She had felt criticized by her family in marrying Mr. L, and they were blaming and relatively unsupportive of her when the sexual abuse was revealed. They expressed both directly and indirectly that she should have never remarried and that if she had put her daughter's needs first, this would not have happened.

Mrs. L presented initially as depressed and overwhelmed. As she worked through the crisis, resolving issues such as housing and income support, she was encouraged to reflect on her relationship with her husband. Mrs. L, shy and inexperienced in her relationships with men and unsure of her own sexuality and what she wanted in a relationship with a man, had been passive in her relationships with men. Indoctrinated growing up into a worldview that dictated that a woman should allow a man to initiate relationships, she had permitted herself to acquiesce to Mr. L's overtures. Her cultural and ethnic heritage reinforced notions about commitment to marriage and family that had contributed to decreasing her self-esteem when the first marriage ended and when the second soured.

With the disclosure of the incest, Mrs. L was helped to think about what she wanted in her life and how to identify and express her own needs. She became more aware of her need to have more control and to be more assertive in expressing herself. She began to look more closely at the values she had derived from her family and reevaluate what she wanted to have as principles guiding her life. She made friends at work with two women, one who was also divorced and one who was single. Through interaction with them and therapy and detachment from the close, everyday connection with her family, she developed a sense of herself as an independent person with choices and decisions that she could and did make.

The third case involves a middle-class White woman who was raised in a strict and abusive home and tried to resolve her conflicts arising from this by marrying someone totally outside her race and culture.

Mrs. Y, 35 at the time of the disclosure of the sexual abuse of her 5-year-old daughter by her husband, had been raised in a Christian Sci-

CASE STUDY

ence home. She described her parents as rigid and often out of control, engaging in screaming and yelling with each other and with the children. She had left home at 18 and attended college where she had met Mr. Y, an African American from a different part of the country. After college, they had married, against the wishes of both families. Her parents had not attended the wedding. He was a practicing Muslim and continued with this practice after their marriage. Mrs. Y abandoned her religion with her husband's encouragement. Mr. and Mrs. Y did not have children for 8 years, and once they did, the "trouble started," according to Mrs. Y. In addition to their 5-year-old daughter, they had a 2-year-old son.

Mrs. Y described a marriage that, although at times conflicted, was manageable before they had children. With the birth of their oldest daughter, differences began to emerge, accentuated by financial constraints. Mr. Y lost his job when their daughter was 1, and Mrs. Y went to work full-time, with Mr. Y assuming much of the child care responsibility. This lasted for 2 years, and after the birth of their second son, Mr. Y found a part-time job. Mr. and Mrs. Y became estranged and were sleeping in different rooms, and the tension level was very high.

After the disclosure of the sexual abuse, Mr. Y disappeared. Mrs. Y believed that he had left the state, if not the country. Mrs. Y moved in with her mother (her father had since died). She needed her mother to help out with the children, as she continued to work, placing herself in a situation in which she was living with another adult who was critical of her. Her mother blamed her for the incest and interfered with the children in a way that was inhibiting and not always helpful to Mrs. Y.

She initially used treatment to complain about her situation. Mrs. Y was able to talk about the details of what had happened to her daughter but did so in a way that suggested that she was not connected emotionally to the meaning for herself. As she discussed the incest, she would become enraged with her husband. She demeaned and vilified him, always trying to engage the therapist in allying with her in regard to what a "bad" person he was.

This reaction had a defensive quality to it. As she was helped to explore this, it became clear that a core belief about herself was that she was inadequate. She harbored deep-seated fears that she must somehow be responsible for the incest. The sense of inadequacy, stemming from her experience in her family of origin, was reinforced by her marriage. Her level of ego development or sense of self as a purposeful, autonomous person was relatively fractured. Reviewing the incest, in her case, provided the pathway to the core, debilitating beliefs about herself.

In Mrs. Y's case, she was encouraged to examine the strengths and abilities she had developed as a result of her success at work. Formerly "put down" by her husband for this and her achievements belittled, she learned to view them as an asset. In treatment, Mrs. Y became more aware of her low self-esteem. As she talked about how her mother had treated her, she became more aware that her mother had been extremely critical and demanding. Mrs. Y had not been allowed to date outside of her religion while at home, and even friends who were not participating in the religion were discouraged. It was expected that she be an excellent student, which she had tried to achieve. When she did not, she was punished, usually by losing socializing opportunities. A by-product of this, as well as a strength, was that Mrs. Y had become a good student, had attended a very reputable college, and developed good work habits and self-discipline. This had contributed to her being successful in the work world, which was a source of satisfaction and self-esteem.

Once she had a better sense of her ability to control her life, attention was turned to the home. Her mother was complaining of the work involved in being available from 6 a.m. to 6 p.m., especially in regard to the care of the young son. Mrs. Y, feeling that her life at home was becoming unbearable, was encouraged to think about options. She employed a baby-sitter to assist her mother and cut down on her own work hours. She also began to make time for herself and her daughter, which helped their relationship, and the daughter's behavior moderated.

All three of these cases illustrate how the mother's negative but entrenched beliefs about herself and her abilities were reactivated in the telling of her story. For all three, an examination of feelings about the incest arose out of an exploration of the nature, duration, and extent of the abuse. As they revisited the incest scenario, core beliefs about themselves, often negative and debilitating, became more apparent, and in questioning these, they were able to reassess and reevaluate their lives.

Phase 5: Identifying Relational Consequences

The identification of relational consequences, as can be seen from the above, is interwoven into the surfacing of the traumatic effects of the incest and cannot readily be separated from that process. It is done so here out of the need to break the healing process down into unique parts, but the parts are interactive and interwoven in the fabric of the woman's life. The relational consequences that I will focus on are the following: the impact of the incest on the woman's relationship with (a) her children and (b) her partner. The relationship with children will be taken up first because it is often the more pressing in the lives of the women who present for treatment.

Consequences of Sexual Abuse on Women's Roles as Mothers

A major underlying issue for many women is their sense of having failed as mothers. This may come out defensively, as it did with Mrs. Y, who attacked her husband without being able to admit to her own feelings, or in depression and anxiety symptoms, when the woman is aware of the feelings of guilt or self-blame and tries to avoid them. This is a difficult and sensitive issue because in many instances, the mother's preoccupation with herself and her own limitations has contributed to a mother-child relationship, but in fact the child's needs have not been fully met. The task for the clinician is to help the mother accept this without turning this into further self-blame, which will only be debilitating. Often, one of the motivations for a woman in therapy is to learn how to be a better parent. It is very difficult to admit that one needs to be a better parent, and this can be successfully addressed only in the context of a "safe" therapeutic environment.

CASE STUDY

Louise was the mother of a 14-year-old daughter, Samantha, who had been adopted when she was 7 months old. The sexual abuse by Louise's husband surfaced for the second time when her daughter confided in a guidance counselor at school. This precipitated a report to CPS and intervention by CPS and the police. Samantha, an emotionally frail and needy child, had a psychotic break, requiring psychiatric hospitalization. Samantha had been in the hospital for 6 weeks when Louise was first referred for treatment for herself.

Early on in treatment, she said that the incest had started when her daughter was 8. Samantha had told her mother what was happening when she was 11. Louise had confronted her father, and they had separated briefly at that time. He had been in treatment with a psychiatrist for a short time but not with someone with experience in treating sexual offenders.

This disclosure also had motivated Louise to seek help for an alcohol problem. She reported at intake that she had been preoccupied with gaining and sustaining her sobriety over the past 3 years and maybe "missed some things with her daughter." Louise had thought that the problem had been solved. Her husband was contrite and remorseful. After a while, they reunited, and she believed that it never had happened again.

In fact, her husband had resumed his molestation of Samantha, and the level of intrusiveness had intensified to the point where he was having intercourse with her. Louise reported that in the 2 years since her husband had been back, her daughter had been "doing terrible in school and very hard to manage at home." Louise attributed this to the start of adolescence.

Lydia had a similar story. Her daughter Elisa, 17 at the time of the disclosure, had been having trouble in school for the past few years. Her daughter had confided to Lydia that her father had approached her sexually, pushing her down on the bed and rubbing her breasts and penis against her. She denied that either had had their clothes off. Lydia blamed others for not figuring out what was going on. As she said, "I took her to the 'best' agencies. She saw the school counselor. She was totally out of control in every aspect—failing in school and everything. Everybody was saying different things: 'You're too strict, she needs this, she needs that,' and not one single person ever asked about sexual abuse." After her daughter was in treatment for a while for the sexual abuse, one of Lydia's ongoing concerns was that something more had happened, that the abuse was more intrusive than initially reported. As she articulated, "My biggest fear is that more had happened." She reported that up until the time of the disclosure, she had been thinking about so many other things that she had not allowed herself to concentrate on what was going on in her relationship with her daughter.

When the incest was disclosed, she reported that she was "going on nervous energy that didn't allow me time to think. I was functioning . . . but it was just a front. I wasn't allowing myself to deal with my feelings. . . . I went through hell; I had to deal with my feelings."

In both these cases, the mothers had seen signs of something very wrong and had even known in one instance of an earlier history of sexual abuse. Yet in both cases, their daughters confided in someone outside the family before they came to their mothers. This compelled Louise and Lydia to examine the relationships with their daughters and what they hoped for in the relationships now. Louise recognized that she had been self-absorbed over the past 3 years. She was able to articulate how her alcoholism had contributed to her not being available to her daughter during the years she was drinking and that the initial disclosure at age 11 had come when she had first obtained sobriety. Since then, her preoccupation with her own recovery and the support of her sponsor and her Alcoholics Anonymous (AA) group to put herself first have contributed to her ignoring some signs. In Louise's case, she needed to accept her daughter's anger at her for not being available and learn how to meet her daughter's needs before the relationship could become closer. Part of her progress came with her understanding that her daughter was functioning on a developmental level below that of her chronological age. This helped her tolerate the neediness she experienced from her daughter.

In Lydia's case, her daughter was older and more distant from her mother at the time of the disclosure of the sexual abuse. Her daughter, Elisa, was on the verge of moving out on her own. Although still living with her mother at the time Lydia started treatment, Elisa was more resistant than Samantha to reestablishing her relationship with her mother. She was oriented outward, to her relationship with a man she was dating and to peers. Lydia had to accept that she needed to let her go, much as her need at the moment was to try to "redo" her parenting. Lydia was trying to be more engaged with her daughter when Elisa needed to move away.

For both these women, accepting how their daughters had viewed them prior to the disclosure of the incest was crucial to their healing. As Louise said, "I think that the reason she didn't tell me was that she saw me as a 'crazy' person—and I was." Lydia articulated her awareness this way: "In the past, I folded under. I could handle some things but not this [the sexual abuse]. My husband saw it and relied on that. My daughter saw it too and didn't communicate with me."

Another woman, Noreen, described her awareness of her daughters' view of her before the incest began in the following way: "They were embarrassed to tell me—they thought I couldn't handle it." She goes on to describe how she could not have handled it—even at the time of the disclosure. It was "too much for me. If they had not taken my girls away, I never would have come here, and I still might not have handled it." In Noreen's case, accepting that her relationship with her daughters was not as close as she wanted it to be, as fast as she wanted it to be, was difficult. For example, Noreen reported feeling alarmed that her daughter had asked her therapist to accompany her to a doctor's visit and not her. Her daughter had many psychosomatic symptoms resulting from the sexual abuse and had refused Noreen's efforts to have her seen by a doctor. The therapist had been successful in negotiating with

Noreen's daughter about this. Noreen was able to articulate how this action on her daughter's part stirred up the feelings that she had not been a good enough mother.

For these mothers, recognizing that they were not emotionally available for their daughters was a crucial step. Grief and sadness accompanied the recognition that they could not go back. Accepting the emotional and developmental consequences for their children and relating in a fashion that met the needs of the children where they were, and not where the mothers would like them to be, were crucial to establishing an ongoing relationship between mothers and children. Some women may have wished that their children had "put it behind them." They would prefer not to see behavior indicating that their children were still struggling with the aftereffects of the abuse. Noreen had difficulty with this dynamic. Wanting a closer relationship faster is another hurdle, as in the situation with both Lydia and Noreen. Learning to accept that being attuned to their daughters' feelings and putting their daughters' needs first was an important accomplishment for both women.

Consequences of the Sexual Abuse on a Woman's Role as a Partner

The consequences of the disclosure of sexual abuse for marriages and partnerships are varied. Much depends on the reaction of the perpetrator. Does he deny the abuse or admit it? Does he accept the idea of treatment? Are there criminal or family court proceedings? Is he the father or stepfather of any of the children? Does he refuse to leave, or does he leave precipitously? Most of the women discussed to date have not wanted to reunite with the perpetrator. But what about the women who do? In the following example, the woman's husband initially denied the abuse but then negotiated a plea bargain in family court, admitting to some allegations of sexual abuse but not all.

Mrs. C was motivated to reunite with her husband after the disclosure of his sexual abuse of their 15-year-old daughter. Married for 17 years, she and her husband had two children, both born before the family immigrated to this country 10 years earlier from Central America. She had learned to speak English but not well. Isadora worked part-time as a housekeeper, and her husband was a manual worker.

After the disclosure by her 15-year-old daughter, Josephina, to her school counselor that her father had been fondling her, masturbating in front of her, and performing "dry intercourse" (i.e., simulating intercourse but not penetrating her), Isadora was shocked and afraid. The resulting intervention placed her in the position of losing her daughter to the foster care system or having her husband move out. She chose the latter.

Mrs. C had resented the imperative to have her husband move out. She complied with the authorities out of fear but was angry and resentful because she felt it made life harder. Although also angry at her husband, after a few months she resumed sexual interaction with him. In exploring the reasons behind her decision, it became clear that her worldview was emphatically shaped by the particular ethnic beliefs associated with being Hispanic and Catholic, as well as with the history of immigration.

In the initial phase of treatment, Mrs. C was still very much involved with her husband. All that the family could afford was for Mr. C to rent a room, without kitchen facilities. Mrs. C was cooking and taking meals to him every day. She also spent time on the telephone with him, as did her son.

Mrs. C's value system did not allow for divorce. Steeped in both religious doctrines that prohibited divorce and ethnic norms that frowned on this, as well as dictating that a woman's place was with her "man," the idea of leaving Mr. C was not one Mrs. C had considered. In addition, the economic realities of her life made it difficult for her to explore this as an option. Primarily reliant on her husband's income, she could not have afforded to support the family, given her training and experience, without his income. This reality fueled her decision to "make it work."

The idea of therapy was alien to Mrs. C initially, and certainly the concept of discussing intimate details of either the sexual abuse or her sexual relationship with her husband was uncomfortable to her. However, her husband was also in treatment, and as time went on, he was able to acknowledge the extent of the sexual abuse and began to take responsibility for it. This acknowledgment, which came after the legal issues had been decided, was a turning point for Isadora in her own therapy.

One major step was the recognition of how the incest had affected her relationship with her husband and her daughter. She had lost respect and standing in the eyes of both. Her daughter was angry because she believed that her mother did not care about her. Her husband, confused and guilty, projected his unhappiness onto her. As Mrs.

C became more aware of the extent and degree of betrayal, learning that both he and her daughter had lied to her about many things, she became angrier. Although at first it was easier to direct this anger toward her daughter, in time and with the assistance of the marital therapist, she was also able to confront her husband more directly.

In this case, the family's goal was to reunite. The principle guiding the process, however, was that reunification would occur at the daughter's pace, not the parents', and only after the father had participated successfully in sex offender treatment. Progress was slower than Mrs. C wanted, and again her initial tendency was to blame her daughter for "not getting better quicker." One task of treatment was helping her focus on the fact that although a speedier reunification would meet her needs for increased financial flexibility and help with both the house and the children, it would not necessarily meet her daughter's needs.

In her individual sessions, she was encouraged to explore her motivations. It became clear that underlying the apparent lack of empathy toward her daughter was her own sense of insecurity and concern about the family's ability to stay in this country. She desperately wanted to have her children attend school in this country, and she was worried about the family's financial security and ability to continue to live here if Mr. C was not able to return home soon.

This was a case in which Mrs. C's dependency on her husband was multidetermined. She had overriding concerns about finances and stability. However, even without these factors, she was motivated by strong cultural and religious norms to stay in the marriage. Mr. C's acknowledgment of the abuse was an important variable as well. A large part of Mrs. C's growth and subsequent ability to assert her own needs and respond more empathetically to her daughter was due to the fact that she became more aware of how frightened and alone she had felt since moving to this country. Before the disclosure of sexual abuse, she had harbored feelings of inadequacy in her role as wife and mother and had chosen, in DeYoung's (1994) words, the path of "intrapersonal role redefinition." Mrs. C had rotated her attention between the demands of mother and wife, never quite meeting the demands of either. This had contributed to her sense of inadequacy as a wife and mother and set in motion a downward spiral in which she withdrew from friends and family out of an increasing sense of worthlessness.

In treatment, she was helped to move to a new position, one DeYoung (1994) characterized as "interpersonal role redefinition." In therapy, especially through the format of couples and family therapy, Mrs. C was helped to develop problem-solving abilities. She was encouraged to seek support from her husband with parenting tasks as the family reunified. These tasks ranged from assisting with the provision and monitoring of discipline to helping with grocery shopping. In addition, Mrs. C was encouraged to eliminate certain behaviors that were stressing her personal resources and could be carried out by others. These included having her daughter assume more responsibility for housekeeping chores and having her husband assist with transportation of her son to and from activities.

Mr. C was engaged in treatment concurrently with Mrs. C and the family. He attended individual and group therapy and worked conjointly with Mrs. C in therapy before he joined the family sessions. He was only permitted to participate in family sessions after he demonstrated the ability to accept emotional responsibility for the sexual abuse and admit that to his wife and daughter (the victim).

Some women choose to stay in relationships with the alleged perpetrators, even when the men do not receive offender treatment or admit to the abuse. In these circumstances, if the child has been determined by either CPS or the court to have been abused, the therapist must keep protective concerns at the forefront—especially if the child is in the custody of the mother. If the child is not with the mother, there may be other professionals involved in the case with whom the mother's therapist can coordinate treatment.

If the child is with the mother and the alleged perpetrator has contact with the child because the mother chooses to sustain the relationship, one condition for treatment for the therapist to encourage is no unsupervised contact between the child and the alleged perpetrator. It is also helpful in these kinds of cases to actively encourage the mother to engage the child in his or her own therapy, so that an additional resource is available to the family. In some cases, the mother's therapist may need to report again suspicions of abuse if, in her work with the mother, the therapist comes to believe that the child is at risk of reabuse.

For a woman who does not want to reunite with the abusive partner, there are other tasks, particularly as she begins to consider becoming involved in new intimate relationships. Louise, described earlier, reacted initially to discussions of dating by isolating herself because she did not trust herself to make a good choice. This insight was actually a first step in coming to terms with some difficult issues. As the reader will recall, Louise was a recovering alcoholic at the time of the second disclosure by her daughter. This disclosure resulted in intervention by the authorities, including criminal prosecution of her husband. She initiated divorce proceedings. Louise's tasks included becoming more aware of the fears and distorted beliefs about herself that contributed to her avoiding and distrusting her own feelings about her relationships.

Noreen's response to new relationships with men was reflective also of the movement from distrust of men to distrust of herself in relationship to men. Like many women, early on after the decision to make the separation from her husband permanent, Noreen felt that she could "never trust a man again," that there were "too many sick people out there" and "how do you ever know what you are getting into?" She moved from this stance to one in which she recognized that she also had had trouble both identifying and trusting her feelings. She became cautious about entering into relationships because she did not trust herself. During this period of her life, she set up rigid and somewhat artificial boundaries with a man she was dating. She would not see him more than once a week and never allowed him to sleep over at her apartment.

Part of her treatment involved learning how to identify who was trustworthy and who might be appropriate to depend on. As her own self-worth increased, she became more confident about making these kinds of judgments. Basic tenets of negotiating relationships, such as learning to express what she wanted, evaluating responses (i.e., did he respond well or with irritation?), taking time to see if he was reliable (i.e., did he follow through, did he promise things he never did?), and so on were critical in helping her learn how to be both more assertive and work together with someone in a reciprocal relationship. These skills are among the most important and take time to accept, practice, and integrate.

Lydia, the mother of Elisa, also had decided soon after the disclosure that the separation from her husband would be permanent. However, in her case, despite the fact that she had put this legal closure on her relationship, she remained emotionally attached to the perpetrator. This is illustrated by an incident she recounted in the group after a year and a half of being in treatment. Her daughter was about to move out of the two-bedroom apartment they shared. Lydia immediately began to think about moving into a studio apartment. When the reasons for this were explored with her, it became evident that she was driven by feelings of helplessness and powerlessness, even a year and a half after the separation from her husband. As she explained it, she expected that with Elisa out of the home, her husband would be "coming around again." She felt that it would be "easier not to give in" and "easier to refuse" him if she did not have the room for him to move in. The strength of her attachment and dependence is evident in this example. With the support of the psychotherapy group, she took steps that were more direct and less disruptive to her own life, choosing to stay in the apartment.

Phase 6:   Working Through and Resolution

As noted at the beginning of the chapter, the process of working through is often one in which the woman identifies an issue, explores the impact on herself and significant others, expresses her feelings directly about this both to herself (and, if necessary, to others), and then works to make changes in a desired direction. This work is often repetitive in that no sooner has one issue been laid to rest, then another appears to take its place. There are ways, however, to identify whether the traumatic effects of the incest have been minimized or resolved. For example, one indication of resolution is the manner in which a woman can talk about the traumatic stimuli without the accompanying involuntary, overwhelming emotions. The following is an example of this process, which, although drawn from a group setting, reflects work done in both individual and group therapy.

CASE STUDY

Noreen was present in the group on the day that a new member joined. As part of the introductory process, each member outlined briefly what had occurred in her family. When it was Noreen's turn, she outlined succinctly but fully what had happened to her two daughters. She elaborated without hesitation when asked a question by a new member, and although she spoke rapidly, some of the earlier signs of anxiety and depression were not there.

Later on in the session, the group was asked to give Noreen feedback about how she had come across during the introductions. One member commented on how different she sounded. She remarked that Noreen always used to get "red in the face and wring her hands" when she talked. Another said that she noticed that Noreen talked more easily, that before she would answer with one-syllable words, and that it had seemed as if she wanted to "disappear into the woodwork." The group also noted that in general, Noreen's presentation was more animated. She was more engaged; in fact, at times, she often led the discussion in the group and was always active. This was in stark contrast to earlier sessions, in which she had sat still, not talking and often not

moving much. The change reflected not only the reduction in anxiety
but also the fact that she was no longer depressed.

Noreen still had issues she was working on, but the traumatic effects were clearly reduced. The ability to articulate past events in a manner suggesting that strong affect no longer accompanies the memory is a good indication of the degree to which an experience has been integrated. A decrease in the impact of the sexual abuse also can be seen in the woman's relationships. One gauge is the degree to which the woman has the psychological energy to devote to her relationships. For women who are substance abusers, control over their addiction is often a reflection of and a contributor to an increase in self-esteem.

One important gauge of the degree of resolutions is the commitment to the process of establishing a closer and, for the mother, a more empathic relationship with her child. In terms of relational consequences with her partner, as illustrated by the case examples, self-examination of one's motivation to be in a relationship and a better understanding of one's own needs and rights in a relationship are two indicators of growth in interpersonal relationships. In addition, the ability to practice negotiating assertive skills in interpersonal relationships rather than resorting to a submissive role, especially if the partner has been physically abusive, is an indication of a better resolution of the traumatic effects. In general, increased comfort in managing the role conflict between the demands of wife or partner and mother signals an improvement in relationship skills that, it is hoped, will serve the woman well in subsequent interactions.

GROUP TREATMENT

Group treatment may occur simultaneously with other treatment modalities or alone. However, the goals of group treatment parallel in many respects the goals of individual treatment. As discussed in the previous chapter, the goals are, broadly speaking, to assist in engaging the woman in treatment, strengthen her coping abilities, address the traumatic effects of the incestuous behavior, and assist the woman in identifying and dealing with the impact of the sexual abuse on her primary relationships. The traumatic effects are traced according to the traumatic dynamics model (Finkelhor & Browne, 1985), and the model itself provides some guidelines for the group process. Issues women have around trust speak to the need to handle "boundary" issues carefully in relationship to group formation, especially membership and confidentiality. The sense of powerlessness women often feel heightens the need for the group to be experienced as a safe space. The therapist needs to establish this by paying attention to boundary issues and by sensitively attending to latent content and relationships between group members. Because of the common stigma felt by women who are mothers of sexually abused children, the group can be a powerful medium in which issues around stigmatization and sexual traumatization in particular can emerge and be processed.

Groups also can be extremely effective in reducing cognitive distortions and increasing problem-solving abilities, strategies that are useful in strengthening coping abilities. Groups can be very influential in helping a woman move from a less adaptive way of handling role conflicts to more adaptive strategies of negotiation and delegating (Levin, 1992). Two primary relationships that are often critical for the woman are her relationship to her partner and her relationship to her children. The modeling and sharing that go on among members around these two issues can be more effective at times than anything an individual therapist can achieve.

As with any group, trust must be developed between members, and as noted earlier, because of the tendency for women not to trust due to the feelings of betrayal, the way a group forms and the manner in which new members are introduced are of critical importance. Strategies that reflect sensitivity to boundary and safety concerns are (a) pregroup interviews with prospective members, (b) pre- and postgroup conferences before each session if a group is co-led, and (c) significant time and attention devoted to confidentiality issues, both between members and between members and the leader(s).

Mothers can be at different phases in their own process and still have a positive group experience if the norms and expectations of the group members are tailored to fit differences. For example, a long-term group in which members are in the mid-phase work of addressing issues around relational consequences can be extremely helpful to a new member who enters in crisis immediately following a disclosure. The old members can validate and problem solve and provide concrete examples to the new member of other women who have lived through a similar crisis. The older group members can have the satisfaction of helping another and of being able to gauge how far they have come from their own crisis. The group, however, has to be open to the process of including new members in crisis because members in crisis are often very needy and may take a good deal of the group's time initially. If the group is educated to the dynamics of crisis, they know that individuals rarely stay in acute stages of crisis for more than 4 weeks and, knowing this, can tolerate the diversion of energy from issues with which longer-term members may be struggling. In addition, as members are added and stay beyond their own crisis, a norm is established that facilitates a group process open to helping new members. In a cohesive, well-functioning group, the curative effect of altruism operates to encourage members to help others as members benefit from the sense of well-being that usually accompanies the knowledge that they have aided another.

If the group is a time-limited, short-term group, more attention may need to be given to selecting members who are at similar phases. An example is a time-limited group that I led in which all of the mothers were past the crisis of disclosure, as this had occurred a minimum of $1\frac{1}{2}$ years earlier for every member. All were separated from their partners, and, in some cases, women were in new relationships. All of their children were or had been in therapy. The women's issues centered on their relationships with their children, and the focus of the group was largely on helping them deal with behavioral problems and the feelings arising from the awareness of the severity of the disturbance in their children as a result of the sexual molestation. In this group, partly because of the time—6 months in duration—it would have been difficult after the group started to incorporate new members, especially if that member was in crisis.

Beginnings

Leadership

A few basics may be helpful. First, a decision needs to be made about whether the group will be co-led. I have had the experience of co-leading groups with colleagues and with students, as well as running groups alone. Each has unique advantages and disadvantages. The advantage of a co-therapist is that there is, perhaps, greater opportunity for a "self-righting tendency" with another therapist present and, to that extent, perhaps a greater capacity to keep the group a safe place. There are many themes and dynamics swirling in any given session, and finding the right balance between meeting the needs of the group as a whole and the individual needs of members is both the challenge and the exciting part of group work. It can be easier if there are two sets of eyes and ears in the room.

In addition, the presence of two leaders provides the group with a model of how two people can negotiate differences within the context of a peer relationship. This can be especially important as the mothers deal with issues around role conflicts in their own peer relationships. It may be especially powerful if the two leaders are male and female because this will present a role model for a healthy male-female relationship. Co-leaders also can ensure more continuity for the group because if one leader has to be absent for any reason, the group can still meet. However, it demands that the two leaders work closely together. They need to commit to developing a working relationship that is characterized by a willingness to share and to confront when necessary. This aspect of co-leadership is not easy to achieve, and when it is not present, the co-leadership can become less than effective.

The nature of the relationship between the two therapists needs to be acknowledged. The rationale for doing this explicitly relates, again, to the extra attention that needs to be given to boundary issues. Given that the group of women have had their own boundaries as well as those of their children violated, clarity in the relationship becomes extremely important. For example, when I co-led a group with a student or a staff member who I was supervising, it was clearer if the relationship between us was defined as leader and assistant. This reflects the true balance of power in the relationship outside the group. Sometimes, leaders have difficulties with this; the assistants may feel that they will not be valued by group members if they are not presented as "equal." However, if the leaders treat the assistants with respect and value their contributions, then the members usually do also, and the feelings can be worked through.

If, on the other hand, I co-led with a peer, it would be important to present us as a team of equals because in reality, this would be the case. The co-leadership between equals has some advantages. There is often a strong degree of confidence that one can rely on the other leader and the sense that the responsibility is, in fact, shared. It also may be easier to deal with conflict between therapists who are peers because each may feel freer to disagree. On the other hand, feelings of competitiveness can be heightened because the two are equal. Whatever the decision, it is important to establish clear boundaries between the two co-leaders and to communicate this to the group.

It is also important to establish a process for ongoing communication between the leaders about the group, its phase of development, and the treatment issues for individual members. In general, allotting time both before and after the group for discussion between co-therapists is critical. The focus of these pre- and postgroup sessions can be on the co-therapist's work together in the group as well as on the issues of the members.

There is also the issue of who interviews prospective members. Ideally, both therapists should interview the woman together. However, this is not always possible. In that case, decisions need to be made. Does the assistant, as in the first model, ever interview members? Are decisions about inclusion always made jointly, or are there instances in which one or the other therapist might decide alone? In general, good practice dictates that if the woman cannot be interviewed by both therapists, the case should be discussed jointly before any decision is made. It is also preferable that if peer co-therapists are not co-leading the group, the person mainly responsible should conduct the initial interviews. However, this will depend on the level of experience of the assistant. In some instances, the less-experienced therapist may be just that—less experienced but still quite able to glean the kinds of significant information that needs to go into a decision about whether to include a particular woman in the group.

Whether it is two leaders or one conducting the pregroup interview, the process needs to be made clear to the prospective member. Is this a process in which the therapist(s) will decide who is appropriate for group? Does the woman's participation depend on her agreement to participate? If the group experience is "prescribed," for example, and the purpose of the interview is to educate her about the type of group and to determine if there are any reasons that the group might be counterindicated, then this needs to be made clear. If, on the other hand, the interview is proceeding on the basis that the woman may be interested but may not want to join at the time, then a different agenda is operating for both the prospective member and the leaders. Reasons for rejection should of course be communicated directly to the woman.

If the therapist chooses to lead a group alone, it may be less time-consuming in terms of the time devoted to working on the relationship with the co-therapist. In addition, some potential benefits to an individual leader model relate to the experiences of the mothers, especially if one has a number of women who are operating as single parents. The single-leadership model will intensify the recapitulation of the single-parent family. It can ideally provide the mothers with a model of how the one in charge can meet the competing needs of a number of people and yet at the same time help each person to feel valued, respected, and cared about. To the extent that these processes in the group become explicit, they can be instructive for group members who are struggling with being single parents. The themes and issues to be addressed in a group are powerful, and it may be helpful for the therapist who is a single group leader to have in place some vehicle of her or his own to assist with the "self-righting tendency" noted earlier. It is easier, without another leader present, to fall into alliances or power struggles with individual members. Whether the vehicle is peer supervision or consultation, it is usually helpful to have some way of processing both one's own feelings and the work of the group.

Membership

Although much has been written in group therapy and group work literature about criteria for starting groups (Brandler & Roman, 1991; Yalom, 1985), it has been my experience that, in general, group members are drawn from the caseload of the therapist or agency in which the therapist is working. Nonetheless, there are some important factors to consider. Traditional approaches to group therapy often suggest that clients be excluded if they are psychotic, are active substance abusers, or carry particular diagnoses such as antisocial or borderline disorders. This may be a helpful starting point, but there are a number of additional issues in working with mothers of sexually abused children. The goal of any group formation is to achieve a balance between similarity and difference that both allows for a dynamic tension that can induce a useful amount of anxiety while generating enough of a sense of universality that the group can coalesce. For these women, issues of similarity have been elucidated in terms of the traumagenic dynamics. That is, the women, in general, will be similar in that they will have experienced the disclosure as traumatic and be struggling, to varying degrees, with feelings of betrayal, sexual traumatization, stigmatization, and powerlessness. Issues of division revolve around the woman's unique coping abilities and relationships with the child victim and offender.

Typically, women who have more positive relationships with the alleged or identified perpetrators may be less willing to confront the reality of the sexual abuse of one or more of their children. They may want to remain with the perpetrators. This perspective may be in stark contrast to a mother who is divorced from the perpetrator who has molested her child. She may be more outraged and angry at the offender. Sometimes, mothers of younger children, who may have less of an investment in a relationship than women with adolescent children, fall into the latter category, whereas mothers of adolescents fall into the former. In a newly formed group, the greater the division among members along the lines of those who ally primarily with the offender versus those who ally primarily with the child, the greater the risk of obstacles that may be too difficult to overcome. This is when the age of the group may make a difference. A long-term group that has a core membership and has been through the process of having members come and go may be better able to tolerate these differences.

A case example may help illustrate this. In an outpatient group of mothers of sexually abused children, five women had been members of a group for more than a year when Aleysha joined the group. She had sought individual treatment following the disclosure by her 16-year-old daughter that her partner had been molesting her for 2 years. However, she was in denial and unsure of whether to believe her daughter at the time she came into treatment. She was recommended to group by her individual therapist and joined somewhat hesitantly. It is important to note that she was the only member at that time in denial, as all the other members were months further along in the treatment process.

At the time she came into the group, she wanted very badly to have a relationship with the alleged perpetrator, and she was not even sure that she believed her 16-year-old daughter. For the first few sessions, she sat very still and did not contribute much, and when she did, it was often to defend her partner. The following describes her reactions in one of the early sessions.

Another member (Laura) talked about how her daughter had been, in effect, prostituted by her husband. She related that her husband had given her daughter money, and now one of the problems for her daughter is that she "thinks she is a prostitute." Laura related this out of frustration, describing how entrenched this belief was for her daughter and how much pain this brought her. She talked about how her husband, despite all that had come out about the incest, was denying that he had abused their daughter. Aleysha, after listening for a while, volunteered that her partner was in therapy. She stated that she did not think "he was ever that bad. He never gave her money or anything . . . maybe a car."

The rest of the group members began to gently confront. How was giving a car that different from giving money? One member, Carrie, tried to empathize, saying that it was really hard to believe and that she still does not know all that happened. Carrie said that for her, listening to a story such as the one Laura told scares her. She admitted that she still gets upset thinking about it and can understand how hard it is to accept that someone could do this kind of thing. Carrie stated that she does not know "how a person could do that . . . knowing you were destroying that child's life."

The rest of the group had been together for quite some time and were comfortable with each other. As Aleysha began to talk more about her situation, group members greeted statements such as "I want to be with him" and "I'm not sure I believe my daughter" with tolerant silence or questions that were asked in a tone that suggested they were seeking understanding and were not out to condemn.

CASE STUDY

The longer that Aleysha was in the group and listened to the other stories, the more she began to identify dynamics that were common to her own situation. For example, another member had an adolescent daughter. As Aleysha heard that mother describe her daughter's predisclosure behavior and what she had come to understand about her daughter's feelings, Aleysha began to note that she too had seen this in her own daughter. As the women talked about the shock and disbelief some of them had experienced when Child Protective Services (CPS) first came to their doors, Aleysha identified more similarities.

After about 2 months of weekly attendance, Aleysha began to take a markedly different position. She began to believe her daughter more and with this entered a period of grieving the loss of her relationship with her partner. A difficult part of this process for her, as for many mothers, was coming to terms with the fact that emotional distance had begun in the relationship long before the incest was disclosed. A relatively serious depression accompanied this awareness for Aleysha. She began having difficulty sleeping and, because of sleep deprivation, was experiencing difficulties at work. With the help of other group members, she was convinced to accept a referral to the clinic psychiatrist for an evaluation. As a result of this, medication was prescribed; she was resistant to taking this. Again, group members were influential in pointing out the benefits of getting some relief through medication, and she eventually had the prescription filled and did experience relief.

In her participation in the group, Aleysha had the experience of learning to talk and get helpful feedback. This is often an eye-opening experience for many women, especially if they start the group feeling shy and have difficulty expressing themselves. The development of trust and the experience of sharing and of both being helped and giving assistance to others are a powerful curative factor. It often has the beneficial effect of helping the woman be more assertive or speaking up for herself in naturally occurring groups—such as family, friendship groups, or work groups. As the woman's self-confidence in her ability to articulate her wishes and positions is strengthened, she experiences a greater degree of mastery over her life.

The tolerance of other group members, some of whom also had been in denial early on, is often pivotal in helping a woman such as Aleysha to accept the reality of the abuse at her own pace. In this case, older group members were successful in incorporating a new member who had been in denial. This may not always be successful, and the amount of time to keep a woman in the group who does not appear to benefit is the kind of judgment call that needs to be made in determining membership.

Another major factor in terms of differences that may be critical is that of mandated clients versus those coming voluntarily to treatment. As discussed earlier, many mothers come to treatment because they have been referred by CPS or have been ordered by a juvenile court judge, usually as a condition of either having their children returned or as a result of being supervised by social services and the court. There are two issues to consider regarding the status of prospective members in terms of this continuum. One has to do with the psychological readiness to engage in the work. For a good group process to occur, it is necessary to strike a balance between members who are prepared to work and those who may need exposure to the process and promise of therapy before they can commit to the hard work of treatment.

The other consideration has to do with the therapist's stance in regard to prescribing the modality or type of treatment provided to the woman. Whether a woman is court ordered to therapy or not, the form that therapy takes—whether individual, group, family, or a combination—is an issue that should be decided by the therapist and the woman. If women have been court ordered to treatment, one approach is to decide that the therapist or treatment program will then prescribe the kind of treatment, and if the therapist feels that a woman would benefit from group treatment even if she is not particularly open to attending the group, she may be encouraged to do so. Another approach, when the therapist thinks that the mother would benefit from group therapy, is to encourage her but give her the choice of whether and when to attend.

Both approaches have their advantages and disadvantages. Sometimes, one will have the experience in which not requiring a woman to attend group against her will results in later concluding that both she and her children would have benefited had she participated. However, it is also possible that women who were initially resistant to the idea of attending a group may become more open to it after time in individual treatment. Leaving the option open and not insisting that the woman start attending the group can work in some instances. These clinical decisions need to be considered and made on an individual basis by each therapist. Although my preference is to encourage but leave the ultimate choice up to the woman, this may be because of my experience with, generally speaking, a treatment-compliant population. Therapists working with hard-to-reach women, who are significantly alienated to begin with from helping systems, may find that conveying the expectation that women attend the group is more effective.

Confidentiality

Even more than with individual treatment, the issue of confidentiality has to be handled especially carefully. Group leaders should plan to spend a good deal of time in the initial sessions of a group and, when a new member joins, in processing these issues. To reiterate, these mothers are typically women who have been betrayed and had their trust in others threatened. Many are survivors of child sexual abuse themselves. In addition to not trusting others, they often do not trust their own feelings, judgment, or abilities. In addition, they may have experienced child protective and court systems as intrusive, and, in fact, these systems may not have intervened in a sensitive manner. Women may have had the experience of having intimate details "bandied" about in court or even in the newspapers, if there is a criminal matter pending. Therefore, there are at least two levels at which confidentiality needs to be addressed. First, there is the issue of trust between group members. Second, there is the issue of trust between the group members and the group leader(s).

Especially critical at the beginning of group is what and how much the group member may reveal outside of the group and how much the therapist reveals to other professionals, both within or outside of the treatment setting. Many times, mothers are in individual or some other form of therapy at the same time that they are in the group. This may be particularly true if the group treatment is part of a specialized treatment program for child sexual abuse, in which individual, conjoint, and/or family treatment are a regular part of the therapy process. Even if this is not the case, mothers are often involved with other systems—such as CPS, social services, and the family or criminal court—as well as other therapists. What they thought was confidential may have been violated.

A few principles are helpful in terms of dealing with confidentiality issues between group members. First, at the time of the initial interview for the group, the possibility that the woman may know someone else in the group should be introduced and discussed. I have had that experience twice; while working in a treatment program in a large metropolitan area, two of seven or eight women had a previous connection. In one case, their children were in the same school, although 4 years apart in age. Although they had not met previously, they did attend common school functions, and the chance of running into each other now was likely. In another case, the women were distantly related—one was married to a man whose niece married the son of a cousin of the other woman's husband. They had only met once—at the wedding—but knew, of course, of each other's family. It helped in the initial processing of this coincidence that they had been prepared for the possibility in the initial interview for the group.

One goal of the initial interview is to process with the woman how she would want to handle the situation if it arose. In most instances, the mother's thoughts usually have been something such as, "Well, she would be there because the same thing had happened to her, so it would be all right." I usually suggest that the woman think about this before the group starts to know more specifically what she might want to request of the other woman or what the other might request of her if the situation should arise. The impact of this discussion on the client is usually to highlight the sensitivity with which the therapist is approaching the group.

Once the group starts, it is imperative that a good deal of time be devoted to a discussion of confidentiality. An important issue to resolve is how much contact members want outside of the group or how much they will interact if they meet accidentally. Even in metropolitan areas, where women may live in fairly widely scattered areas, they may run into each other. In small towns or rural areas, this is much more likely. Issues to be addressed can often be posed in questions. Would they want to acknowledge the other person? Would it make a difference if they were alone or with someone else? These questions usually stimulate women to think through issues such as who in their families and social networks knows about the sexual abuse and how they feel about identifying themselves as members of a mothers group. In addition, and perhaps more important, the issue of whether and how the group members want to have contact outside the group usually arises. If there are group members who want to initiate contact immediately by exchanging phone numbers or the like, I suggest that they wait until they know each other better. I find that some of the women's issues around lack of boundaries and the need for connection sometimes impel them to reach out prematurely.

It may be counterproductive to have a hard and fast group rule that says no contact outside of the group, but it is usually effective to suggest waiting because some members consider it too threatening to exchange telephone numbers or establish contact outside the group in some other way. With long-term groups, I have found that at some point, some of the members may have had contact. As long as this is known to the group and its impact processed, I have not found this to be a problem. With short-term or time-limited groups, I have found that it generally works well to establish the same kind of boundary. Some groups may become comfortable with contact outside before the end of the allotted time, but often they do not. I view the decision to have contact not necessarily as a measure of cohesion but rather as a reflection of the composition of the group.

Equally important is the degree of confidentiality that group members bring to discussions with other family members in treatment. For example, at one time I was the co-leader of a mothers group, and a number of the mothers had spouses or partners in treatment in the same agency. One of the women in my group went home and told her spouse about a group session—specifically, events, thoughts, and feelings of individual members. Her spouse brought one of these issues up in his group, which was attended by the partner of another woman in the mothers group. This man went home and talked with his wife, who then became outraged that something she had said or a thought she had expressed had ended up in the men's group. This incident highlighted the importance of processing with the mothers that although they can share their own feelings about the group or insights they came to, it is not permissible to talk about other members' families or any identifying characteristics of group members with anyone outside the group.

A second factor, directly related to how the member is going to learn to trust the therapist, is the degree to which the therapist can and will keep information confidential. This necessitates work on the therapist's part in clarifying how communication will flow between her or him and other professionals and other family members. As noted earlier, mothers often enter therapy while there is an ongoing CPS investigation or an ongoing court process, either in the juvenile or criminal court. The woman may have been required to sign a release of information for CPS, for example, which enables the therapist to communicate with CPS. The mother needs to know what and how information will be communicated. The same holds true for the court. If the therapist or treatment team is required to submit reports to the court or another supervising body (e.g., the local department of social services or, in some instances, criminal probation), the mother likewise needs to know what and how that information will be processed. I have found it particularly helpful to review written reports first with the mother whenever such a report relates to her treatment. No matter which procedure is used, however, the important factor lies in the discussion with the mother so that she knows what is being said and why and to reiterate these norms for the group.

Increasingly, mothers of sexually abused children are seen in clinics or agencies where their children or partners also may be in treatment. Commonly, therapists work as a team, or even if they do not have a specialized sexual abuse treatment team or program, they may meet to discuss cases. I have found that it is helpful if the client knows from the beginning if the therapist is part of a team that shares information. It is also important to describe the kinds of information that is discussed, why it may be important to share information, and to whom this information goes. I have had mothers who thought that other family members in treatment might learn of something they said through their therapist. For example, a mother was concerned that her child's therapist, on learning about continued contact that she was having with the perpetrator, might communicate this to her daughter. From a treatment perspective, whether or not the therapists believed that the daughter should know, both therapists would need to respect the mother's wishes. It was reassuring for the mother to learn that the daughter's therapist would never tell the daughter something like this.

In fact, information gained from treatment of one family member may influence how a case is approached or an issue is dealt with in therapy with other family members. This can be acknowledged while ensuring that particular thoughts and feelings of the mother will not be shared. The use of group time to do this is often instrumental in solidifying trust between group members and the therapist(s).

The Treatment Approach in Group Therapy

The six-phase treatment approach outlined earlier is applicable to the group therapy process as well. Because mothers can benefit from the group at any stage of treatment, it follows that the stages in an individual woman's process of healing will need to be interwoven with the group process. Thus, part of the assessment of prospective group members needs to revolve around identification of where the woman is in her process and how the group can address this. If the group is conceptualized as a short-term, time-limited process, it may not accommodate members who are in vastly different phases.

However, if one starts a group with mothers who are first coming into therapy just postdisclosure, the stages of the treatment approach can guide the process. A group that has just formed will deal with the group issues of engagement of group members and the strengthening of their ability to cope with their current life situations. Similarly, as trust and cohesion develop, group members become more open to dealing with the difficult issues of identifying the traumatic effects and relational consequences. The group forum is well situated to problem solving and growth around these relationship concerns. For a short-term, time-limited group, members who start out in generally similar phases may only get so far in the process, much as indicated in the approach when it was introduced for individual treatment. If they are at the point of the disclosure crisis, getting through that and developing better adaptive capacities may reflect the measure of a successful group. If a short-term group is formed with women who are past disclosure, work on identifying traumatic effects for themselves may prove very useful, and the problem solving around relational consequences may only begin. That also would be a success. With an ongoing, long-term group, each time a new member joins an existing group, it provides old members with the opportunity to review their own growth or to revisit issues that need fuller or more complete resolution.

Early Intervention Around Traumatic
Effects and Enhancement of Coping Capacities

Group can be a logical extension of, or instead of, individual treatment. However, if a woman comes to treatment at the time of disclosure and has not had any individual treatment, the group needs to be formed around crisis intervention purposes and strategies. Once past the acute crisis of disclosure, which is typically, in my experience, when women come to therapy, the group can meet the demands of the engagement and empowerment phases of treatment. Engagement in the group process parallels the affiliation stage of group development. Members must feel that they have enough in common so that they view themselves as "like others" who will understand them and their issues. Discussions around confidentiality, as detailed earlier, are one way of engaging members in the group. In such a discussion about confidentiality, they are sharing and testing the waters and problem solving around rules and norms they wish to establish as a group before being asked to share intimate details.

Implicit in the affiliation phase is that group members know enough about each other to make the determination that they do indeed have something in common. Although they know that they are coming into a group with other mothers whose children have been sexually abused by a spouse or partner, linking individual mothers with particular children by name, age, and sex at a minimum is very helpful to the process of individualizing and making concrete the reality of the experience they share. Introductions need to include some detail about the family sexual abuse. The degree of detail is left up to the individual woman. Some women may wish to be as vague, stating, "My husband sexually abused my 5-year-old daughter and I found out."

Others may give more details about the nature and duration of the abuse, as well as their feelings about it.

In addition to having common experiences, women are also looking, in the early stages of the group, for reactions that are similar to their own. They are particularly attuned to the nuances introduced regarding the relationship with children and partners. When a group has a number of women who have made the decision to stay with their partners, it is important that they feel free to express their preferences. This means that it is important for the therapist to help create an atmosphere in which it is safe to express feelings even if the other members do not agree with them. In this fashion, the group experience can aid in the development of ego strengths that help the women function more effectively in the world.

Surfacing Traumatic Effects

Another benefit of the group is its ability to help women identify traumatic effects. The group is particularly effective because of the sharing of experiences and reactions that typify the interactions among group members. One member's story may trigger a memory, thought, or feeling in another, and a member may use the forum of the group to develop and share insights. The following example from a group session with Maureen illustrates this. In this example, Maureen becomes more connected to the feelings of despair and loss that follow the disclosure of sexual abuse and the dissolution of her marriage.

As discussed earlier, Maureen's husband had been imprisoned for 5 years following the conviction of child sexual abuse. His family had sided with him, against her, and she had difficulty believing her daughters herself at first. She came into treatment only after the court ordered it as a condition of her children being returned home. Thus, she was one of the "mandated" clients who came into therapy as a result of "reduced choices." She had trouble at first accepting responsibility for having made a choice, wanting to believe that she was there because of outside forces that "made" her come.

Two years after the disclosure and about 20 months into treatment, Maureen came into a group session and disclosed that she has gotten a letter from her husband in prison. In his letter, he continued to minimize the sexual abuse. This is the first time she had heard from him or been in touch with him in more than a year. Maureen stated that she

CASE STUDY

was going to write him a nasty letter and tell him not to write anymore, saying that it was important for her to do this now. She was motivated to do this because of her concern for her children. She spoke at some length about a current problem that her oldest daughter is having, which she relates directly to the sexual abuse. Her discussion revealed that she realized even more now how hurt her children have been. She expressed feelings of being depressed, describing how she is more depressed and functioning less well now in some ways than in the first year after the disclosure. For example, she was no longer working, having given up her job and gone back on public assistance out of the feeling that she wanted to be more available to her daughters.

At the same time, she was aware that she is probably doing a better job with her children. As she notes, "I am stronger, more outspoken . . . I am speaking up more for the kids." She also identified an expanded awareness of her inner process. She noted that "feelings I should have had 2 years ago are coming up now. . . . That's why I have to write back and say, 'Don't come here—know you did it.' Before, I would have let it go, been passive."

Maureen did experience a relatively serious depression. She was having difficulty getting out of the house and, in the 2 months previous to this session, had missed 4 or 5 weeks of therapy in a row. The letter, as well as her daughter's continued difficulties, had triggered a new awareness in Maureen of the emotional ramifications for herself as well as her daughter. As she said, she was going through feelings now that she could not experience 2 years earlier. At the time of the disclosure, she was emotionally quite fragile. This fragility had been reflected in a presentation characterized by rigidity and an overreliance on denial as a defense against being overwhelmed. Throughout the year and 8 months of therapy, she had accepted her daughter's story at a cognitive level and was able to function on a day-to-day basis. The security of having reestablished her family without her husband and the ongoing support from individual and group therapy had helped give her a sense of control over her life and liberated her to move to a place where she could begin the internal process of grieving. The identification of the degree to which she felt stigmatized, guilty, and inadequate had not been fully processed earlier. The increased awareness of these feelings contributed significantly to her depression. Examined from the perspective of growth-producing events, the depression, given that it could be managed and not become debilitating, was a milestone in the movement to a different level of ego development marked by greater self-awareness and decreased reliance on denial as a defense.

The feedback to Maureen at the end of the session, described earlier, was very positive and exemplified how a cohesive group can be supportive. A newer member said to Maureen, "I'm glad you came . . . it was helpful to me. . . . At first I felt like I was the only one in the world this happened to, and you had a bad story, like me. We think we aren't important to other people, but we are." This was helpful for Maureen to hear, and near the end of the session, she stated that she often does not feel like coming to the group but that she always feels better when she does.

A session with the same group a couple weeks later highlighted the members' group cohesion and ability to process difficult issues. The discussion turned to more openness about sexual relationships, and the women talked about how often they did or did not have sex with their partners, the perpetrators. Three members revealed that they felt rejected by their husbands because their partners were not interested in them sexually. One member admitted to often feeling that there was something wrong with her and talked about how her partner would avoid coming to bed at night. Another identified a similar pattern—she commented on how her partner would sometimes be gone for 4 nights at a time. She stated that they "only had sex about once a month" and talked about her frustration with that. This had been infuriating to her, but her ambivalence about the relationship had kept her from taking a stand.

The women also talked about how, in learning more about the details of the abuse, they felt increasingly betrayed. Maureen mentioned that before she knew about the incest, she always used to wonder why her husband would keep one of her daughters home from school whenever he was off from work. She did not realize until after the disclosure that this was when her husband had abused her daughter. Another woman had a remarkably similar experience. Her partner did the same thing—asked to keep her daughter home from school when he was off from work. The excuse he would give was that he was going to visit his son from an earlier marriage who liked to see this woman's daughter. These too were the times when the husband molested the daughter.

One woman noted that her husband (and stepfather of her daughter, whom he had abused) used to make comments such as, "When I married you,

I married Annette." She said that this had always bothered her but that now, knowing about the abuse, it all made sense. In addition to sharing the experience of having been tricked by their partners, another common denominator in their relationships with their partners was the degree to which the women either felt like their partners' mothers, or, conversely, their partners acted as if the women were the mothers. For example, one woman stated that she felt like her husband's mother and noted that people used to say to her that she looked like her husband's mother.

Two other women described behavior on the part of their partners that made them feel that the men acted more like children than like adults. One woman said, "My husband was always playing games and running around the house like he was one of the kids. I would say to him, 'Stop running around, you're getting them all riled up,' but he wouldn't." Another woman identified similar dynamics, noting that her husband would play music that was popular with kids her daughter's age. She described him "like he came down to her level."

As this woman talked, she became upset and began to cry. As she tried to hold in the tears, group members responded empathetically. In an explicit connection to the betrayal, members noted that this woman was mourning the loss of trust and of the relationship. One asked if she had "cried with other people," saying that this had made a difference for her, and encouraged her not to "stuff" her feelings. I was impressed by the degree to which the others members showed strength and concern yet were matter-of-fact in their advice. Throughout this discussion, the woman was helped to articulate her feelings. She said, "When I did see him, all I could think was, 'He slept with my daughter and how could he, how could he?'" In an anguished voice, she went on to say that she had "loved him so much . . . I would have died for him, you know? . . . and when I think about how hard I tried to make a life. . . . I worked, I worked, I worked . . . and for what?" Group members listened, allowed her to talk, and made supportive comments such as, "I felt that way too at first." In this manner, the group was helpful in both comforting the member and instilling hope. This was extremely useful for this woman, who was prone to depression and a sense of a foreshortened future.

Identifying the traumatic effects of powerlessness, stigmatization, betrayal, and sexual traumatization for women is thus an important aspect of the group process. In the case of all the women mentioned in this section, they were in individual therapy as well, so it was impossible to completely distill the effects of group treatment. However, the group session described earlier illustrates how reviewing the details of the relationship with partners, in the safety of other women who have had the same experience, can trigger feelings that lead to greater awareness and insight.

The treatment guidelines presented so far have focused on surfacing and working through traumatic effects for the mother before concentrated attention is turned to the impact on significant relationships. However, it should be noted that reality often intervenes. Sometimes, this is in the form of a family crisis, which demands that attention be paid to mother-partner relationships. In other instances, protective issues arise and present a need to turn to mother-child relationships, sometimes before the mother is fully ready to do so. In these instances, the interventions may need to be framed more like crisis intervention, with more direction and support from the therapist and other professionals than normally called for at a time.

Identifying Relational Consequences

As with individual treatment, an important phase of the progress in therapy is the ability to move beyond the discovery of the depth of the impact on one's own life into a phase in which there is enough psychological energy to address the issues that one has in relationships with significant others. With most of the women in the group described earlier, their relationships with their partners or spouses were in the process of dissolution, if in fact they had not already been dissolved through divorce or permanent separation. Nonetheless, residual issues still needed attention. One of the benefits of group therapy is that it decreases the stigma for a woman around the topic of having been in a sexual relationship with a man who molested her child. It also allows for fuller disclosure of dynamics in that relationship, especially ambivalent feelings.

The role of group therapy in this phase of treatment is to help women identify issues in intimate relationships. Effective modeling and problem solving are functions of group therapy that help women become more adept in modulating their relationships. Ventilation of feelings helps women gain perspectives on their relationships. Conjoint, mother-child, and/or family therapy may still need to be employed to help the mother put into action concepts or insights she arrives at in group therapy.

In the group session detailed below, one of the members, Laura, started out in the group by discussing her latest meeting with the district attorney. Her daughter, 14 now, had first made a disclosure when she was 10. Laura had confronted her husband at that time, and he promised never to do it again. She then sought counsel from her religious leader, who encouraged her to stay in the marriage. Laura talked in this session about the impact of her religion on her life, noting that she could not allow herself to be in a sexual relationship outside of marriage. She felt that her marriage was not that satisfying but was conflicted because she believed that she should stay married both for her child and because it was supported by her church.

CASE STUDY

> Laura informed the group that it looked as if the trial was going to go forward because her husband was not admitting to the abuse and was not willing to enter into a plea bargain. She described the double bind for her daughter, saying that part of her loved him as a father. Laura admitted that part of her did not want to see him imprisoned either. She noted that she "still had feelings for him but hated his behavior . . . [when] she learned what he did; it was horrible."
>
> She drew the distinction between her husband as a person and his behavior. Despite her belief for a number of years preceding the disclosure that the marriage was not succeeding, she appreciated certain aspects of their relationship. For example, her husband had supported her through her recovery from alcohol. He had undertaken a great deal of the child-rearing tasks while she was "under the influence" and continued to do so. She had been able to attend Alcoholics Anonymous (AA) meetings a number of different nights a week, for example, because her husband was willing to be at home with her daughter. Although she now also recognized that this gave him the time and opportunity to molest her daughter, Laura was aware that his assuming so much of the day-to-day tasks had assisted her in her recovery from substance abuse.

In the session described above, other members identified with Laura's ambivalence. One mother—who, like Laura, was closer to the disclosure of her child's abuse—revealed that lately she had the urge to see her partner. She reported that she had not seen him for 3 months. Earlier in the week, she had driven by his job site in the hopes of catching sight of him. Although she had not made contact, this type of honesty about her mixed feelings was ultimately helpful to her in sorting out feelings about her partner. It also helped set a norm in the group that these kinds of feelings were not taboo and that the group was a safe place to process them.

Another group session illustrated how intertwined the lives of these mothers are with their ex-partners and how complicated and difficult it can be to separate.

Rosa revealed that her partner and father of her youngest child was "coming around all the time." Rosa had an order of protection because of his violence, but because the court also allowed supervised visitation with her youngest daughter, her partner came to the home two times a week, usually accompanied by another family member, to pick up his daughter. Both she and her partner are first-generation Puerto Rican Americans, and the cultural norms to stay together and the value on "family" are powerful incentives not to separate. Rosa acknowledged that she was having difficulty separating and maintaining boundaries. She noted that his attitude is still, "This is my family." Although she described herself as fundamentally motivated to stay separated, she also acknowledged that both her youngest daughter and her son still very much want to see their father, and this created a very real conflict for her.

This was a very difficult and conflicted relationship for Rosa, who was still somewhat undecided about how much to invest in the relationship when she left treatment about a year later. She was unable to make a permanent separation from her partner, even though he never received treatment. The motivation to stay connected was multidetermined. As with many Hispanic women, the pull of traditional Hispanic values around the woman's role of wife and mother, as well as the religious imperative to stay with a child's father, affected her decision. The impact of economic realities was important as well. The perpetrator continued to contribute to her financial support, and she had no viable means of supporting herself and her three children. The lack of legal intervention in this case also was confusing for Rosa. There had been no criminal prosecution and no adjudication in juvenile court because she was not married to the perpetrator, who was the father of her youngest child but not the father of her daughter who had been victimized. The significance of legal intervention, or lack of it, is taken up more fully in Chapter 8. Suffice it to say that in Rosa's case, the message she received was that there was some doubt about his commission of the sexual abuse because the legal system had not been involved.

In addition to the issues that surface around reunification, there is the issue of how women who separate relate to potential new partners. Here, confusion around creating boundaries, negotiating roles and responsibilities, and choosing someone who is trustworthy are all aspects of relationships that call for attention.

Another major focus in group therapy is on the mother-child relationship. This relationship is often an area of ongoing conflict as well as an opportunity for reconnection. An important dynamic to be aware of is the fact that the child often blames the mother for sexual abuse. Sometimes, daughters blame their mothers even more than they blame the offenders.

With young children, an area of difficulty for the parent is a child's sexually acting-out behavior. In many instances, the child's behavior may become more pronounced or fail to decrease at the rate expected by the mother. Finding strategies for handling this acting-out behavior is a major concern of many mothers. This is especially true when the behavior involves masturbation or sexual inappropriateness with other children (or adults).

Group therapy can be one of the modalities where skills in managing sexualized behavior are introduced or reinforced with women. Deblinger and Heflin (1996) discussed a number of strategies for working with the nonoffending parent in this regard. The reader is referred to their work for a full description. However, to summarize briefly, they suggested focusing on educating parents about normal phases of child sexual development, encouraging parents to respond calmly to sexual questions and behavior, identifying inappropriate sexual behavior, and using behavior management techniques to decrease sexual behaviors.

The manner in which mothers can assist with problem solving is illustrated in the group session described below.

CASE STUDY

J brought to the group's attention that she was having difficulty with the frequency and manner in which her 6-year-old daughter was masturbating. She was disturbed by the fact that her daughter would do this many times during the day at home, usually when she was watching television but also when she was engaged in play, usually parallel play, with her 4-year-old brother. Another mother joined in that she also had had that problem with her 5-year-old daughter. In her case, the daughter would go behind the couch and masturbate because she had learned that her mother disapproved if she did it in public. This brought a response from some of the other mothers, and the group engaged in a problem-solving discussion with the two mothers.

Two principles emerged from this discussion: (a) that whatever the mother did, it was important to stress that masturbation was not bad. The first goal with each child, therefore, was to help him or her get the behavior out of the public living spaces and into the privacy of their bedrooms. The second idea that emerged addressed the compulsory nature of the behavior. Here, the leader suggested that this reflected a degree of anxiety and preoccupation on the part of the child. The mothers again problem solved and agreed that it might be helpful to give the child some reassuring attention at the time they were found masturbating and also to introduce or try to get the child involved in some other kind of activity to distract their attention.

Each mother was then asked to think about exactly what they could do. The first mother had a hard time, saying that it often happened when her mother (the daughter's grandmother) was taking care of the child and that she would have difficulty getting her mother to do anything but yell at her child. The second mother, however, thought that she could sit down with her and play a game of the daughter's choosing for a few minutes, hoping then to get her interested in continuing on her own. With this example, J was then able to envision a scenario in which she or her mother responded empathetically to the child ("I see you are maybe worrying or thinking again about what Daddy did") and then try to engage her in some activity, even if this was helping the adult in kitchen.

The mothers were doing most of the problem-solving work in this example, with the leader facilitating interaction, presenting information about the possible roots of some of the behavior, and identifying potential behavioral management techniques. The latter include strategies such as positive reinforcement, active ignoring, giving effective instructions, and the use of time out. With that, as with other difficult behaviors that members brought in, the women in this group were able to help each other with these difficult issues. The suggestions were not always carried through or, when they were, did not always work, but there was enough success that members were motivated to continue to work with each other in seeking help with their children.

For the child who is an adolescent at the time of the disclosure, the relationship can become more conflicted. The adolescent who has been sexually abused may not have experienced the mother as an emotional resource during childhood and distrusts that her or his mother may be that now. In addition, social norms are often beginning to push adolescents—boys, in particular—toward association with peers as the source of status, identity, and interpersonal gratification. Thus, when a mother may be more available to her adolescent emotionally (as she works through the traumatic effects of the incest for herself), her child may feel the connection as too much of a regressive pull and resist it.

The degree to which the mother-child bond can be reestablished may be related to the age and gender of the child as well as the nature and duration of the sexual abuse. From my experience, women whose children have reached adolescence and had been molested over a period of time often seemed to have histories of significant disruption in the mother-child relationship prior to disclosure. In these cases, the children have felt seriously abandoned by their mothers and harbor deep-seated feelings of distrust and anger. If the sexual abuse had begun and been disclosed in adolescence, the confusion about developing sexuality and the pull toward identification with and reliance on peers often contribute to the adolescent distancing from the mother.

A case example may help to illustrate this dynamic. Laura had a relationship with her daughter that was characterized by these dynamics, as her discussion of her relationship with her 18-year-old daughter in the following group session illustrates. The incest had been longstanding, starting, as far as Laura knew, when her daughter was about 9. Laura's husband left the home, and she subsequently divorced him. There was no family or criminal court intervention. Laura had been in treatment for about a year at the time of this group session, although the disclosure of incest between her husband and the then 15-year-old daughter occurred 3 years previously. Unfortunately, her daughter had never been in treatment.

CASE STUDY

In this group session, Laura brought up difficulties she is having with her daughter, who is skipping school. She described with resignation in her voice how she drives her to school on her way to work and then how her daughter obviously does not go to class. She talked about how there was a counselor at school who was invested in her daughter and called her every morning at 7:00 to get her up. Laura said that she had given up on being a taskmaster and had put the responsibility on her daughter for getting herself ready.

She then described the context of the relationship with her daughter within which this behavior occurs. Her daughter was about to graduate from high school, and Laura told her that she would have to move out. Laura felt that she "had to have a separation from her daughter . . . there is no turning back." She said that it has been a very difficult 3 years, escalating into "worse and worse." She felt that her daughter was on "a self-destructive schedule," and although it hurt her to see "this person do things that are so destructive," she acknowledged that she felt very helpless.

Group members suggested to Laura directly that her daughter may need her and that the behavior might be her way of saying that she does not want to leave. One group member described her own daughter's antisocial behavior, saying that she learned from this that her daughter was trying to reach out and was asking for help in the only way she could. Trying to reach out to Laura to convey how it could be important that Laura look beyond her daughter's behavior, the group member described how desperate she felt at that time and how painful it was to watch her daughter struggle. Laura responded that she used to feel upset all the time and questioned the direction that her daughter was going but said that now she "felt nothing . . . I planned this [her daughter moving out] . . . this is going to happen. . . . I detached myself."

This interchange reflects the degree of distance, 3 years after the disclosure, between Laura and her daughter. From all accounts, her daughter was a very troubled young woman who was not succeeding academically. The sense of detachment from her daughter that Laura conveyed in this session reflected the compartmentalization of feelings that Laura had resorted to in response to the overwhelming feelings of guilt and helplessness she was experiencing in relationship to her daughter. In fact, she had devoted a great deal of time and energy to her daughter's problems prior to as well as following the disclosure, with varying degrees of success.

Having accepted the fact of the abuse at the cognitive level, it was not until Laura entered therapy that she began the slow process of identifying and resolving the emotional effects. She was just at the point in this group session of beginning to be ready to turn her attention to the relationship with her daughter. Laura was a woman who had been abandoned by her own mother and raised by a grandmother whom she experienced as distant and strict. She had not had her own dependency needs met as a youngster and felt like she had "raised herself." Impaired as a result in her capacity for empathy, Laura struggled to respond with more empathy to her own daughter. She stayed in the group for another year and a half and did begin to work on her relationship with her daughter. The relationship remained conflicted and not close, but Laura was able to function more effectively as a parent. Her daughter graduated from high school after going to summer school the summer after she turned 18 and then stayed at home for another year. When she left, it was to go into a marriage that Laura did not approve of, but it was clear that this was her daughter's choice, and the mother supported her, knowing that her daughter was going to have to make her own mistakes and learn from them.

The mother-daughter relationship between Rosa and her 11-year-old daughter reflected a different dynamic. As noted earlier, Rosa's daughter was molested by her live-in boyfriend of 5 years. This man, who was the father of Rosa's 4-year-old daughter, was physically abusive to Rosa. Following the disclosure, Rosa did get treatment for both herself and her children. They had been in treatment for about a year at the time of the following group session.

In the first part of the group session, the women had been discussing the impact of their relationships with the offender on their children. The theme changed to a focus on how their children were functioning. Rosa volunteered that her daughter was doing much better. The biggest change, according to Rosa, was that her daughter was "not quiet anymore . . . she is always running around the house. She speaks right up for herself, and she wants to do all these things now that she never did before, like having friends over after school." Rosa reported that her daughter "talks back to me now . . . she is changing the way she is acting." Rosa talked about how this was hard for her; it put extra demands on her that she did not have before.

Rosa was describing an increase in her daughter's self-esteem that was manifested behaviorally in her increased assertiveness in her relationship with her mother. Rosa, having had a withdrawn, compliant daughter who had reacted to the sexual abuse with depression and isolation of affect, was experiencing the response of an active, developing 11-year-old who wanted to move outside the circle of the family.

Rosa was feeling that the demands of parenting all three children while coping with her boyfriend (who was visiting her third child on a weekly basis) and dealing with the effects of the incest in therapy did not leave much energy for this new development. Part of her wanted to respond to her daughter, and this was the part that the group focused on. She was helped to see that she could be an effective parent if she was supportive at the same time that she set limits.

Rosa, also like Laura, stayed in the group for a year past this session. In her case, the struggle in the relationship with her daughter revolved around finding a way to stay connected with and nurture a child who, in a sense, was outpacing her. This called on strengths that she was just developing, and Rosa continued to need assistance in sorting out and prioritizing parenting conflicts. She did achieve a healthier relationship with her daughter that better prepared both of them for her daughter's entering adolescence.

CASE STUDY

Summary

In this chapter, I have focused on the ways that group therapy can be beneficial for mothers who are struggling with the impact of the incestuous behavior of their partners on their own lives, on their relationships with sexual partners (the perpetrators or new partners), and on their relationships with the victimized children. The next chapter examines the role of family therapy in evolving new relationships among family members.

FAMILY TREATMENT

F amily treatment, like individual and group therapy, can be useful at any stage of the treatment process. In this chapter, I will focus on family treatment at the initial stage of engagement, when the family may be in crisis, and on mid-phase treatment issues dealing with relational consequences. Although family treatment can serve to highlight traumatic effects for a mother, the modality is best suited to working on relationship issues between family members because a major purpose of family therapy is to decrease dysfunctional patterns of interaction that support the incestuous relationships in families. Family therapy with the mother and children—the emphasis in this chapter—is relevant whether or not the mother chooses to reunite with the offender. Issues regarding reunification of an offender with a family will be briefly touched on, but family therapy with the offender is a topic deserving of special attention. The reader is referred to the work of Gil and Johnson

(1993), O'Connell (1986), Palmer (1997), and Salter (1988) for specific attention to the issues in family reunification.

Friedrich (1990) does an excellent job of summarizing the work of family therapy with incestuous families. He identifies two important issues surrounding family treatment of incestuous families. The first is the division between two groups of clinicians, both of whom have been involved in treating victims and their families. One group is family therapists, who, coming from a systems perspective where causality is viewed as circular, have viewed each family member as influencing each other as well as the family system as a whole. Consequently, the responsibility for the incest is viewed as resting with the family system as a whole, in which all members share responsibility. In opposition to this is a group of victim advocates who place the responsibility for incest solely with the offending parent. They have felt that the family systems therapists risk holding other family members responsible for the offending parent's behavior, a position with which they strongly disagree. Inherent in this position is the notion that the organization of men and women in society places men in the nuclear family unit in a more powerful position than women. Our social structure supports the dominance of men, and therefore the marital partnership is inherently unequal, much as is the parent-child relationship.

In this chapter, I attempt to reconcile these two positions. Although believing that incest is supported by families in which there are dysfunctional family interactions and patterns, it is unclear if this dysfunction is a cause or a result of incestuous behavior (Salter, 1988). It must be acknowledged that principles guiding our definition of *dysfunctional* have not been historically informed by an understanding of the power differential between men and women. Thus, the family systems explanation is, in my opinion, inherently flawed. This is supported by the growing evidence from both clinical practice and empirical research that incest does not occur unless there is an adult in the family who is motivated to sexually abuse a child. This position has been adopted by others in the field, most notably Mowrer (1987), who has stressed the need to combine a family systems perspective with a sexual deviant approach. Friedrich (1990) advocates an approach to family treatment that keeps the protection and validity of the child victim position paramount while working with the whole family.

The second major trend that Friedrich (1990) traces in the field of family therapy is the move from a tendency to view incest families as homogeneous in nature, thereby characterized by certain predictable dynamics, to a view of incest families that is more heterogeneous. Thus, not all incest families are patriarchally organized and characterized by a rigid control and emotionally distant family members, as was initially believed (Friedrich, 1990). Although not homogeneous, there exists a fair amount of consensus in the clinical literature about some characteristics common to incest families. Friedrich, in looking at 15 authors who described work with incest families, found a high rate of agreement about the presence of social isolation, poor communication, poor conflict resolution skills, homeostasis enmeshment, and a history of loss. Additional variables, about which there was a fairly high degree of consensus in the literature, were high levels of stress (Gordon, 1989; Justice & Justice, 1979), an exaggeration of patriarchal norms (Herman, 1981), substance abuse (Barnard, 1983; Gordon, 1989), and an absent or incapacitated mother (Herman, 1981; Justice & Justice, 1979).

There are families who are socially isolated, have poor communication among members, have difficulty resolving conflict in a healthy way, and have a history of loss and members who are substance abusers. Yet, incest does not occur in all these families. Many alcoholic families, for example, may fit this profile. However, the presence in the family of an adult who is motivated to sexually abuse children turns this family into an incest family.

Motivation to Sexually Abuse

What do we know about the motivation to sexually abuse or, in family system terms, the intent of the incest? There have been topologies proposed by both family therapists (Abbott, 1995) and sex offender treatment specialists (Cole, 1992). One typology from the family systems field is that proposed by Larson and Maddock (1986), who outline four types of incest families, differentiated by intent of the incestuous behavior. They divide families into four groups, depending on the degree to which aggression, eroticism, and affection affect the intent. A second schema is provided by Finkelhor (1989). He conceptualizes offending behavior as resulting from four preconditions. These are motivation to sexually abuse, the lack of internal inhibitors if the motivation is present, the presence or lack of presence of external inhibitions, and the resistance of the child. All four preconditions must exist for the abuse to be carried out in this conceptualization.

It would be beneficial if assessment of families and decisions about separating offenders were routinely undertaken using clinical topologies. However, until such topologies are empirically validated, this is unlikely to be the case. Practically speaking, the sophistication of the response system (or lack of sensitivity to the issue) regarding sexual victimization, coupled with the victim's characteristics (the age of the child, how verbal the child is, etc.), the nonoffending parent's attitude at disclosure, and whether the offender admits guilt, are typically the deciding factors in determining whether the offender is removed from the home.

Treatment needs to be focused on both the treatment of the deviant response pattern in the offender and the family's dysfunctional patterns of coping. It is beyond the scope of this book to focus on offender treatment because a wealth of clinically and empirically based literature addresses these issues (Groth, 1979; Horton et al., 1990; Pithers, 1988; Salter, 1988; Schwartz & Cellini, 1997). In this chapter, I will focus on offender treatment only as it pertains to the process of family reunification, assuming that the sexual deviant issues will be addressed in individual or group treatment of the offender.

In the following pages, a variety of issues that characterize the initial and mid-phase stages of family treatment will be highlighted, with the assumption that gender-sensitive family therapy (see Barrett, Trepper, & Fish, 1990) first will be conducted with the mother and children. Beginning stage factors that often need to be addressed include (a) communication between all nuclear family members about the sexual victimization of one or more children and (b) the crisis of parenting given that the offender has been part of the family and is extruded from the family. The mid-phase issues that will be emphasized include the mother-victim and mother-child relationships in general and the relationship between the mother and her spouse or partner, including reunification issues. A framework for evaluating successful family treatment is a final subject that will be discussed briefly.

Beginning Treatment

Constellation and Choice of Therapists

As indicated earlier, family therapy with the mother and children can coincide with individual and group treatment if there are enough treatment resources to do this and if family members can attend a number of therapy sessions in a given week. Alternatively, initial family sessions with the mothers and children may be employed as part of the initial assessment if resources are limited. If the family is coming to treatment in crisis as a result of a protective services or law enforcement intervention, it may be important to treat the family initially from a crisis intervention standpoint and see them more than once a week.

Ideally, the family therapist should be one who is viewed as neutral by all family members—that is, not allied with one family member over another. This is difficult to achieve if the family therapist is also the individual therapist for one of the family members. If the family therapist is also involved in individual treatment with a family member, the best choice is probably the victim's therapist because this person, although needing to avoid overidentification with the child, is also likely to be the most sensitive to and aware of the victim's needs. Attention to the victim's concerns must be paramount because of the power imbalance in parent-child relationships within the family. However, as both Gelinas (1983) and Gil and Johnson (1993) emphasize, although it is crucial to believe and support the victim, the family therapist must develop an empathic stance toward each family member to be effective.

Another model, which dilutes the impact of a therapist alliance with an individual family member, is the use of co-therapists in the family sessions. Even if both therapists are treating individual family members individually, the impact of an alliance between a therapist and an individual family member is lessened, thereby reducing the possibility of that family member's perspective dominating family therapy objectives and session content. However, even in this case, one might want to ensure that the victim's therapist be involved as one of the family therapists (see Coulson, Wallis, & Clark, 1994, for a description of a diversified team approach to family therapy in intergenerational cases of incest).

Many of the issues raised in the discussion of co-therapists in group sessions also apply, such as ensuring that the relationship between the two therapists is explicit to the family. This is especially important because one of the major issues in incest families involves difficulties maintaining boundaries, as has been noted by many family therapists (Friedrich, 1990; Gelinas, 1987; Gil & Johnson, 1993). The value of having a male and female team involved in family work is that the opportunity exists for modeling functional adult relationships, in which boundaries are respected, as well as adult to child relationships in which children are listened to but treated as children.

Another major issue for the therapist to address early on in the relationship with the family is confidentiality and its limits. If, as in most family situations, there is involvement with protective authorities, the therapist will need to develop an alliance with Child Protective Services (CPS). Most family therapists have noted the importance of this liaison (Fish & Faynik, 1989; Gelinas, 1983; Gil, 1993; Trepper & Barrett, 1986). As in work with family members in other modalities, the nature of what is shared and the process for conveying information are important to delineate.

There are often protective or safety concerns that the family therapist needs to be cognizant of, particularly if the disclosure and involvement of CPS and the court system have been recent and the offender has just left the home. The mother may not enforce restraining orders or allow telephone or supervised face-to-face contact if an order has not been effectively specified. Sometimes, women misinterpret a "no-contact" order to mean only no *unsupervised* contact between the victim and offender. The victim's well being can be compromised if the intent of an order is to prevent all contact.

One of the first factors to evaluate is the referral route. As Gelinas (1987) points out, the manner in which the family comes to treatment will affect their openness and ability to participate in a meaningful way in therapy. There are fundamentally three routes: (a) the family seeks help voluntarily; CPS may or may not already be involved. In these cases, the nonoffending parent is usually already separated or divorced from the offender. (b) The family seeks help as a "condition" imposed by protective authorities. Typically, this occurs when CPS has agreed not to remove a child if the alleged offender leaves the home and the mother is willing to seek help. (c) The family comes as a result of a court mandate. The route will affect the family's orientation to treatment and the approach that the therapist needs to take in rapport building or "joining" with the family.

Regardless of the route, important issues to be assessed include the mother's control and authority over the children, the degree of parent-child and child-to-child conflict, the mother's management of role conflict, and the meaning of the incest to the family system, both in terms of the implicit or unconscious intent of the incest and the conscious ascription of responsibility by family members for the incest. Information obtained by DeYoung (1994) in her study of role conflict in mothers in incest families can be helpful here. Questions to be asked might include the following: How active is the woman in problem solving? Does she seek support for her role from her partner and from her social network? Is she able to delegate role responsibilities effectively? If so, she may be toward the more functional end of the continuum. If, on the other hand, she has resolved role conflicts by overlooking one or both roles, rotating attention between roles, neglecting her role responsibilities, working harder to meet all demands, or assuming a passive or helpless orientation, then she may fall more toward a dysfunctional end of the continuum.

Communication Between Family
Members About the Incestuous Behavior

A common dilemma presented by many families at intake is that the nonoffending parent—sometimes influenced by the offender, sometimes by the victim, and sometimes by her own issues—may not want some or all of the siblings of the victim(s) to know about the incestuous behavior. The ostensible reasons presented by the mother for this may be that the siblings are "too young to understand" or that the knowledge would unnecessarily damage the relationship between the children and the offender or the victim and other siblings. Often, this camouflages the mother's need to limit the exposure of the incest because of her sense of betrayal and shame, which she may be struggling consciously and unconsciously to avoid. If she has a history of childhood sexual abuse herself, she may want to avoid concrete discussion of the abuse because it is too painful. In other instances, it reflects the mother's ambivalence about either the fact of the abuse or her relationship with the offender. A mother who does not believe that the abuse occurred or feels that she may want to stay in a relationship with the offender, even if it is true, may be resistant to opening up a discussion with siblings of the victims.

Processing the fact of the incest with all the children presently living in the family unit should be a goal of early intervention (Gelinas, 1987; Gil, 1991; Trepper & Barrett, 1989). The need to develop a therapeutic alliance with the mother may lead to a negotiation about how soon this is done, but it can nonetheless remain a goal. Gelinas (1987) suggests that the therapist adopt an active stance early on in therapy to develop this alliance. Trepper and Barrett (1989) advocate for an approach that provides education in the early stages of therapy—specifically, about how families function. For this explanation, he draws heavily on the structural theory of Minuchin (1974).

Deblinger and Heflin (1996) provide a useful framework for working with nonoffending mothers and children, stressing the need to open communication by suggesting to parents that they encourage questions, reinforce the sharing of problems, and encourage the expression of feelings in an appropriate manner. In this process, however, they stress the need to encourage dialogue gradually and naturally, avoid "catastrophizing," and help the parent to understand that the child may not share the parent's view. They also emphasize the need to evaluate readiness for parent-child sessions, noting that "a parent who is not emotionally ready may not only fail to facilitate the child's progress but may actually hinder the therapeutic process" (p. 213).

The notion of educating the family about the impact of the family system on individual behavior is an important one. However, an explanation needs, in my view, to be cognizant of a woman's role in the family. Walters, Carter, Papp, and Silverstein (1988) do a very good job of sensitizing clinicians to gender-based definitions of family roles and the manner in which sex role socialization creates the structure and culture of marriage, child rearing, and the family.

The benefit of opening up the discussion, if the mother has not done this on her own, is threefold: (a) It demystifies the reason that the offender is out of the home or has limited or supervised contact with the victim or other siblings. (b) It allows the siblings to express their feelings and reactions to the abuse and the resulting consequences of the disclosure. (c) It provides an opportunity to place responsibility for the separation of the offender from the family, or other consequences of the system intervention, squarely with the offender. In addition, the presence of this new "secret" (i.e., the reason that the offender is not in the home) in the family operates much as the secrecy of the incest itself did—whether that was to isolate family members emotionally from one another, express hostility, or maintain a dominant position by one or more family members over others. Opening up the secret dilutes the power of the secret and frees family members to address safety issues more directly.

How does one approach this topic with the mother? It is helpful to do an "inventory" of interactions within the family that result from the siblings being purposefully kept in the dark. Often, one finds that the secret is keeping a family's level of anxiety unduly high. For example, a mother who is trying to keep the secret will find that she is monitoring or censoring her telephone calls or other conversations she is having in front of the children who do not know. Looks are exchanged between the mother and victim in the presence of the siblings, which let them know that "something is going on" and usually that something is connected to the offender. The mother will find that she is unable to have important conversations with either the victim or offender if the other children are present. All of this creates additional stress for the family, especially the mother. Reviewing the effects of the sexual abuse in her daily life and eliciting her support in the decision to broach the topic with the children are the necessary steps.

Another approach may be to discuss with the mother the possibility that the siblings already know the "real" reason for the absence of the offender or, if not, that they may have a distorted understanding of the current family activities. The mother has often not thought of the latter, in particular, and may find this persuasive. Another reason that one might want to have this discussion is the possibility that some or all of the other siblings were also victims. Depending on the mother's stance at the time of the initial engagement, this possibility may or may not be a motivating factor, and thus how explicit the clinician might want to make this is a matter of judgment. If resistance continues, exploring for a history of childhood sexual abuse that has not been shared may be an important route to take.

Because it is recommended that all the children be present, including the victim, it is important to have the mother or the victim's therapist (sometimes both) discuss this process with the victim, including the reasons for it as well as exactly what is expected in the session or sessions in which the abuse is discussed. Specific elements to include in the session would be (a) a discussion of exactly what had occurred, at a level that could be understood by the youngest child present; (b) an exploration with the children for clarification and assurance; (c) a linking of the offender's behavior to the consequences for the family; and (d) a clear statement by the therapist that it is not the victim's fault.

In regard to the discussion of exactly what has occurred, this can be done in any number of ways. The approach will depend partly on the age of the children and partly on the mother's ability to articulate and direct the discussion. In some families, mothers can take responsibility in a session for informing siblings of the victim, and, in other families, the mother may feel inadequate to the task and delegate that to the therapist.

With young children, it may be appropriate to approach the facts from the point of view of "touches" that bothered or upset the victim. Even with older children, it is usually not appropriate to go into the details of what occurred. For one thing, this may be embarrassing to the victim (and here is where the victim can have some input about how much is disclosed). Second, it may be overstimulating or overwhelming to young children. Thus, it may be helpful to use concepts such as private parts of the body being those covered by a bathing suit and the notion of good touches and bad touches. As illustrated elsewhere (Strand, 1991), it may be possible to make a game of discussing good and bad touches as a prelude to describing the interaction between the offender and victim.

Once the children clearly understand what has happened, it is important to convey that this is unacceptable behavior and a crime and that this is why CPS and the police have intervened. Children, especially victims, may have questions about why they have to come to therapy if it is the offender's fault. It is useful to emphasize that there has been a secret that has had a negative impact on all family members. Part of what will be done in family therapy is to understand that impact and perhaps help family members to get along better with each other.

It is important to obtain each child's reaction to the disclosure of the sexual abuse. Here, not only can the therapist check for whether the child already knew but also explore if other siblings have been victimized. It is not uncommon for siblings of the victim to make disclosures, perhaps not only about the offender but also about other siblings, including the victim, who might have acted out against them or others outside the family who may have touched them sexually. Finally, this session or sessions should provide siblings with an opportunity to express how they are feeling about the offender's behavior, both in terms of what it means to them and how it makes them feel about the victim, the offender, and the mother. In the initial session where this is discussed, one may not be able to get much further than identifying issues that will need to be returned to later.

The third factor to cover is the connection between the offender's behavior and the resulting consequences for the family. Thus, if the offender is out of the home and perhaps not supporting, so that the mother is concerned about finances, it is important to clarify that mother would not be worried if the father (or the father-surrogate) had not behaved the way he did. It is important to make clear that the negative consequences arise from the actions of the offender, not the disclosure of the victim.

This leads into the fourth issue, which is a clear statement that it is not the victim's fault and that any negative consequences have occurred because of the offender's behavior. Often, siblings are aware that their mother or the offender is very upset as a "result of what the victim said." Siblings may have strong positive relationships with the offender that have not been compromised by his abuse of them. In these instances, the children may miss the offender, especially if he is their father, and resent and blame the victim for his absence from their lives. The therapist can empathize with the feelings of loss while maintaining support for the victim. Adopting this stance can offer a particularly helpful model for the mother in her interaction not only with the siblings but with the victim as well. Although these issues cannot be resolved in the initial processing of the facts of the abuse, it can begin here.

The Crisis of Parenting

Another common dilemma facing the therapist and the family at the beginning of treatment, especially if this coincides with early postdisclosure phases of intervention for the family, is the crisis of parenting that the mother may be experiencing. This results when the offender has taken an active role in parenting and otherwise structuring the family. The degree to which this has been a functional stance has to be assessed. Sometimes the offender has maintained control though coercion, threats of physical abuse, or outright violence; other times, the offender may have maintained control in more functional ways. There is an assumption that he has been pivotal in the establishment of some structure and routines in the family. With him gone, there is often a power vacuum.

Two dynamics are important to assess relative to this issue: (a) the degree of respect and authority held by the mother in relationship to the children and (b) the degree to which the victim now has an inappropriate hold over the family in terms of power. Others have noted these dynamics and the importance of addressing them early on in the family treatment process. Trepper and Barrett (1989) identify "abusive family relationships" as an important focus of treatment. Gelinas (1983) describes power imbalances between family members as "high-risk constellations," one of which is the parentified child phenomenon.

In regard to the mother's authority, it is not unusual, as delineated earlier, for the mother to be immobilized in the early stage of her response to the disclosure of sexual abuse. This may make her ineffective in carrying out the normal roles and responsibilities associated with parenting. One pitfall for the therapist to avoid is characterizing the mother as chronically ineffective or inadequate if her response is in fact exaggerated or amplified by the crisis following the disclosure. Although the therapist will want to assess the degree to which this is an acute response versus a chronic pattern of parenting, if there is a void in the family at the time of initial referral to treatment, this is an issue that the therapist is going to have to address.

In regard to the issue of the mother's authority over the children, the crisis usually manifests itself in a lack of order and discipline in household routines: Children do not get up or go to school on time, meals are haphazard or not made, laundry is not done, fights go on endlessly between siblings, or the mother is always screaming or even resorting to physical punishment to achieve results. As Gil and Johnson (1993) have identified, the mother's lack of authority sometimes flows from failures of omission (i.e., the failure to intervene) rather than abusive interventions or an act of commission. Two principles direct the interventions relative to this issue. The first is that the current situation must not be allowed to continue. It is important to communicate to the mother that as a result of being the adult (sometimes the only adult) in the household, she is responsible for establishing control, and the therapist's job is helping her to do that. Second, the mother may need help with specific strategies to make those necessary changes. Sometimes, these strategies can be modeled in the family sessions themselves; sometimes, they will need to be addressed also in individual therapy or in parenting classes that may be offered as a corollary to treatment.

The second part of the crisis, that of the victim holding an inordinate degree of power over the mother or other siblings, may be an outgrowth of patterns that have emerged as a result of the incestuous behavior, or it may be a result of the impact of the disclosure. In the first instance, the child (especially if this is the oldest daughter) may have been involved in a cross-generational alliance with the offender that undermined the power and authority of the mother. This will have eroded the mother's authority over the victim and possibly contributed to the mother being disrespected by the other children. If the family was one in which the mother was being physically battered or emotionally abused by the offender, then the message of disrespect toward the mother's role may have been reinforced by the offender's behavior. In addition to the mother's role authority being undermined by the offender, his behavior is likely to have affected the woman's own view of her role and her power in the family. Not only may she be perceived by her children as ineffective, but she also may feel that way herself. She may, for example, view her daughter as more effective in handling siblings.

An important role that family treatment plays is to provide a forum for helping the woman and the child victim learn different ways of interacting and coping and experience these in the session, with the goal of helping them transfer these new patterns to family interactions outside the therapy office. The victim's anger at the mother may contribute to her difficulty in accepting any authority or discipline from the mother and inhibit the mother from trying to assert her authority with the victim. The victim needs to be helped to see that by giving up some of her age-inappropriate responsibilities (emotional and behavioral) around the house and with siblings, she will be freer to pursue her own interests. This usually has a positive appeal. At the same time, the mother needs to be helped to take on these responsibilities. If she views these as a way to reassert control, restore routines, and lessen the stress she is experiencing, she may act accordingly. These goals are important in the early stages of therapy with the mother and children, and the strategies that the therapist uses to obtain these goals will result from his or her particular training or orientation.

As the therapist is involved in the crisis management aspect of the early stages of family work, important assessment functions also can begin.

Trepper and Barrett (1989) identify a number of patterns that they believe are important to evaluate. In addition to the range of abusive relationships, family structure, coping and adaptive patterns, and the manner in which family members communicate are among the factors that are important to identify. Gil (1996), although describing family therapy with families in which an adolescent is the molester, nonetheless provides helpful information. She believes that it is important to evaluate the manner in which family members inadvertently supported the problematic sexual abuse, the level of denial, family of origin impact, the rigidity of prescribed gender roles, and cultural and religious attitudes and beliefs. Steen and Monnette (1989), although also describing family treatment with families of adolescent offenders, make some important observations about issues that need to be addressed. These include how families make decisions, how disagreements are processed, the strength of the sibling system, and how affection is expressed.

Middle Phases of Family Treatment

Relational Consequences and the Mother-Child Connection

The composition and sequencing of issues must be left to the individual therapist because they will be dictated by the particular dynamics of the case. What follows is a discussion of issues of middle-phase work that typically arise in family treatment and goals for intervention. A major issue to be confronted in the middle phase of family treatment is the relationship between the mother and child victim, which most family therapists recognize as a pivotal treatment issue (Deblinger & Heflin, 1996; Friedrich, 1990; Gelinas, 1987; Gil & Johnson, 1993; Trepper & Barrett, 1989). This may be handled in sessions with all children present, or the therapist may want to have sessions with just the dyad of mother-victim to address some of the issues. If there is more than one victim, sessions with the mother and each separately, as well as the mother and victims separate from other siblings, also may be warranted at times. Again, this will be up to the family therapist, as dictated by the needs of the case.

As a prelude to this discussion, it is important to emphasize that the nature of mother-child relationships in incestuous families varies enormously. To a greater or lesser extent, however, they are characterized by a degree of estrangement. The age of the child and the length of time the child was victimized will always be important factors. At one end of a continuum may be families in which the mother has been physically separated from her children for months or years preceding the sexual abuse within the family unit. This separation could have resulted from immigration patterns, in which a mother came first to this country, for example, and did not see much of her children for years, or from the mother's incarceration. At the middle of the continuum might be the mother whose children were removed, and she had not been living with the children but had frequent contact. Mothers whose children are in foster care, especially kinship care, might fall into this category. Mothers who were out of the home for prolonged periods due to substance abuse treatment or hospitalization would be other examples. At the other end of the continuum are those families in which the mother was physically present throughout the child's childhood. Although the degree of physical separation will affect the mother-child bond, the distance between mother and child is often due to two other factors: the difficulties experienced by the mother in dealing with the emotional demands of parenting and the secrecy surrounding the sexual abuse. An important indicator of the mother-child bond may be the child's disclosure to the mother.

If one believes that it is not the inadequacies of the mother that cause the sexual abuse but the manner in which the offender's behavior shapes the family environment and colors the mother-child interaction, it is critical to inventory how, in a given case, the power of the male partner has emerged. Is this a family in which the mother was a battered woman? Does her cultural heritage affect her adherence to more rigid sex role norms that in turn inhibit her ability to challenge her mate? Is her immigration status an issue in the degree to which she feels that she can assert herself in the family domain? These and many other issues need to be evaluated in coming to a determination about the degree to which the woman is disempowered in the family. The degree to which she feels powerless will directly affect the messages she conveys to her children about her effectiveness. Her partner's attitude and behavior toward her will be evident to the children as well.

One specific contextual issue that affects the mother-child relationship is the manner in which the offender has coerced the child victim into keeping the abuse a secret. Although the mother may be overwhelmed with her own issues, the offender usually has actively schemed to have the children keep the sexual interaction a secret from the mother. This drives a wedge between the child and the nonoffending parent. As with any secret, an alliance is inexorably made between the keepers of the secret, excluding those family members who are not in the "know" in a way that has powerful reverberations in their relationships. Children, in their dependent state, do not have the ability to make sense of it all—they just become distant from the nonoffending parent.

In the initial stage of treatment, issues in the power imbalance between mother and children may have begun to be addressed. As noted earlier in the section dealing with the crisis of parenting, one consequence of the disclosure and system intervention, particularly if the offender has been removed from the home, is that the victim may feel an inappropriate sense of power (often oscillating with the feelings of powerlessness). The feelings of powerfulness can result in a grandiose view of oneself and behavior that reflects a sense of omnipotence on the part of the victim. At the same time, the mother's feelings of powerlessness in relationship to her child may be intensified because of the abuse. This dynamic will vary with the nature of the attachment between the mother and child.

One major task in the work with the mother and victim is to foster age-appropriate nurturing on the part of the mother and age-appropriate dependence on the part of the child victim. The subtasks that need to be accomplished include both the mother and child expressing their feelings of anger, remorse, and sadness for what the child went through. It is important that neither assume responsibility for the sexual victimization but for their own relationship. As the adult, the nonoffending parent must take the lead with the child and take responsibility for whatever gaps or lack of attunement may have been present.

A format for beginning this work is to have the mother listen to what the victim has to say about her feelings toward the mother for what the child perceives to have been a failure to protect. The therapist's job is to assist the mother in hearing the child without becoming defensive, at the same time ensuring that the mother does not take responsibility for the abuse that rightfully belongs to the offender.

An example is the Rodriguez family. In this case, 6-year-old José had been molested by his father, Mr. Martinez, who was divorced from his mother. Mr. Martinez took care of José after school on many days, for example, because both Mrs. Rodriguez and her new husband worked. Although José had told the police investigator in very explicit detail what had occurred, enabling them to make an arrest (and, in this case, obtain a confession), José had not told his mother and stepfather the details of what had occurred. In individual and conjoint sessions with Mr. and Mrs. Rodriguez, it became clear that their guilt prevented them from facing the full fact of what had occurred and, consequently, the path for José to communicate the full range of his feelings to them. They blamed themselves because Mrs. Rodriguez's return to work had resulted in the arrangement in which the father took care of José for a few hours every afternoon after José came home from school.

A second subtask is to begin to develop new ways of relating. This can be begun in the therapist's office with the child victim and mother. There are as many activities that could be undertaken by the therapist with the mother and victim. I have found the activity of play particularly fruitful. Many children and mothers have not spent much time playing together. Having the mother and child begin to do this within the context of therapy serves a number of purposes. First, it aids the mother in relating to a child using a medium through which the child is usually comfortable communicating. Second, it provides a means of interaction that is easily transferable to the home environment.

Although the nature of the play activity that can be used is vast, I have found that board games serve this purpose well. A number of games, both those developed specifically for therapeutic purposes as well as general games commercially available, work well. Board games can be used with children ages 4 to 14. Some of the specific, therapeutically focused games include *Speak Out About Sexual Abuse* (*SASA*) and the *UNGAME.* These highlight emotional concerns and relationship issues. More general games (*Candyland, Clue, Chutes and Ladders,* etc.) can serve the purpose as well.

The dynamics between the mother and child generally emerge rather quickly in playing a game. An example is the case of a mother and her 9-year-old daughter who had been molested by her biological father. The mother had subsequently divorced him, although he continued to have supervised visitation. Also living with the mother were a 5-year-old and a 4-year-old, both sons and both products of the marriage. In this case, the *UNGAME* was used in mother-child sessions. The family dynamics included a mother who was overburdened with the responsibilities for her family, having had no financial support from her ex-husband who had left the state 6 months earlier following a report of sexual abuse. The mother, who manifested borderline personality features, could be unempathically attuned and verbally abusive to her children. The victim, a daughter in this case, adapted to the family dynamics with oppositional or defiant behavior vacillating with withdrawal. A depressive demeanor characterized her presentation.

In this case example, the incest increased the emotional distance between the mother and daughter, a relationship already strained because of the mother's difficulty in responding to the emotional demands of her daughter. The daughter felt increasingly that her mother did not care about her and blamed her for not being aware of the incestuous behavior. The mother's re-action to the daughter's defiant behavior was to feel deeply rejected.

The following interaction took place while playing the *UNGAME* during the second month of mother-child sessions.

> L: [Her turn involves her making a statement or asking a question to a person in the room] To mother: "I feel bad about my behavior."
>
> Mother: (Nods her head, no real response)
>
> Therapist: [When her turn allows for making a statement or asking question to a person in the room] To L: "Was it unusual for you to say something like that to your mother?"
>
> Both child and mother acknowledge that it was.

This resulted in a short discussion in which the daughter identified that it was unusual for her to take the risk of sharing this feeling with her mother. The mother was then able to acknowledge the daughter's attempt to move closer by sharing her feelings. In this case, as the emotional relationship deepened over time, the mother was able to move into a more caring, nurturing role. Her daughter was able to give up some of the defiant, antisocial behaviors that had characterized her defensive reaction to feelings of abandonment and rejection.

A second major objective in dealing with the relational consequences of the sexual abuse in the mother-child relationship is to increase developmentally appropriate sibling relationships and increase peer relationships between children and peers outside the family. This can be achieved by working with the mother and all children in family sessions. The format used in achieving this may depend on the needs of the family. It can take the form of weekly family sessions or variations of that. Hines (1989), for example, has described a multiple-impact model that she suggests is appropriate for low-income African American families. In this model, the developmental needs of the family are attended to through an intense daylong intervention followed by case management services and half-day follow-up sessions. Other innovative family approaches may work best with different families, depending on the need (see Deblinger & Heflin, 1996, for additional specific strategies and techniques).

Regardless of the format, the goal is to support healthier relationships between siblings and between children in the family and their peers. For example, in the Carson family, 8-year-old Rebecca had been molested by her father on overnight visitation. She lived with her biological mother and 4-year-old half-sister, Leah. The sibling relationship was characterized by jealousy, anger, and resentment, not in small part motivated on Rebecca's part by her belief that her sister had it "better" because she had not had to suffer the sexual abuse. (Leah's father had died when she was 2.)

Mrs. Carson treated the children in developmentally inappropriate ways. Both had the same bedtime, for example, despite the 4-year age difference, and Rebecca had no privileges that reflected the difference in age. Interventions with the mother and children helped rectify this. The mother was encouraged to have the bedtimes spaced half an hour apart and to spend time playing with the children at home, both together and individually. The mother was encouraged to allow Rebecca to watch TV and other movies that were age appropriate for her but inappropriate for Leah. Her adjustments in her routine in this fashion worked to reduce the sibling rivalry and promote more developmentally appropriate interactions between Rebecca and Leah.

Likewise, the example of the Wilson family illustrates the need to facilitate interaction between the children in the incest family and their peers outside the family. In this case, Rashona, age 9, had been molested by the mother's partner of 3 years. During that time, Rashona had become withdrawn, and her grades at school had declined. With the disclosure and subsequent removal from the home of the offender, Ms. Wilson was helped in therapy to encourage Rashona to meet her needs for companionship with peers. She was enrolled in the local cheerleaders group, which she enjoyed immensely, and her mood improved. This encouraged Ms. Wilson to search for other outlets. With the support of the therapist, she arranged for Rashona to become involved in Girl Scouts.

The secret of family sexual abuse affects family functioning and individual members' relationships both inside and outside the family. It can affect everything in a family, from sex role expectations and identifications to conflict resolution and the handling of intimacy, not to mention sibling as well as parent-child relationships. One can assume some level of distortion in all these areas, depending on the nature and duration of the sexual abuse and the strengths of the family in coping with that. As the family moves toward a healthier level of functioning, with both children and the mother supported in their needs for companionship, support, and pursuit of individual talents and interests outside the family as well as within, many of the distortions can be addressed.

Relational Consequences and the Marital or Partnership Relationship

In this section, the nature of the work in the marital pair or partnership relationship will be discussed along with the issues for family sessions in which the offender is planning to reunite with the family. A major part of the work within the context of family treatment can involve the relationship between the woman and the alleged offender if the mother is choosing to sustain that relationship. In this instance, couples work may be an important phase in the process (Palmer, 1997). If the mother is going to reunite with the alleged offender, he will need to be integrated into the family sessions with the mother and children. Before this can happen, it is necessary to have sessions with the woman and her husband (or the woman and her partner) alone.

The nature and scope of treatment of the offender are beyond the scope of this book. However, therapists undertaking family therapy that includes an offender need to be cognizant of the issues the offender must deal with in his own treatment before reunification with the victim and family can be attempted (see Schwartz & Cellini, 1997, for a comprehensive coverage of offender treatment issues).

Trepper and Barrett (1986) identify a number of issues that will probably need to be addressed in marital sessions. These include communication problems, conflict resolution skills, enhancement of intimacy, and the sexual relationship. Couples, for example, may need help learning not only how to listen better but also how to express themselves, make requests constructively, and provide positive feedback. Depending on the degree of sexual dysfunction in the relationship, the therapist may want to refer to a specialist or work with the couple directly. In general, most therapists are now aware of the cornerstones of sex therapy, which include the acceptance of mutual responsibility for the sexual relationship, basic education about sexuality, reduction of anxiety about sexual performance, and specific skill enhancement. In addition, work on family of origin issues may be needed, both in couples work and the family sessions as well.

A specific event that marks the move from couples work to family sessions that include the offender is the apology or clarification session. A number of offender therapists have now written about such sessions (Salter, 1988; Trepper & Barrett, 1986). Some of the preapology work needs to be done with just the couple, and some can be done with the mother and children in family sessions. Part of the work for the couple should involve a detailed disclosure by the offender to his partner of the nature and frequency of the sexual abuse. This is to ensure that the offender is ready to take both emotional and intellectual responsibility for the abuse and that the mother is aware of the full extent of the abuse and has time, prior to being in a session with the children, to process this. In some instances, the mother may have protected herself from this awareness as a way of defending against guilt, anger, or feelings of inadequacy. Going through this allows both parties to fully explore and understand the range of their own emotions, so that they are more emotionally available for the meeting with the children.

The purposes of the apology session are, first and foremost, to consolidate what the family has learned so far in treatment. As noted at the beginning of this chapter, it is not recommended that reunification be pursued without the offender having been in his own treatment (O'Connell, 1986; Palmer, 1997; Salter, 1988). If he has, the family therapist can work with his individual or group therapist to help gauge his readiness to reenter the family. In his own therapy, the offender should, at a minimum, have participated meaningfully, owned the responsibility for his offense, developed both intellectual and emotional understanding of the reasons for his behavior, and begun to make some behavioral changes (Salter, 1988). Ideally, he also will have begun to work on relapse prevention (Pithers, 1988). In this process, he should have begun to identify with great specificity the factors precipitating his abuse, family dysfunctional patterns, communication problems, and the way in which he probably avoided discussing problems, held emotions in, did not listen, did not assert needs, and did not provide time for the partnership relationship to unfold (Steen & Monnette, 1989). He should have identified high-risk situations for himself, developed some skills in avoiding these situations or learning how to handle them, learned how to monitor his affect, and exercised the ability to make choices about behavior that could lead to a lapse or relapse (Pithers, 1988).

The disclosure to his wife should reflect growth in all these areas. It can be viewed as an opportunity to consolidate what he has learned about his offending behavior. For the woman, it can be an opportunity to learn more about her partner as well as to monitor her own reactions to the detailed information about the abuse. Time should be allotted for her to ask questions about the specifics of the molestation as well as to reflect on her relationship with him. Often, for example, the woman has not asserted herself, has been satisfied with less than the intimacy she wanted, or has allowed outright abuse, whether emotional, physical, or both.

In addition to this work with the couple, preapology work needs to be done with the victim and other family members as well. The victim and other siblings need to have the opportunity to discuss their own expectations about the apology session and what reactions they anticipate both in themselves and other family members; they also need time to anticipate and practice through role-plays or other techniques. In the apology session itself, the offender should go first, apologizing to the victim for the abuse and to the other family members for putting them in the situation that perpetuated dysfunctional relationships and was not a healthy environment for them.

The mother's position is a complicated one. For reasons enumerated earlier, the woman's position in the family is usually gender prescribed; as such, she is perceived as the one who is responsible for the protection of children. In fact, this expectation of women is in some regards overdetermined. This leads to a tendency on the part of the children, as well as on the part of the mother herself, to blame her for the molestation.

Many therapists argue that the mother should be included in this apology session (Trepper & Barrett, 1986) and take responsibility for the lack of better communication or a better relationship between herself and her children. This would have, as the thinking goes, then permitted the child victim to communicate to her the abuse experience. Although she may want to take responsibility for not recognizing or working on the need for a closer relationship with her children, especially the victim, it is imperative that this be separated from taking responsibility for the abuse. Consequently, it is recommended that any apology that the mother may give should occur in a separate family session. In many families, the mother-child relationship is less than ideal, but the children are not sexual abuse victims. This only occurs when there is an adult in the household who is motivated to sexually abuse children. It is necessary to clearly separate the issue of the mother's relationship with the children from the sexual abuse, lest family members (as well as the therapist) be lured into the trap of overlooking the power of the male in the family and the specific strategies he may have undertaken to have the child keep the secret and deflect the mother's attention away from the true nature of his interaction with her child.

Following the apology session, the work of helping the family reconstitute itself begins (Gelinas, 1987; Trepper & Barrett, 1986). It is difficult to generalize an amount of time because every family is different; a year for this phase of the work is probably realistic. One of the major issues as the therapy goes forward is how much responsibility the therapist encourages the spouse or partner to take in helping the offender with relapse prevention. On the face of it, having the offender inform his partner about the kind of irrational decisions he may make that could lead toward a lapse, having her know what the high-risk situations are for him, and helping him monitor affect and identify abstinence violation effects seem to make sense (Pithers, 1988). It may be that this is part of the "price" the woman has to be prepared to pay for staying in a relationship with a man who has the motivation to sexually abuse children.

However, it seems that, in return, certain demands should be made of the man vis-à-vis his relationship with the woman. For example, as the woman identifies her needs for intimacy, her tendencies not to assert herself, and the situations that are most likely to cause her to avoid problems and fail to communicate emotions, he should likewise be made aware of these and asked to work with her on strengthening herself as well as their relationship. In addition, the husband or partner should be encouraged to help the woman with her goals in her relationship with her children. If this is a family in which the daughter, for example, has been parentified, the mother is going to need support to reestablish herself in the position of authority with the children. The father (or father-surrogate) can be very effective if he lends his support to the mother rather than undermining her authority as he may have done while he was abusing one or more of the children. Although this may be difficult to achieve while he is out of the household, the family sessions that include him (which ideally take place before he returns to live with the family) provide an excellent opportunity to begin to practice this stance, identify resistance to it, and address this.

In addition to supporting her authority, another issue that family sessions can address is extending what the parents have learned about being in a relationship to the whole family system. Thus, better ways to resolve conflict—such as focusing on the present rather than fighting battles from the past, taking small steps in healing relationships, and working for solutions in which all family members involved in a conflict can be "winners"—are some of the strategies that can be enhanced and reinforced in family sessions. Encouraging constructive requests, listening skills, and direct expression of feelings are others. In general, the work with the family system should be geared toward establishing a healthier structure in terms of the functioning of the family system as a whole and with individual subsystems. Thus, boundaries between generations will probably need to be strengthened and boundaries between the family and others redefined. Once the power of the secret is no longer there to support isolation and distancing of members from friends and peers outside, the interactions with those outside the family should gradually create a flexible and permeable boundary that encourages healthy and more functional interactions. Likewise, as communication increases, conflict and tensions should diminish, making for a more peaceful and less turbulent family environment.

There are many families in which the mother is not going to reunite with the offender. However, as she begins to pursue new relationships, many of the factors noted earlier will apply. In addition, she can be helped to identify characteristics in men she dates that indicate that they are trustworthy, sincere, or respectful of her. She may wish to incorporate this individual into the family, and it is appropriate then to include him in the family sessions as well. All of the issues identified earlier for healthier family functioning in situations in which the incest offender is reunited with the family would still apply here.

In general, if the incestuous behavior has terminated and if there is a healthier family structure in place, the family is functioning in a healthier fashion. Also, if there is an improvement in the marital relationship or relationships between the mother and a new partner, and the daughter and/or other children are less parentified, this is the formula for a good prognosis.

Case Coordination

One of the most important tasks for the therapist in the treatment of the mother in the incest family is to coordinate the treatment with other intervention systems that are involved with the family, especially the legal system. The point has been made earlier that the families in which children have been sexually abused are, by definition, affected by both civil and criminal justice systems. Mental health treatment is but one in an array of systems that become involved with children and families once a report has been made of suspected child sexual abuse. Consider the following example.

The Marks family consists of Charlotte Marks (age 33), Ralph Marks (age 40), Tamara Rollins (age 14), Brendon Rollins (age 10), and Eva Marks (age 5). Charlotte, who had Tamara and Brendon as a result of an earlier relationship, has been married to Ralph for about 7 years. Eva is their daughter.

Tamara has made a disclosure to her guidance counselor at school stating that her stepfather has been coming into her bedroom at night, fondling her breasts, inserting his finger into her genitals, and recently had attempted vaginal intercourse. Assume that there is a joint response team for the investigation of child sexual abuse allegations, a model that is widely used. This team usually consists of a Child Protective Services (CPS) worker and a police officer.

The system responds to the report of suspected child sexual abuse by sending a CPS worker and a police officer to the school to interview Tamara. Following this interview, her mother is contacted and interviewed by the CPS worker and the police officer. Following this, Tamara and her mother are taken to the local hospital emergency room by the CPS worker, and the police officer goes off to interview Mr. Marks. At the hospital, Tamara is interviewed by both the pediatrician, with the nurse present, and the social worker. Mrs. Marks is also interviewed by the social worker.

Based on the results of the medical exam and Tamara's statements, Mrs. Marks is asked by the CPS worker if she will ask Mr. Marks to move out of the house. Mrs. Marks, scared and overwhelmed, becomes defensive and says that she needs to talk to her husband and that she does not understand what is happening. CPS decides to remove Tamara and places her in a group home for the night. Tamara meets two new staff at the group home.

The following day, the case goes before the judge in the juvenile (or, in New York, the family) court. The liaison from the district attorney's office sits in at the hearing, as the district attorney's office has automatically received a copy of the CPS report. Also at the hearing is the county attorney (or, in some jurisdictions, the attorney representing CPS), the Marks's attorney, the caseworker, and the caseworker's supervisor. The family is told that a law guardian is to be assigned.

Mrs. Marks learns from CPS that although the original caseworker will stay involved, because Tamara is now in foster care, there will be a worker from the foster care unit who will need to become involved. This worker eventually will take over the case if the child stays in care. A detective from the police department goes to speak to Tamara and other family members and obtains recorded statements.

By the end of the first week, the number of individuals already involved with the family include the following:

CPS worker
Police officer
Nurse

Pediatrician
ER social worker
Group home staff (five in all)
CPS caseworker's supervisor
Parents' attorneys
County attorney
Law guardian
Juvenile (family) court judge
Liaison from the district attorney's office
Detective
Foster care worker

Fourteen (or more) professionals are now involved with this family, and it would not be unusual for the mother to feel confused, overwhelmed, and somewhat powerless with all the professionals involved.

If the case is now referred for local mental health services, the mother's therapist will be at least the 15th person she has met with in one capacity or other since the report to CPS (given that she has only talked with one of the staff at the group home).

This scenario should alert the clinician to the overwhelming nature of the system's intervention from the family's point of view. Therefore, at least initially, it may be extremely difficult for the mother to differentiate the therapist's role from that of others. Although the therapist will be one of the only professionals who has contact with the mother on a regular (probably a weekly) basis, this is not necessarily evident to the mother at the beginning. In fact, however, the therapist may be best positioned to assist the mother with navigating the other systems that are involved with her family because the therapist is likely to become one of the professionals who knows the mother the best.

A conceptual framework useful in working with families is one in which coordination is approached from the point of view of the chronological phase of the case (the beginning, middle, or end) in terms of its involvement with the system. At the beginning, the agencies most involved with the family are charged with *investigation* functions. This includes, from the civil side, CPS and, from the criminal side, law enforcement. If the city or county had an interdisciplinary team, mental health professionals from a crisis unit may be involved. The county attorney and his or her designee might also be involved in the investigative phase if there is a more coordinated response.

The second phase can be characterized as the *litigation phase.* The case may move quickly into this phase if the child is removed from home as a result of the CPS intervention. In most states, the juvenile (or family) court must review the reasons for removal within a matter of days. This marks the move into the litigation phase, which may overlap with the ongoing investigation. The systems and individuals involved in this phase are the county attorney's office, the respondent's attorneys, the law guardian or guardian ad lidem, and the family court judge. The investigative agents or any service providers may be called in as witnesses in this process.

The third phase is the *supervision* phase. To move to this phase, the case must have had a legal disposition. On the civil side, if successfully adjudicated in juvenile (or family) court, the public child welfare agency is usually charged with ongoing monitoring of the family. This occurs though the foster care system if the child is in care and through some branch of the public child welfare agency, often a preventive services or a court-ordered supervision unit if the child is not in care. Treatment agencies and other service providers relate to the public agency caseworker, who functions as a case manager and case coordinator, funneling information back to the juvenile court at the time of judicial reviews of the case.

If the offender has been convicted in the criminal system, the probation or parole (depending on whether the offender will spend any time in jail) system will supervise the offender. Although the juvenile court system may function on a parallel track, the criminal justice system has the most impact on the offender. The juvenile court, on the other hand, may have the biggest impact on the nonoffending parent and the child victim. As in the civil system, mental health professionals and other service providers may provide feedback either to probation or parole or to the court directly.

Investigation

Generally, CPS and law enforcement are charged with the responsibility for establishing what has occurred and if there is enough evidence to bring either a petition in juvenile (or family) court or to file a complaint in criminal court.

If the therapist for the mother is engaged in treatment while the investigation is still under way, two issues are paramount. One is that the mother may need help in negotiating the CPS and law enforcement systems. Mothers often raise questions such as, "Why is both a CPS worker and police officer interviewing my child?" or "If CPS thinks that something has happened, why hasn't my husband been arrested?" It is critical that the therapist understand the purpose and procedures of these two systems to be able to assist the mother. What follows is a brief description of each based on my experiences in two states. It is recognized that these systems vary, depending on state laws, and the reader is encouraged to become familiar with the particulars of local practice.

Child Protective Services

CPS began to be widely established as part of the public child welfare system in the 1960s, in response to the developing awareness of the abuse and neglect of children. This movement was spurred by the publication in 1962 of an article about the *battered child syndrome* (Kempe, Silverman, Steele, Droegemueller, & Silver, 1962), a movement first concerned with the physical abuse of children. In 1974, with the passage of the *Child Abuse Prevention and Treatment Act,* that concern widened to include child maltreatment, including sexual abuse, and emotional neglect. This federal law stimulated the passage of mandated reporting laws in all states, as federal funds were tied to states having such a reporting system in place.

CPS was institutionalized to *respond* to the reports of suspected abuse and neglect. Sometimes, therapists mistakenly assume that this system is staffed by graduate-level social workers. Historically, with a few notable exceptions, CPS has been staffed by caseworkers with a bachelor's degree.

The purpose of CPS is to conduct an investigation and come to a determination about the credibility of the report. In most states, this means interviewing the child and other family members. It may mean obtaining access to school, psychological, or medical records (and/or personnel); coordinating with law enforcement; and preparing a petition for the juvenile court alleging abuse or neglect. There are basically three outcomes of an investigation: (a) The case is unfounded, in which instance no further action is taken. (b) The case is indicated, but no juvenile (or family) court action is initiated. This occurs when CPS feels that the report is credible, and the family is cooperative in pursuing referrals to recommended services to address the condition noted in the report. In this instance, a juvenile court petition is not deemed necessary to motivate the family to engage in services. In some cases, although the report is indicated, there is not enough evidence to pursue a juvenile court petition. In the latter case, because referral to services is voluntary, the family may or may not follow through with the referral. (c) The case is indicated, and there is enough evidence to warrant filing a petition in juvenile court.

For the purposes of our discussion of the mother, the significant issue to note is that without juvenile court intervention, CPS cannot mandate a family to attend *any* kind of services. Furthermore, because only a juvenile court can place and keep a child in foster care, even if a child has been removed in an emergency placement, if there is not enough evidence to file a petition in juvenile court or the judge does not agree that there are grounds for removal, the child will be returned home. Another possibility is that a child may be left in the custody of the nonoffending parent if the alleged offender is out of the home. Often, CPS will ask the nonoffending mother to take out an order of protection to keep the alleged offender away from the child. A juvenile court petition alleging sexual abuse can be filed if the child is in their own home; being in foster care, in other words, is not a prerequisite to having a petition alleging sexual abuse filed in juvenile court.

If the therapist is familiar with the role and function of CPS, it is possible to (a) educate the mother about this, (b) help the mother predict what is likely to happen next, (c) help prepare her for the consequences of the CPS intervention, and (d) intervene more effectively with the system on behalf of the mother.

Law Enforcement

Law enforcement proceeds from a different premise than the CPS system. CPS is concerned with the protection of the child and rehabilitation of parents and children, if necessary. Law enforcement is conducted when appropriate. Although CPS is concerned with protecting the child from the offender, law enforcement is concerned with protecting society from the offender. Although this may seem to be a small difference, it has enormous implications for the respective intervention systems.

The main role of law enforcement is to investigate the report of a criminal incident. Although the process varies from state to state, generally the filing of a complaint initiates the investigation and arrest process. In New York, if and when an arrest is made, a formal complaint is drawn up at the police station for the purpose of charging the defendant with the crime committed. A legal statement of the facts (called an affidavit) will be drawn up and signed by the parent or child. For the purposes of our discussion, the important consideration is that law enforcement personnel are aware that the standard of evidence necessary for prosecution in the criminal court system is much higher than the standard needed for adjudication in the juvenile court matter. Thus, they are concerned about the nature and quality of the evidence. For example, it is critical to pinpoint dates and times. Because the accused has the constitutional right to be confronted by his accuser, these specifics must be present for the accused to defend himself.

The ability of the child to be a credible witness is another issue because in many child sexual abuse cases, the testimony of the victim may be the only evidence. Without going into detail here about the kinds of evidence and what makes a good witness, in general it is fair to say that if a child is younger than 12 (and particularly if the child is younger than 6), it is very difficult to obtain sworn testimony that will be credible. (An individual cannot be convicted on the basis of unsworn testimony alone.) Because of the nature of child sexual abuse, there are often neither witnesses nor medical evidence, making prosecution difficult. If a case goes to trial, often the child witness is the main source of evidence, and if he or she is vulnerable to being discredited, the case may be a weak one from a criminal justice perspective.

In addition, the inability of law enforcement to establish precise dates and times of the alleged offenses can present barriers to prosecution. Because the accused has the right to defend himself, it is necessary that specific dates are indicated. The ambivalence of the child about testifying in open court against the family offender is another barrier. Taken together, these factors can present obstacles that are impossible to overcome for the prosecution.

Police, in conjunction with a district attorney, often find that they cannot proceed with an arrest or enter into prosecution because of the need to rely on the child witness. Family members, including the nonoffending parent, may resist having the child victim drawn into the system. Some families, because of their own involvement in illegal activities (e.g., drug dealing), may be reluctant to be involved with law enforcement. Other families, because of a history of insensitive interaction with formal governmental systems in general, may be apprehensive about how the criminal justice system will treat them. They may be reluctant to cooperate with law enforcement in this family matter.

There are two major implications for the therapist dealing with the mother in the incest family. First, it is unlikely, although not impossible, that the alleged offender in the juvenile case will be prosecuted within the criminal justice system. This has to do with the difficulty of developing the sufficient level of evidence as well as with the resistance of the family to such action. When the mother wants to see criminal justice intervention and the prosecutor believes that it is not possible to go forward, the therapist may need to help the mother deal with the resulting confusion, disappointment, and discouragement with the criminal system. If the reverse is true, and the system wants to go forward and the mother is resistant, different challenges are presented. The most appropriate course for the mother's therapist, in this case, is to ensure that the mother is making an informed choice in her determination of whether to support the criminal prosecution.

The second implication revolves around the leverage over the offender. If the criminal system is involved, there are usually much stricter controls. Orders of protection may proceed from the criminal rather than the juvenile court. If the offender is successfully prosecuted, there are often constraints regarding his movement imposed, including his contact with the child and family. These controls stem from the fact that the ultimate sanction in the criminal system is loss of personal liberty (i.e., someone may go to jail). In the juvenile court system, the ultimate sanction is loss of contact with the child victim. The juvenile court, essentially, has jurisdiction over the child and has a great deal to say about who has custody, visitation, and even parental rights. The criminal court has jurisdiction over the offender and can control his movements, as opposed to controlling the movement of the child.

The relevance of this for the therapist treating the mother of a sexually abused child is that if the mother is struggling with her relationship with the offender, the nature of the relationship and even how much she believes the fact of the abuse may be colored by the legal context. If there is no criminal prosecution, what is the message being sent to the nonoffending parent as well as to the offender and victim? The meaning of this message may differ for each mother and is an important issue for the therapist to explore. Conversely, the prosecution of the offender also may affect the mother's thinking about her relationship and will also need to be processed with the mother.

An example is the case of Mrs. R, a mother whose 5-year-old daughter had allegedly been orally sodomized by her biological father. At the point of intake for mental health treatment, Mrs. R. had a difficult time with the fact that the police had not arrested her husband. In her case, a report had been made by a baby-sitter after a disclosure from the daughter. CPS, in turn, had notified the police, who had interviewed the father and taken a signed statement from the mother. Although the child's story was credible to the CPS investigator, there was no medical evidence or any other evidence tending to corroborate the child's out-of-court statements. The police, in consultation with the district attorney, determined that they could not in good faith pursue an indictment because the only evidence was the child's statements. The child was only 5, there was a question about whether she could provide a sworn statement, and when the district attorney was making the decision, the child was not willing to talk with anyone else about the abuse. The significance for our discussion was the impact on Mrs. R. She was very confused about what she perceived as conflicting messages. On one hand, CPS was telling her they believed her daughter and had filed a petition in the juvenile court to alleging sexual abuse by the father. On the other hand, there was no arrest and no consequences from the criminal court system.

Her husband maintained his innocence and conveyed to his wife that the whole intervention was a big mistake. He suggested that perhaps their daughter, if she had been molested, had been molested by the man across the street, who looked somewhat like him, and that their daughter had been afraid to identify him so had named her father instead. Mrs. R, assuming that the stance of the police meant that they did not believe her daughter, found herself wondering if the allegations were true.

One role for the therapist in this case was to help her sort through her feelings (part of her wanted to believe this had not happened). Another role was for the therapist to share her knowledge about the function, limits, and constraints of the criminal justice system. In this case, as in all cases, however, the best source of information about the legal system is an attorney, and clients should be encouraged to talk to the prosecutor about their concerns.

In another case, another mother, Mrs. M, was also deeply affected by the role of law enforcement. In her situation, her 14-year-old daughter, Nina, had made a report to the police that her stepfather, Mrs. M's fourth husband, was sexually abusing her. Mrs. M did not believe her daughter. She had a history of a very hostile relationship with Nina, who she viewed as a troublemaker. Nina resisted her mother's efforts to set limits, was often truant from school, did not pay attention to curfews that were set for her, and was using drugs and alcohol. Her stepfather was the only one in the family who seemed to have any control over her, but they often fought verbally. Mrs. M viewed her daughter's report to the police as the latest in an attempt to resist his control.

Her husband adamantly denied the allegations and made a suicide attempt, for which he was psychiatrically hospitalized. He went from the hospital to jail, where Mrs. M began to visit him. The definitive position taken by the criminal justice system, however, and the forced separation from her husband (and his influence over her) contributed to her ability to develop a different perspective. Gradually, she began to rethink her position, as the system remained firm and her oldest daughter joined the younger one in her own allegations. In this case, her initial denial turned to ambivalence as she dealt with the ramifications of the criminal justice intervention. The role of the therapist was largely in helping her to come to terms with her disappointment about her husband's behavior, as well as helping her predict what the steps in the criminal process would be.

Litigation

Although it is difficult to draw a clear line between the initial investigation phase and the second, or litigation phase (as the investigation may be ongoing as the litigation begins), the litigation phase takes on a life of its own and is important for the therapist to understand. One of the most important distinctions for the therapist to understand is the different purposes of the two legal systems. In the criminal justice system, the severest remedy is the loss of liberty or freedom (i.e., being incarcerated) or, increasingly as the death penalty is reinstated in many cases, in the loss of life. In addition, as more states pass statutes such as Megan's law in New Jersey, the possibility that the offender convicted through the criminal justice system will have to register his whereabouts becomes increasingly possible. This may have a significant impact on the family, whether or not the offender reunites with his family. Because the consequences of being found guilty are severe, the standard of proof—beyond a reasonable doubt—is high.

In addition, elements in our Constitution form the cornerstone of our legal system and play an important role in the criminal process. For example, the Constitution guarantees the right to be confronted by one's accuser. In the case of family sexual abuse, this means that the offender has the right to be confronted by the child victim or witness. For this reason, the Supreme Court ruled that although closed-circuit TV can be used in cases in which the judge so rules, it is not an absolute right. (In fact, in the cases in which a judge does decide that a child can testify via closed-circuit TV, it may be a two-way closed-circuit TV system. The offender's presence is therefore in the room, via the TV screen, where the child is testifying. Although it would be incorrect to say that two-way screen is the norm in the United States, it does occur and, in my opinion, may undercut the safety the child might otherwise feel if he or she is not in the same room with the offender.) Thus, in the criminal system, the standard of proof is high, and the constitutionally guaranteed right to be confronted by one's accuser is not waived because of the potential serious consequences to conviction.

It is a different situation in the juvenile or family court system. The juvenile court was founded in the early part of the 20th century to deal with juvenile delinquents and abused and neglected children. Because it was initially established to deal with the juvenile offender, who was thought to be more amenable to rehabilitation due to age, legal sanctions were often less severe, and, consequently, the standard of proof was less. Also, because a major motivating impetus was rehabilitation and protection of children, the constitutionally guaranteed right to be confronted by one's accuser was not as assiduously guarded. Over the course of the 20th century, two things happened that have driven our juvenile court system as it responds to child sexual abuse cases today. The first has to do with the movement into the juvenile court system of huge numbers of cases involving allegations of abuse and neglect. Again, the rationale in bringing these cases to the juvenile court was that the purpose in removal was not to punish families but to protect children. Therefore, because the consequence of an adjudication was not a loss of freedom for the offender, the standard of proof (in New York state) became a "fair preponderance of the evidence." This means it is easier to "prove" a case in juvenile court than in criminal court. In many states, it may even be possible to have a case adjudicated without having the child testify. It is extremely difficult in the criminal court situation to prove a case that goes to trial without the testimony of the child.

The second major reform of the juvenile court system evolved as a result of *in re Gault,* a decision of the Supreme Court that, in effect, stipulated that juveniles had the right to be represented in the court. This has led to the widespread practice of appointing *guardian ad lidems* or *law guardians* as the child's representatives in court. Thus, in most instances, if an abuse or neglect petition is filed, the child will be assigned a lawyer or a guardian ad lidem. Although myriad issues surround this role, the guardian ad lidem or law guardian can be an additional resource to the child in a sexual abuse case. The mother's therapist should be familiar with the position of the law guardian in the case because it may have an impact on the juvenile court case.

In addition to the differences in purpose, the courts also differ in their procedures. What follows is an attempt to make some of those differences clear.

Juvenile Court

The process in juvenile court can be thought of in three phases: filing of a petition, fact finding, and disposition. A juvenile proceeding is initiated by the filing of a petition alleging specific sexual acts, usually within a specific time frame. This is filed by the attorney representing CPS. This attorney may be the county attorney or an attorney hired as counsel to the local department of social services. In New York, the petition alleges specific instances of abuse or neglect and identifies the accused—the respondent. In other states, the petition may allege that the child is dependent and in need of the intervention of the juvenile court for protection. In any case, the filing of the petition is followed by a fact-finding hearing. At this hearing, the juvenile court judge, acting as the trier of fact as well as the one to determine what the law dictates, will make a finding. The distinction between trier of fact and law is significant only in that there is no jury in juvenile court. In the criminal court, the role of the trier of fact is relegated to the jury, and the judge makes the determinations about what can be admitted, whether objections can be sustained or overturned, and so on. In the juvenile court, the judge has both roles.

CPS, as the petitioner, will be represented by an attorney. It is important to note that the attorney represents the agency, not the child. Although the argument may be made that the agency has the child's interests at heart, the legal interests of the agency may at times be different from that of the child's.

The attorney for the child (which in New York is the law guardian) is the one who represents the child's interests. There is an important caveat about the role of the child's attorney. Most therapists, like most lay individuals, assume that the attorney for the child will represent the child's *best* interests, which for social workers and other professionals often means the child's best interests as determined by adults who know the child. Many times, mental health professionals are called on to provide evaluations that speak to the child's best interests. However, the child's lawyer must weigh his or her ethical duty to be a zealous advocate for the child's *expressed* interests against any argument to operate instead as a *best-interests* advocate. *Best interests* has a particular meaning in the legal arena. When a child's attorney decides to substitute his or her judgment for the child's expressed interests, there must be compelling grounds for the attorney to do this. The attorney may do this in cases in which the child is judged incompetent. Competency also has a particular meaning under the law. The meaning of *incompetent* in this instance refers to the child's inability to provide the attorney with direction, due to age or other circumstances.

For example, a child may tell his attorney that he wants to go home to a family that, from the point of view of a guardian ad lidem and other professionals, may be judged unsuitable. Given the child's age, the determination about the child's competency, and a host of other factors that the child's attorney may need to take into consideration, the child's attorney may nonetheless believe that his or her ethical duty lies in representing the child's wish to go home in any juvenile court proceeding. This might be in opposition to the determination of the child protection agency and other professionals involved with the family.

For example, let us take the case of a 10-year-old girl who has been removed from her family based on two younger siblings' report of sexual abuse by their father. The father is adjudicated for the abuse of the younger two only, but under the statute in New York that allows other children to be removed based on a derivative finding, the 10-year-old was placed in care also. She was adamant with her law guardian that she wanted to return home, denying that her father had ever abused her. The law guardian, believing that the child was competent to give instruction, felt compelled to represent the girl's interests to the court, despite the opposition by the caseworker and child's therapist.

The significance of all this for our purposes is that the therapist needs to be aware of the complexity of some of the legal issues (for additional information regarding the complex subject of child representation, see "Ethical Issues," 1996; Myer, 1985). Familiarity with these issues is an important way to better predict and prepare the mother for her interface with these systems. Of course, referral of the mother to an attorney for further clarification is always useful as well.

Typically, the respondent in juvenile court is represented by one attorney, and the nonoffending parent is represented by another. In some cases, it is not so obvious that there should be two different attorneys. However, it is often the case that the mother's interests are not the same as the alleged offender's, and she can benefit from her own attorney.

For example, returning to the case of Mrs. R, discussed earlier, Mr. and Mrs. R initially had one attorney representing them. This resulted from the fact that Mr. R convinced his wife that they could not afford two attorneys, and because he was innocent, there was no need. It was important for the therapist to understand the legal distinctions identified earlier and to help Mrs. R with an informed decision about whether she wanted her own attorney. The attorney originally retained was mostly concerned with defending Mr. R. Then an issue arose because CPS was also going to name Mrs. R in the petition as neglectful because she "knew or should have known" about the sexual abuse. Mrs. R began to feel that the attorney was not operating as zealously in defending her rights and began to see that her interests were different from those of her husband. In fact, as the case proceeded, she made the decision to retain her own lawyer.

At the fact-finding hearing, the petitioner presents his or her case first and typically calls the CPS worker, a physician if there is any medical evidence, and other witnesses who could tend to corroborate the child's out-of-court statements. In New York, if that is sufficient to prove the case, the child will be adjudicated as a sexually abused child. A point to note here, briefly referred to earlier, is the concept of out-of-court statements. In New York, as in many states, the juvenile court act allows for the child's statements to be admitted as an exception to the hearsay rule. The hearsay rule is a rule of evidence that usually requires that a witness appear in court to present the evidence, so that the witness can be cross-examined. Otherwise, the evidence cannot be tested for reliability by cross-examination.

In child abuse and neglect cases in New York, as in many other states, out-of-court statements made by the child, coupled with other evidence tending to corroborate, can suffice to meet the standard of proof needed by the juvenile court to make a finding of abuse or neglect. If the therapist knows this and is familiar with the particulars of the case, she can be helpful to the mother in predicting whether the child will have to go through testifying as a witness in a juvenile court prosecution.

Based on the evidence presented by the petitioner and countered by the respondent's case, the judge will make a decision. The decision can be either that the judge finds that the petitioner has proved its case, in which case the respondent is found to have committed one or more of the acts alleged in the petition, or the case is dismissed. Another possibility, at least in New York, is a middle ground. This is an admission in contemplation of dismissal (ACD). With this provision, the respondent does not admit to the allegations but agrees to the court's adjourning the case for a period up to 1 year under specified terms and conditions. If, over the course of the adjournment period, there are no new violations of the conditions and the respondent complies with the court's orders, then the case will be dismissed.

The latter finding can be particularly problematic for mothers of sexually abused children, unless the court orders are clear and very specific as to what is expected of the offender and other family members. A case example may help to illustrate this point. In the Miller case, Mr. Miller agreed to an ACD after a petition was filed alleging that he had abused his 11-year-old daughter. Mrs. Miller, tired of continuing court battles and feeling overwhelmed by the financial drain, agreed to this. The county did not insist on specific court orders mandating Mr. Miller to a sex offender therapist for an evaluation or mandating treatment with a sex offender specialist. The court ordered supervised visitation and that Mr. Miller was to "attend therapy" for a year. At the end of the year, the case was dismissed, and Mr. Miller had the right to unsupervised visitation, despite the fact that he had not been evaluated or treated specifically for the alleged sexual abuse. In this case, it is questionable whether the juvenile court disposition of ACD was useful in protecting the children from sexual abuse.

There may be a period (in New York it can be weeks or months) between the finding of abuse and a disposition hearing. The purpose of the delay is to allow the public child welfare agency, ideally in conjunction with their attorney and the law guardian, to develop a rehabilitation plan to be presented to the judge. At the time of the disposition hearing, the judge will listen to the plan presented by both sides. Often the attorneys, including the respondent's attorney, have reached an agreement about the plan, in which case there will not need to be a formal hearing but just an appearance before the court.

The relevance for the mother's therapist, as for the other family member therapists, is that he or she often can have input into the plan that will be approved by the court. Even in those jurisdictions in which the disposition follows immediately on the fact finding, if the therapist is aware of this, he or she can assist the mother by ensuring that the mother takes the necessary steps to have input prior to the time of the hearing.

After the court orders are in place, the family will not be back in court until the case is scheduled for a review, which is usually a year later. The courts can order treatment for the offender, for other family members, for preventive services, and for substance abuse treatment and put permanent orders of protection in place. During the time between disposition and review, the offender and other family members will have been ordered to attend a number of services. Various agencies may be involved in their implementation. One remedy that is available to the court if the offender or other family members do not comply with the court orders is the ability to invoke legal sanctions. Although the most extreme sanction (again, in New York) is 6 months in jail for violating the juvenile court order, it is nonetheless a remedy that may be helpful in controlling the offender. It is sometimes necessary for the mother, and sometimes the therapist can help with this, to confer with the county to get a violation petition of the existing court orders filed. The therapist who knows what legal remedies are available in his or her jurisdiction will be in a better position to refer the mother appropriately.

Criminal Court

The process leading to criminal justice involvement with a family is more complex. In New York, there are basically four phases: indictment, pretrial, trial, and sentencing. They are discussed in general below to aid the therapists in their advocacy work with clients.

Indictment

A felony prosecution is initiated in two ways. The district attorney can file a charge at the local court level, in which case there will be a preliminary hearing to determine reasonable cause for the grand jury unless waived by the defendant. If the district attorney is going to take this route, the time limits from the point of notifying the court to the hearing date are short and often specified in state statutes. The purpose of this hearing is to inform the defendant of the charges, set bail, and schedule the next court appearance. An important issue to underscore is that the purpose of bail is to ensure that the defendant comes to the next hearing. It has little to do with the nature or severity of the crime and mostly to do with whether the court feels that there is any reason to believe that the defendant would flee the jurisdiction.

At this hearing, the victim probably will have to provide sworn testimony and be cross-examined by the alleged perpetrator's attorney. This is also a public hearing and thus open to the press and the public in general. This means that early on in the criminal phase (at least in New York), the offender's attorney will have an opportunity to hear the evidence and to cross-examine, a process that may be overwhelming to a child victim early in the process following disclosure. If the judge decides that reasonable cause exists, the case is referred to the grand jury, which may indict the defendant (i.e., authorize a felony trial of the defendant). If the crime rises only to the level of a misdemeanor and not a felony, the case may be tried in the local court, or the complaint may be dismissed.

To avoid putting the child through this kind of public hearing, the district attorney may decide on an alternative route by submitting the charge directly to the grand jury in the first instance. This can be done before an arrest is made. In New York, this means that a group of 16 to 23 individuals (the number may vary by state law) hear the case and make a decision about whether to indict the alleged perpetrator. The advantage of this process for the prosecution is that the only person to question the child is the district attorney, who, it is hoped, will have established a relationship with the child and have prepared the child for the hearing by that time. Although the offender's attorney is present, he or she is not permitted to ask the child any questions. The alleged offender is not allowed to be in the room.

In addition, the child may not have to appear in person at this hearing. The law may permit a child's videotaped statement to be used as the evidence brought before the grand jury to request an indictment. The advantage to this, of course, is that although the child will still have to answer specific questions about what has happened, the child can do so without having to sit in front of a large group of adults. If the mother's therapist is knowledgeable about this process, he or she is in a position to help the mother make a more informed decision about whether to go forward with a criminal prosecution.

Pretrial

Perhaps one of the most crucial details about the criminal prosecution is to know that in child sexual abuse cases, as in all criminal cases, only a minority ever goes to trial. What happens in the pretrial stage is just as important as what may happen at trial because it is during this time that the contours of a plea bargain may be decided. (It is important to note that a plea bargain may be entered into at any time in the process.) In general, the two issues that are significant for the purposes of this discussion are the discovery process and the pretrial hearings. The point to be made about the discovery process is to underscore that this is the legal procedure by which each side has the right to query the other side about the nature of the evidence they will produce at trial. This is a fundamental principle of the law. One of the most fascinating issues is the failure of the opposing sides to use this mechanism in a timely fashion.

For the therapist's purposes, however, the relevance is that records can be subpoenaed. This means that in cases of child sexual abuse, the therapist should anticipate that their records of the mother's treatment could become the subject of a court hearing and keep notes with this in mind. Ethically, one cannot compromise the treatment record keeping, but remaining aware that diagnoses as well as the description of the mother's psychodynamics and relationships both within and outside the family may need to be defended can help therapists be precise in their record keeping.

It should be noted that if the subpoena is a compulsory legal process, the therapist has to comply. However, a therapist should never turn over a record until his or her own attorney or the agency's attorney has had a chance to review it. The subpoena may be defective in its form or method of service, there may be portions of the record that can be omitted, or a treatment summary can sometimes be substituted.

In terms of the second issue, pretrial hearings, the significance for the therapist is that these hearings are usually arguments over the admissibility of evidence. It is likely that they will occur, and if the therapist knows this, he or she can help prepare the mother for the fact that there are likely to be many delays between the indictment and possible eventual trial. It is also the case that as a result of one side or the other not being able to have evidence admitted, the motivation to settle can be accelerated. Although plea bargains that do not include a conviction for some degree of sexual abuse (i.e., a reduction to endangering the welfare of the child or aggravated assault) can result in sentences that do not include sexual offender treatment, in many instances, a plea bargain is preferable to going to trial. The problems with convictions for other than a sexual assault may be similar to those that arise in the case of the ACD in juvenile court—there may be no mechanism to compel sex offender treatment, a condition that is usually always preferable.

The reason that a plea bargain may be preferable from the family's point of view—given that there is still a sexual abuse conviction, albeit a lower degree—is that it saves the child from having to testify. It also prevents the possibility of the therapist having to testify. In the case of the therapist working with the mother, this is always an issue. If the therapist has to testify, it is difficult to avoid making any statements that the mother might view as negative, and the implications for the treatment process are obvious. If the case goes to trial, it means that supporting the mother through the criminal process needs to be integrated into the treatment.

Trial

The trial in a child sexual abuse case is, in general, an extremely anxiety-provoking experience for the mother as well as the child victim. It is helpful if the therapist, knowing this, can be alert to the mother's ability to cope with anxiety and be prepared to focus on skills to aid her with this during the trial. At least three issues are involved in supportive therapy during the trial. One common dynamic is the mother's focus on the child as the trial goes forward. It is usually crucial to highlight for the mother that she will have issues independent of the child. Many mothers find that they are triggered by the substance of the trial proceedings far more than they had anticipated. Although they may have difficulty anticipating this, if the therapist is sensitive to these dynamics, he or she is better positioned to help the mother. For example, negative statements may be made about her, either by the attorney for the offender or the prosecutor. The prosecutor's main focus is the child, and to accentuate the child's vulnerability, sometimes there is a tendency to vilify the mother as well as the offender.

While supporting the mother, the therapist will need to help the mother to support the child. The preparation, waiting, and actual testimony at trial are extremely stressful for the child, and the mother may need to be helped to put aside her own issues to be available for the child. The third issue has to do with the mother's reaction to the therapist being called to testify, if that is the case. Time will need to be devoted to preparing the mother for the therapist's appearance as well. This can all become quite time-consuming and over-shadow other treatment issues. Although it is imperative to do this work, one has to be careful that it does not become the raison d'être of the treatment process.

In addition to the conviction of a defendant, there are three other possible outcomes: acquittal, mistrial, or a hung jury, which usually means a re-trial. What happens if the offender is not convicted and the charges are dismissed? This also can set the stage for a depressive reaction or a reaction of rage on the part of the mother. To mitigate against this, it can be helpful if the therapist keeps the possibility of a dismissal before the mother as a good reality check.

Sentencing

Sentencing can be a critical time for the mother as well as the child. Most times, the sentence is for less time than the mother (and others) may feel is warranted. Often, the family has gone through the ordeal of a prosecution that may have dragged on for years. To learn that an offender is only going to get 6 months or a year and probation and that the jail time has already been served if the offender was incarcerated up to or during the trial can be very disillusioning for family members. Sometimes, the maximum sentences for the crime feel insignificant to the mother. Family members, including the mother, may experience a depressive reaction to the finality of the criminal justice system if the penalty seems too light.

On the other hand, the mother may feel that the sentence is too long. This is more likely to be the case if the offender has admitted the charges and the mother feels that rehabilitation rather than incarceration is what is indicated. In either case, these issues may require considerable time in processing with the therapist.

Supervision

The supervision phase of the case can be the longest. The agencies that have the authority for supervising or monitoring cases include the public child welfare agency on the juvenile court side and probation or parole on the criminal justice side. The role of the supervising agency varies depending on its auspices. It is useful for therapists to have a basic understanding of how the system works so that their own expectations are realistic, and they can help the mother predict, cope with, and advocate for herself with these systems.

Supervision in Juvenile Court Cases

If an offender has been adjudicated in juvenile court for child sexual abuse, the juvenile court judge will have issued orders for the family and its members. These orders are usually to be implemented under the supervision of the department within the public child welfare agency that is responsible. If the child is placed and remains in foster care as a result of the juvenile court adjudication, then the division responsible for monitoring foster care cases will probably be responsible. One very important fact for the mental health professional to know is that public policy in child welfare demands that the agency work on reunifying the child with his or her biological family as quickly as possible. This means that the biological parent or parents responsible for the care of the children will be directed toward services that ameliorate the problem for which the children were placed. It is only after the agency has made diligent efforts to provide appropriate services and the parent has failed to respond that the agency can consider a plan other than return to the parent as a goal for the child.

With the passage of the *Adoption and Safe Families Act* (1997), child welfare agencies will be under even greater pressure to reunite families quickly when the child has been removed from the home. If a child is not in kinship care, unless the agency can present a compelling reason, agencies will be required to initiate termination of parental rights actions once a child has been in care for 15 out of the last 22 months. From a mental health treatment perspective, this may be an unrealistic time frame, considering all of the issues that typically need to be resolved before a child can be returned home, particularly if the offender is still in the home. Nonetheless, it is critical for the therapist to be aware of where the family's case is in the system and to aid the child welfare system in supporting grounds for extending beyond the 15-month limit if they support that position. Otherwise, termination of parental rights may be initiated.

In New York, as in most states, permanent neglect is the ground most often to terminate parental rights. In New York, failure to plan—which means that the parent has not cooperated with the public child welfare agency in the planning and execution of the service plan—is the most common ground. In sexual abuse cases, this can translate into an offender's parental rights being terminated if he did not comply with offender treatment. It might be applied to the mother if she did not obtain substance abuse treatment or engage the child in therapy if that was ordered by the juvenile court. The relevance of this information for the mother's therapist is to highlight the need to become informed about the realities of the child welfare system and what the mother has to deal with if one or more of her children are in foster care.

If the child has not been placed in foster care, with a juvenile court finding of child sexual abuse, the public child welfare agency will probably be ordered to follow the family in supervision. The unit or division generally responsible for this is a court-ordered supervision unit. Preventive services are often utilized. Sometimes, the agency will handle preventive services cases itself. Other times, it will have contracted with private, not-for-profit agencies to provide preventive services. In those instances, the duties are the same, but two levels of administration are involved—the voluntary agency and the public agency. The latter has the responsibility of monitoring the work of the private agency.

It is helpful to the mother's therapist to identify the worker in the respective agency who is responsible for case management functions in the client's case and to establish a liaison with her. This person will be responsible for assisting the mother with entrée to programs that provide government benefits and services (i.e., public assistance, food stamps, child care) as well as for engaging and monitoring the family's engagement and participation in the court-mandated personal social services (substance abuse, psychiatric evaluation, sex offender therapy, etc.). This is also the person to whom the therapist may have to report about the mother's progress in treatment. The therapist, with the information and knowledge she will have about the mother, also may be able to influence the worker's report to the court in a way that is helpful to the mother and the family.

Supervision in the Criminal Justice System

A conviction in the criminal justice system results in one or more public agencies being involved in ongoing supervision of the offender. The distinction between the supervision that goes on in this system and that which goes on as a result of the juvenile court adjudication is that this system is solely concerned with the offender. If the offender is sentenced to prison, when he is released he will be on parole, and that system will be responsible for super-

vising his movements in the community. The expectation of parole is that
the offender has served his time, and although his movements and activity
may be monitored, additional requirements for service may or may not be a
condition of parole. Because only some states have few prison-based treatment programs, one hopes that with the sex offender, community-based sex
offender treatment is a condition of parole.

The other, more common institution that is involved in the supervision
of the offender is the probation department. Often, a family offender may
have a sentence that involves some limited amount of jail time and probation.
In these instances, sex offender treatment, as well as other services, is often a
condition of probation.

Although the therapist for the mother may have less reason to be involved with this system than with the public child welfare agency that is
monitoring the juvenile court cases, it is nonetheless useful to know how the
system works. In some instances, the mother may have a restraining order or
order of protection through the criminal court. The order may be either to
restrain the offender from contact with the mother or with the child. The
probation officer can violate the offender's probation if he or she has information from the mother or therapist that the offender is not complying with
this condition. This means that the offender might have to return to jail or be
sentenced to prison. This can be a powerful incentive to help keep the offender away from the family or mother, if that is indicated. Thus, if probation is active with a case, the therapist may want to assist the mother with appropriate contact with that agency.

Summary

In addition to mental health treatment, many other systems usually are
involved with the family when child sexual abuse has occurred. Regardless of
whether the therapist becomes involved with the family at the beginning,
middle, or end of the intervention process, it may be very important for the
therapist to interact with other agencies. These systems have a powerful impact on the family, and it cannot be stated strongly enough that the therapist
has an obligation to know what the responsibilities of the other agencies are
so that one is aware of the context in which mental health treatment of the
mother is occurring. Second, with that knowledge, the therapist can help the
mother predict what may happen. Third, the therapist will be better positioned to intervene directly or help the client advocate for her interests.

It is a sad statement, but too often the reality is that the interventions by
the staff of formal systems supposedly established to help families are not car-

ried out in the sensitive, knowledgeable, or thorough manner that one would wish. Therefore, as the individual professional who may know the mother the best, the therapist is ethically compelled to be knowledgeable and to do what is in her or his power to shape that experience with formal systems for the mother in a positive manner.

WORKING WITH MOTHERS INVOLVED IN CUSTODY AND VISITATION DISPUTES

One of the most difficult areas of practice involves a woman whose concern about sexual abuse has arisen within the context of a custody or visitation dispute with a current or ex-husband. This is a particularly troubling area because the task of establishing whether a child is sexually abused is a forbidding one in these circumstances, especially when preschool-age or very young children are involved. Children of this age are often not able to provide a coherent verbal account of their experiences because of cognitive and developmental limitations. This can present a barrier to the clear determination of the "fact" and then to effective intervention by either Child Protective Services (CPS) or the courts. Sometimes, it can be established that the child has been abused, but it is not possible to identify the perpetrator. Other times, it remains unclear at the end of an evaluation period whether abuse has occurred.

A major obstacle to the determination of child sexual abuse is the bias against the mother when an allegation arises, particularly after a separation (Abel, 1989; Faller, 1988b). Abel (1989) in describing custodial mothers who believe their children have been sexually abused. He stated, "The perception that the legal system is against the custodial parent is probably accurate; the belief that the custodial parent must protect the child because the court system will not is a real one" (p. 261).

Third and perhaps most important, the problem of child sexual abuse overwhelms the traditional approaches to problem solving in instances of custody and visitation disputes. Some of those most adamant about the "suspect" role of the mother, for example (Gardner, 1987), come from a mental health generalist background with experience conducting child custody evaluations as a particular method of practice. Those mental health professionals who have a background in child sexual abuse often have not had this history of evaluation within the context of a custody dispute, and although they are perhaps more knowledgeable about the dynamics of child sexual abuse, they are just beginning to address the special needs of families involved in marital dissolution or custody battles.

This inability of our approaches to successfully resolve this problem is perhaps most visible in the legal system, which operates on the principles of fault, liability, and individual rights. Yet this system serves as society's main vehicle for resolving family disputes. As Awad and McDonough (1991) have argued, a system that operates from a paradigm of needs, interests, and functioning of the family would probably prove more effective. Others have argued that an approach that embodies the notion of continued mediation over time to resolve conflict, as opposed to one that proceeds from the idea of a "final agreement," would be more effective (Abel, 1989).

The Problem With the "Blame-the-Mother" Stance

The problem, simply stated, is that the lay public, the legal system, and some mental health professionals attribute vindictiveness on the part of the custodial spouse, usually the mother, as the motivation when allegations of sexual abuse arise in the midst of a divorce, especially with very young children. Gardner (1987), for example, has described what he calls the "parental alienation syndrome." This syndrome attributes the emergence of child sexual abuse symptoms to the emotional enmeshment and overinvolvement of one parent with a child, rendering it difficult to separate her needs from those of the child. Others, most notably Blush and Ross (1987), have advanced the sexual allegations in divorce (SAID) syndrome. In this syndrome, the mother's presentation is characterized as one typified by

> a fearful person who believes she has been a victim of manipulation, coercion, and physical, social or sexual abuse in the marriage. She has tended to see herself as a powerless victim . . . and the man as being a source of physical threat. Another type of hysterical manifestation is the "justified vindication." In this instance a hostile, emotionally expansive, vindictive and dominant female. (Blush & Ross, 1987, p. 4)

Experts in child sexual abuse generally agree that these are not acceptable perspectives from a scientific point of view. In fact, the research that has been conducted to date with large samples, often drawn from the court system, reveals that there is little basis to these claims that mothers in divorce or custody battles can be characterized in this fashion. Thoennes and Tjaden (1990), in their study of more than 9,000 cases of divorce, found that not only were custody disputes involved in only a small minority of cases but also that the number of custody disputes involving sexual abuse allegations (163) accounted for only 2% of the total sample, hardly reflecting a massive increase in the problem.

Second, of the cases involving child sexual abuse in their study, more than 50% were deemed to be valid cases, approximately 25% were unable to be determined, and less than 25% were attributed to "false allegations." In the latter category, the allegation was attributed to misinterpretations or misunderstanding by the parent of a child's behavior or statement. This has contributed to the understanding that when false allegations do arise, they often emanate from an adult in the situation and not the child.

Another landmark study, that of Jones and McGraw (1987), investigated the abuse allegations of children. They reviewed 576 complaints of possible sexual abuse made to the Denver Department of Social Services. Findings revealed that more than 50% of the allegations were substantiated, but only 8% were found to be fictitious. Again, 24% had insufficient data to make a determination, and the remainder, although unfounded, were confirmed as representing justifiable suspicions. Faller et al. (1993), in their review of the research on false allegations of child sexual abuse, made the point that the most valid studies are those with larger, more representative samples. Small clinical samples drawn from the practice of individuals tend to be less reliable in terms of generalizing to the larger population.

The timing at which allegations arise does appear to affect the perception of true or false allegations. Faller (1991) has suggested four categories for classifying different case situations, based on her research at a University of Michigan clinic. These are the following: (1) disclosure of a history of child sexual abuse that precedes the mother's decision to divorce, (2) a pattern of longstanding abuse that is revealed only after the marital separation, (3) marital dissolution that precipitates the onset of sexual abuse, and (4) allegations that turn out to be unfounded or false. In her study, she found that women who had independently chosen to end the marriage after learning that their children were sexually abused (Category 1 and 2 cases), in cases in which the authorities were not involved, were more likely to have their motives about visitation questioned. When the authorities have addressed the sexual abuse situation before the divorce action, this was less likely to be the case. The largest proposition of cases in Faller's study fell into the situation where the marital dissolution precipitated the sexual abuse. This group of women is most vulnerable to having ulterior motives attributed to them.

Theories about the dynamics involved in situations in which the divorce precipitates the abuse stress the emotional vulnerability of the offending parent following divorce. It is suggested that the loss of family structure, the emotional loss experienced by the offending parent, and the anger at the spouse contribute to the emergence of offending behavior. Research into the characteristics of paternal caretakers also provides some useful information. Based on her research with 196 paternal caretakers, Faller (1988b) found that the victims of the noncustodial biological fathers were the youngest, with a mean age of 3.6 at onset. This supports the notion that in cases of parents who have separated, in which the onset of abuse occurs with children on visitation, they are among the youngest victims, contributing to the difficulty of establishing a clear fact pattern.

This context forms a major dilemma for the treating therapist. What stance can the therapist take when a mother presents herself or her child for treatment when there is a concern about sexual abuse but no legal finding has been made, and the alleged offender still has access to the child?

Treatment Approaches

There is no easy solution or set of recommendations that apply to all case situations. However, from my clinical experience as well as a reading of the literature, some principles or clinical standards can provide some guidance in these most difficult situations. First, it is important to advocate for the therapeutic management of a case when sexual abuse has been alleged, but it is impossible to make a determination of whether sexual abuse has occurred. A second type of case is one where it is determined that abuse has occurred but is impossible to identify the perpetrator. *Therapeutic management* means involvement by a therapist over time with the child and family, with a family or juvenile court and or social service agency having some oversight responsibility.

Most who have written about these dilemmas (Awad & McDonough, 1991; Breese, Stearns, & Bess, 1986; Hewitt, 1991) stress the need for ongoing involvement by a therapist who is perceived as neutral and is open to working with all family members. Although the recommendations in the literature differ as to the number of therapists who need to be involved (one, two, or a team), the gender of the therapists, and the focus of their work, all agree that there needs to be one person whom the children views as "theirs." The best possible situation for therapeutic management is where, even though an initial evaluation has resulted in an inability to determine whether allegations are true, the therapist is involved as a result of the referral by a court or other official. If the family has been court ordered to treatment, it is possible for the therapist to have more control over the ensuing process. A number of models have been promulgated for therapeutic intervention when a family has been directed to a clinic or therapist. Hewitt (1991) outlined a step-by-step process that involves the therapist initially supervising contacts between the child and alleged family perpetrator and moving to a stage where supervision is first undertaken by another third party, and then, ultimately, visitation is unsupervised. The cooperation of the noncustodial parent or court-ordered supervision of visitation would clearly need to be achieved in this model.

In a more recent book, Hewitt (1999) described a revised protocol for the therapeutic management of cases, suggesting that such involvement should always be court ordered. She reviewed recent research on sexual recidivism to arrive at a list of variables associated with a low risk to reoffend. Risk assessment of the alleged offender is an important step in her process, and she suggested that these factors be used as guidelines, augmented by clinical data on the alleged offender. Noting that little research has been done on child risk factors, she maintained that "most risk factors for children are embedded in their families and their surroundings" (Hewitt, 1999, p. 252). She then described a process for therapeutic management in court-ordered cases, and the reader is referred to her work for an excellent description of detailing a structure and process that can be useful in such cases.

Awad and McDonough (1991) advocated the engagement of families in long-term treatment as a method of therapeutic management. This model also rests on the assumption of cooperation from all attorneys about the need to resolve the dispute therapeutically and, subsequently, the involvement of both parents. This also is not always possible. If it is possible to have the parties, through their attorneys, stipulate to accepting and working with a therapist, this also can be a helpful way to proceed.

Therapeutic Management in Non-Court-Ordered Cases

From my experience, however, what often occurs is that a mother presents either herself or her child for treatment following one or more interactions with CPS or the family court, in which the outcome is inconclusive in regard to the allegations of child sexual abuse. There is no supervision by the court, the department of social services, or any other authority. Although it is best to involve the father, the therapist chosen by the mother is often suspect just because of that fact, given the acrimony that can exist between the parents. Although an ideal approach to problem solving would incorporate both the needs and protection of children and the maintenance of the integrity of the family system, this is not always possible. If the above models cannot be implemented, the goals become to facilitate the engagement of the child and mother in therapy and actively explore the potential of involving the noncustodial parent (alleged offender) with the child's therapist. This may be easier to achieve if the therapist for the child is not also the mother's therapist or if the choice of therapist for the child is agreed to by both parents. Other goals include working with the mother to help her understand the importance of retaining a lawyer and working to establish an "oversight" authority that can provide leverage for keeping the family involved in treatment. This may be achieved through mediation by the parents' lawyers, through the vehicle of a hearing in the divorce action, or, if appropriate, through the reactivation of the CPS system and family court.

Case Examples

Case examples may help to illustrate this approach.

The Gideon family included mother and father, who were separated at the time of referral for treatment, and their two daughters, Laura (age 10) and Sarah (age 5). This was a White working-class family in which both parents had been employed throughout the marriage. In this case,

CASE STUDY

Mrs. Gideon separated from her husband following the report of her 5-year-old, Sarah, that her father was coming into her bedroom at night and touching her. This case therefore falls into the first category proposed by Faller (1991)—a case of when the disclosure *precedes* a divorce action. Following the disclosure by Sarah, Mrs. Gideon talked to her 10-year-old daughter, Laura, to ascertain if anything similar had happened to her. Although Laura denied that anything had happened, Mrs. Gideon was concerned about her reaction. When Mr. Gideon was confronted by Mrs. Gideon with Sarah's statements, he denied having done anything. Mrs. Gideon sought legal advice and, on the advice of her attorney, made a report to CPS. Sarah repeated her story to the caseworker, but Laura continued to deny that anything had occurred. On the suggestion of the child protection agency, Mrs. Gideon obtained an order of protection, and her husband reluctantly moved out of the house.

There was an automatic referral to the local district attorney's office by CPS, but Sarah had, by this time, become reluctant to talk further about the abuse. The district attorney's office decided that it did not have grounds to move forward and that CPS would need to handle the matter.

Mrs. Gideon initiated divorce proceedings almost immediately, and the CPS agency, finding Sarah's report credible, indicted Mr. Gideon for sexual abuse. However, because of Sarah's recantation, the agency decided to let the judge who was going to hear the divorce handle the sexual abuse allegations and did not file a separate petition alleging sexual abuse. Although the reader may find this scenario difficult to believe (how could CPS fail to file an abuse petition, even if the case could not go forward in criminal court?), in my experience, this pattern is all too familiar. Due both to the large caseloads demanding attention and the difficulty in proving these cases even in family court, CPS often feels compelled to move on to "stronger" cases, in which there may be more evidence to facilitate the filing of a petition in family court. In this case, the agency wanted to believe that the matter could be constructively handled by the divorce judge, but in fact that court has no ability to adjudicate a sexual abuse matter and, at most, can take the CPS finding into consideration in its ruling.

In the hearing before the divorce judge, the allegations of sexual abuse were highlighted by the mother's attorney. However, the father's attorney made a very strong case that the allegations were false and motivated by Mrs. Gideon's desire to keep her husband out of the children's lives. She was accused of using the allegations as a ploy to get him out of the house, as divorce had been pending for a number of months. Mrs. Gideon did not want Sarah to have to testify in court, so other than the fact of the indicated CPS case, the court heard very little evidence regarding the sexual abuse allegations.

The net result was that Mr. Gideon had unsupervised visits while the divorce matter went forward. Mrs. Gideon then brought Sarah to treatment. At the time I met Mrs. Gideon, the girls had unsupervised visitation with their father. The therapeutic contract arrived at with the mother was that Sarah would be seen in individual treatment, and the mother would join a group for mothers of sexually abused children. Mrs. Gideon was leaning strongly toward disengaging her attorney and representing herself in court due to financial constraints. She was encouraged to retain her attorney. In addition, Mrs. Gideon had to agree to my attempt to engage Mr. Gideon in collateral contacts.

During the therapy, Sarah did begin to reveal what had occurred. There were no new allegations of any sexual contact on visitations, but she did confirm the earlier report about Mr. Gideon's behavior while he was in the family home. The divorce settlement involved disagreements over finances and property as well as custody. Mrs. Gideon was encouraged to talk with her attorney about what could be done, given the information that was emerging from Sarah in therapy. In this case, an experienced attorney was willing to be an advocate for the mother. However, she was expensive, and Mrs. Gideon needed continued therapeutic support to make the financial sacrifices that enabled her to retain this lawyer.

I then developed a relationship with the mother's attorney, with the mother's permission. She helped the attorney develop a case for supervised visits and was successful in having the court temporarily instate supervised visitation pending the settlement of the divorce. Although the supervised visitation legally extended only to Sarah, it in fact became the practice with both girls.

Concurrently with the legal settlement, which actually proceeded over the next year and a half, I engaged the father. He was invested in having visitation in as "neutral" a setting as possible, and I was able to facilitate the hiring of an M.S.W. in private practice who was willing to supervise on weekends and evenings. This supervisor was also open to providing the supervision in neutral but public settings such as parks, malls, and restaurants. This clinician entered into a contract with both parents that, in keeping with the court order, forced both parents to split the cost of the supervisor's time. Mr. Gideon was pleased with this arrangement; Mrs. Gideon was not.

Mr. Gideon was able to be engaged by taking an approach that sought his perspective on the family situation. Rather than taking a position about whether Sarah's statements were the "truth," he was asked his opinion about why Sarah would say this if it were not the truth. This led to ventilation on his part about his angry and resentful feelings toward his wife, who he viewed as manipulating him. He was then more open to interventions from me after this. An important agreement emerged around visitation with Laura, the older daughter. Although Mrs. Gideon was concerned about the possibility of her husband abusing her, she recognized that Laura was significantly older than her sister. At first, both girls were together with the supervisor and their father, primarily because it was easier for him to see them together. Eventually, there were visits once a month with Laura by herself.

Ultimately, the divorce settlement granted the mother sole custody, with the father having supervised visitation with Sarah until she was 10. There was no requirement of supervised visitation with Laura. This was possible in this case because the mother was willing to give up some financial support in exchange for the father's acceptance of the limitations on visitation. This is a condition that a woman is not always in a position to adopt.

Following the settlement, the family remained in treatment. There continued to be crises around visitation and lack of financial support by Mr. Gideon. Threats of continuing legal action were brought up by both parents, but usually disagreements were settled without resorting to further court hearings. Over the course of 3 to 4 years, the paid supervisor moved out of the picture as a maternal aunt (by marriage to Mrs. Gideon's brother) became the supervisor. Sarah made progress in regard to the effects of the impact of the sexual trauma. Not surprisingly, issues around her relationship with her mother began to dominate, and part of the therapy involved mother-daughter sessions for about 6 months. Although the resolution was not "perfect," therapeutic involvement on an ongoing basis was successful in the protection and gradual evolution of a father-daughter relationship and mother-daughter relationship that provided needed nurturing to Sarah.

A second case example illustrates the category of families in which a pattern of ongoing abuse was revealed after a separation.

The Robertses, an African American family, consisted of Mr. and Mrs. Roberts and one daughter, Jennifer, age 4 at the time of referral for treatment. This case fell into the third category outlined by Faller (1991), in which the separation preceded the disclosure of sexual abuse allegations.

In the case of the Roberts family, Mrs. Roberts was the parent who worked outside the home and provided the major financial support for the family. Mr. Roberts worked on and off but was at home and assumed responsibility for much of the care of their daughter, especially when she was a toddler. Mrs. Roberts described becoming unhappy with the marital relationship about a year after she married Mr. Roberts. She later reported in treatment that he was emotionally and verbally abusive to her, possessive, and jealous of her time at work and with other adults. At the same time, he was unable to sustain a full-time job. She suspected crack cocaine use on his part. Mrs. Roberts also reported that she was not happy with their sexual relationship, as Mr. Roberts was rarely interested in sex, and when he was, he preferred oral-genital sexual contact. It became unusual for their sexual repertoire to include intercourse, which was frustrating for Mrs. Roberts. After 5 years of marriage, she initiated divorce proceedings. Her daughter Jennifer was 4.

The separation was opposed by Mr. Roberts, who did not want to divorce and was alternately despondent and angry at the prospect. He moved out reluctantly about a month after the divorce action was filed and returned to his parent's home in an adjacent city. He still provided child care for Jennifer in the family home, leaving when Mrs. Gideon returned home from work.

After the separation, Jennifer began to talk to her mother about her father's activities that were suggestive of sexual abuse. For example, she told her mother about "Daddy tickling her vagina" and that "Daddy's pee pee gets big" when he does this. Mrs. Roberts began to realize that during the months preceding their separation, Jennifer manifested behaviors suggestive of sexual preoccupation, including excessive masturbation, using stuffed animals as well as her hand to manipulate her genitals. There had also been one incident when Jennifer grabbed at the genitals of teenage cousins when she was with extended family members for a holiday visit.

Mrs. Roberts made a report to CPS and sought therapy for her daughter and herself. Jennifer would not talk with the CPS caseworker but did confide in the therapist after a number of sessions. This information, along with the behavioral evidence reported by Mrs. Roberts, resulted in a CPS indication of the case. However, because of the age of the child and the lack of specificity about the nature of the abuse, the case was not presented to the juvenile (family) court. Therefore, there were no court orders requiring supervised visitation with the father or, indeed, any other services.

The case was heard in the civil court that handled divorce actions. Here, although the indicated CPS case carried some weight, the judge did not feel that it was sufficient, without a court adjudication of abuse, to warrant limiting the father's contact with the child. Subsequently, he ordered unsupervised visitation to continue but allowed no overnight stay with the father.

Attempts to engage Mr. Roberts therapeutically were unsuccessful. He came in one time to talk with the therapist but would not return. At the therapist's urging, the mother resorted to emergency room visits on two occasions when Jennifer returned from visits complaining that her father had hurt her genitals. Neither hospital visit resulted in any medical findings, but on the second visit, Jennifer did disclose to the nurse who was part of the examination team that her father had fondled her vagina. This, along with the therapist's report of the continuing statements to her by Jennifer, as well as the child's emotional and behavioral presentation, did result in the mother's attorney being able to present a stronger case for sole custody and supervised visitation.

Mrs. Roberts had been on the verge of giving up the fight in court due to the financial stress of retaining her attorney. With the help of the therapist, she identified extended family members who might be able to help her financially. This meant, however, confiding to them the real reasons for her concern about Jennifer visiting with her father. She had been unwilling to do this up until this point because of her feelings of shame. When she took the step to approach her older brother and confided to him her suspicions and reasons for separating, he proved to be very resourceful. He was willing to help her financially and also suggested that his wife, Mrs. Roberts's sister-in-law, help out with child care. With this assistance, Mrs. Roberts was able to continue to retain her attorney and was able to take on additional work, knowing her daughter was well cared for by a family member.

In this case, as in the Gideon case, the father gave up his right to unsupervised visitation in the divorce settlement when the mother dropped her request completely for financial support. He agreed to supervised visitation and exercised that right erratically for about 2 months. He then dropped out of sight, and although Mrs. Roberts did not know precisely what had occurred, she believed that he had had a "brush" with the law due to illegal drug activities. He did not reappear during the period that the family continued in treatment.

Both family situations present the therapist with very difficult treatment challenges. Both mothers were involved in divorce actions that entailed custody disputes, and in both cases, the alleged perpetrators continued to have unsupervised contact with the children. These situations present dilemmas for the therapist who is engaged with the child or the mother. Engagement of the child and family in therapy cannot be accomplished at the expense of abandoning the protective concerns. At the same time, the lack of any legal determination must be respected in terms of the rights of the noncustodial parent. The principles summarized below attempt to address all of these.

For mothers who come to the attention of a therapist with the kinds of issues illustrated earlier, treatment must include a focus on helping the mother protect the children. In the two case examples, there were indicated cases of child sexual abuse, giving some credence to the fact that the abuse did in fact occur. At intake, both Mrs. Gideon and Mrs. Roberts felt rage at their husbands and the system, despair about their inability to protect their children, and guilt for what the children had suffered and were suffering. These feelings were fueled by each mother's individual issues—including her own history, the nature of the marital relationship, her ability to support herself economically, and her feelings about the sexual abuse. Each situation was complicated by the response of the system, including the sensitivity or insensitivity of the CPS worker, the reaction of the legal system, the mother's interface with law enforcement if that had occurred, and the mother's ability to engage an attorney.

Summary

In the two cases discussed earlier, the mothers came into treatment when their children were not protected from unsupervised contact with the alleged offender. In both situations, the mothers had initially believed their children but found themselves at times questioning this because of the adamant denial by the children's fathers as well as the failure of the legal system to take any action. They believed that their hands were tied, and the repeated experience of sending their children off to be with men they suspected had abused the children seemed to have a numbing effect on the mothers. They reported similar reactions—although they believed their children, they began to hope that maybe it was not true and, especially, that it was not happening any-more. One can see how denial can become an adaptive response. Much as hostages in violent terrorist situations begin to identify with the outlook of the terrorist, the mothers were subject to being drawn into the offender's or system's view of the situation.

Given this, it can be difficult for the therapist to help the mother adopt a protective stance. However, as the cases above illustrate, a number of strate-gies can be adopted. First, it is important for the child to be in therapy with a mental health professional who is experienced in working with child sexual abuse. This strategy of engaging the child with a therapist who specializes in treating child sexual abuse may be self-evident. If children come to trust the therapist, they may be able to share the experience of true sexual abuse or enough about their feelings about visitation with the alleged abuser to make it possible for the therapist to be helpful with the juvenile or other court sys-tem. It is critical that the mother understands the need to find the right thera-pist. Usually, this person must be willing to testify or report to the court, even though it will not be needed in most cases.

Second, it is important to attempt to engage the noncustodial parent or alleged offender in therapy. Sometimes, the alleged offender can be encour-aged to engage in his own individual therapy to work on parenting or rela-tionship issues. As noted earlier, sometimes the child's therapist, especially if this person is not also the mother's therapist, can sensitize the noncustodial parent to the child's needs and concerns. In some cases, the therapist may be able to effect helpful changes in parenting approaches. At a minimum, if the alleged offender knows that the child is in treatment, it may act as a disincen-tive to reoffend.

Third, it is critical for the mother to have an attorney. Mothers often have real financial constraints that make it difficult for them to afford an at-torney. Yet, because of their husbands' incomes, they may not qualify for a court-appointed attorney. Even if they do qualify, it may take a while for one to be appointed, and the attorney may have very little time to devote to the mother's case because of caseload sizes. It is crucial that the mother have a good attorney. She may need to be encouraged to make this a priority, even if she has to work an extra job (thereby sacrificing time she may want or need with her children) or borrow money. The latter strategy may involve her sharing with extended family members the true nature of her concern for the children (as was the situation in the Roberts case), a step she may not have wanted to take because of her feelings of shame and stigmatization. Part of the therapist's approach may need to be helping her work this through so that she can adopt a more proactive stance for herself and her children. In the Gideon case, the mother did engage Sarah with a therapist who specialized in treating sexually abused children. This therapist, sensitive to the contextual, legal issues, encouraged the mother to continue to retain her attorney.

Last, the therapist can help the mother work to establish an "oversight" authority that can provide leverage for keeping the family involved in treatment. It is important for the mother to continue making new reports to CPS each time she becomes concerned about a new incident. Often, it is important for the mother to see that the child is evaluated medically as well. Even though the chances of getting any physical evidence are slim, the child may verbalize his or her experience to a health care professional, establishing another professional who has statements from the child that may become useful in future legal proceedings.

In reference to the need to keep CPS involved, it is important to point out that in some instances, the child continues to tell the mother about incidents of alleged sexual abuse while the child is visiting with the father. It is important that the mother be encouraged to report again to CPS. Although this may again result in unfounded cases or even indicated cases in which there is no family court action, it can help the mother develop an official record. In New York, as in other states, unfounded reports of suspected child sexual abuse are kept for a period of time and not purged from the information tracking system. Although civil libertarians concerned with parents' rights (and there are important issues here) may object to this practice, it can afford additional protection to mothers and children in cases of real sexual or other abuse.

There are risks, for instance, that a bureaucratic system, once it has unfounded a case, will develop a negative posture toward a family that makes repeated reports. However, there is also the possibility that the child will, in true cases, eventually be able to recount a credible story that will either move the case beyond "unfounded" to "founded" or from the CPS "indicated" level to family court. Having the mother's or child's therapist involved in providing interpretations to the child protection agency about the child or mother's behavior also can be helpful.

Working with mothers who are involved in custody or visitation disputes and with children who have been sexually abused by noncustodial parents will continue to present many challenges to the clinician. The best of all possible situations is to have the family court ordered to treatment, with conditions set forth that allow for optimal protection of the child if the allegations turn out to be true. If therapeutic management of a case is not supported by court orders, keeping protection as a major treatment concern, ensuring that the child is treated by someone experienced in working with sexually abused children (so that if further allegations emerge, the professional will have knowledge about how to proceed), and assisting the mother in obtaining competent legal assistance are key principles to treatment planning.

FUTURE DIRECTIONS

This book has centered on treatment for effects of a specific event in a woman's life—the uncovering of a history of child sexual abuse by her husband or partner. To this end, the disclosure of child sexual abuse has been conceptualized as a traumatic event. A set of specific traumatic effects has been hypothesized as flowing from this, captured in the dynamics of betrayal, powerlessness, stigmatization, and sexual traumatization. To treat these effects, a treatment approach encompassing six phases is presented: (1) beginning engagement and assessment, (2) intervening early around traumatic effects, (3) enhancing coping strategies, (4) surfacing traumatic material, (5) dealing with relational consequences, and (6) working through and resolution. The contributions of individual, group, and family treatment modalities to ameliorating the traumatic effects have been described. Presented as discrete phases of treatment, it is hoped that the reader has understood that, in practice, the six phases or stages are overlapping and described as distinct only for the purposes of at-of attempting to capture in a linear medium—a book—what is by nature a circular and multifaceted process.

A number of interrelated dynamics have been accented in an attempt to depict the context as well as process of treatment. Countertransference issues, particularly as they relate to gender, have been highlighted in an effort to bring the backdrop against which intervention and treatment proceed into the foreground of the therapy session. It has been hypothesized that in our society, women's socialization to undertake caretaking roles so permeates our cultural view of the role of women that it is difficult for the clinician to untangle the social imperatives from their clinical judgment unless they pay specific attention to these issues. An alternative view of the psychological development of women has been emphasized—one that stresses the development of identity and self-concept in the context of self-in-relationship—as a counterpoint to a more traditional view that has tended to pathologize the nonoffending parent. The more traditional view, it is believed, has contributed to a perception of the woman as collusive, narcissistic, and nonprotective, a stance militating against effective engagement. The alternative conceptualization, which accentuates the socially derived underpinnings of a woman's psychological makeup, has been explicated with the hope of encouraging clinicians to undertake an assessment of the manner in which their own socialization experiences may inadvertently negatively affect their reactions to the nonoffending parents.

In addition to the impact of gender, additional efforts have been made to underscore the contextual issues of race, ethnicity, and class, again with an eye to articulating the significance of social forces in a woman's life, not only at the time of initial assessment but throughout the treatment process. It perhaps has not been emphasized enough that for women of color, oppression because of race and ethnicity may, in certain circumstances, override concerns with gender oppression. The need for particular sensitivity by White clinicians in working with women of color has been stressed because of the typical power differential between clinician and client. Not only does the therapist represent an authority figure (and culture may dictate particular *transference* reactions because of this), but as a member of the dominant group in this society, the therapist also represents a culture that may have myriad ways of actively discriminating against the client. Becoming cognizant of the manner in which these social forces may play out in the transference and countertransference reactions in the therapy session will help the clinician be more attuned to the client's needs.

The influences of gender, race, ethnicity, and class are inextricably inter-woven into a life pattern that is a composite of childhood experiences, adult relationships, and social forces. These can interact with the particular effects of the trauma of the disclosure of child sexual abuse to overwhelm the mother. Although the therapist may view the disclosure of child sexual abuse as the precipitant to treatment and a determining life event for the client, life experiences and circumstances may militate against a woman reacting the same way. Family and cultural norms about mental health treatment, partic-ularly the use of formal systems, may make it difficult for a woman to appre-ciate the value of therapy. An effort has been made in this book to pay atten-tion to intervening variables whose presence demand flexibility. A woman's agenda on entering treatment, which appears at first blush to counterindicate a successful treatment process and outcome, must not automatically be viewed as resistance. It is hoped that in the attempt to articulate what is spe-cial and specific to a woman's experience as a mother of an incest victim, the need to attend to the larger context also has come through.

A number of topics warrant further inquiry. Increasingly, the popula-tion coming to the attention of the child welfare system, which identifies many family sexual abuse situations, has serious substance abuse or intimate partner violence as co-occurring problems with family sexual abuse. Crack/cocaine and heroin, as well as alcohol, are the substances about which mental health providers need to be knowledgeable, both in terms of pharma-cological effects and in terms of the implications for treatment. Mental health treatment approaches for sexual abuse increasingly will need to incorporate strategies and techniques that address these problems. Substance abuse treat-ment services, as noted earlier, may be moving toward a harm reduction ap-proach and increased emphasis on assessment, realizing that a "cookie-cutter approach," which offers the same abstinence-oriented intervention for every client, has resulted in high dropout rates from programs. Mental health pro-viders will need to understand how their intervention can complement a harm reduction approach and vice versa. These interventions need to be de-tailed and studied.

In addition, women whose children are in care may present special needs. They undoubtedly present challenges to the clinician, starting with the potential for stimulating especially problematic countertransference reac-tions. As articulated earlier, our culture socializes us all to define women's worth according to their caretaking role as mothers. Women who have their children either removed from their care or who have voluntarily placed their children are anomalies and threaten our sense of order. Beyond that, the psychological needs of this group may be particularly formidable. Their histories of childhood abuse, neglect, and other traumatic experiences have often contributed to attachment disorders and character difficulties that will be lifelong challenges. Sometimes, services that can help them grow and sustain a healthier adjustment often call for the kind of intensity (multimodalities) and duration that are difficult to provide in the current climate of short-term behaviorally oriented treatment. Even with that kind of capacity, some women will not be able to overcome addiction or the effects of severe histories of deprivation to enable them to parent. In these cases, what may be best for the women as well as their children is to make life adjustments that do not demand that they assume a parenting role.

Intimate partner violence is another problem area that has a high correlation with family sexual abuse and not only in the population coming to the attention of the child welfare system. The presence of intimate partner violence has a number of implications for the clinician treating the nonoffending parent. First, the therapist needs to be knowledgeable about these abuse dynamics to fully assess for safety. If the strategy of Child Protective Services (CPS) in child sexual abuse cases is to press for the removal of the alleged offender, this can afford protection that is congruent with the safety needs of the battered woman. Beyond safety, however, additional assessment is necessary. How, for example, have the traumatic effects of intimate partner violence intertwined with the traumatic effects of the disclosure of child sexual abuse? To what extent can these issues be treated concurrently, or to what extent does there need to be a focus on one before the other? These are the kinds of questions that future research and study need to address.

There are also some lessons to be learned from the family violence field. One, it seems, is a more effective use of legal leverage. The battered women's movement, maybe because it has been fueled largely by grassroots efforts, has been more successful in some cases in moving law enforcement into a protective stance vis-à-vis the victim. Automatic arrest laws that set in motion an arrest of the alleged batterer when his partner makes a call to the police are an example. Not only are such interventions potentially helpful to the nonoffending parent who is also a victim of intimate partner violence, but they are also a prototype for family sexual abuse situations. A parallel set of laws in the area of child sexual abuse (i.e., automatic arrest when allegations arise) could be supportive to women as well as to children and not only when the nonoffending parent was a victim of intimate partner violence.

This speaks to the issue of the role of the legal system in family sexual abuse cases. Further inquiry into the differential impact, if any, of the criminal justice and juvenile and family court system interventions would be useful if studied in regard to treatment motivation as well as treatment effectiveness. There is a special need for both the provision and evaluation of services geared to assist women who suspect that a child's father has sexually abused him or her and who are in the throes of a custody or visitation dispute. The prevailing attitude of suspicion and distrust of a woman's motives in such cases is unwarranted, making it imperative for those who are knowledgeable about the dynamics of family sexual abuse to advocate for and provide therapeutic management of such cases. Legal rights of a parent who is an alleged offender cannot be ignored, but the protective issues should prevail. Therapists who are willing to become familiar with the court system and to tackle the challenging task of working with family members who are in adversarial relationships with one another would not only be of great assistance to the court but to the children and parents as well.

More needs to be known about the population of nonoffending parents. Research to date has suggested that the length of the relationship between the nonoffending parent and the perpetrator has an implication for maternal support at the time of a disclosure of child sexual abuse. Further knowledge about this would help clinicians target interventions. The nature and duration of the relationship between the child and nonoffending parent and how that affects treatment needs following disclosure are another area that cries out for further study. For example, in my experience, there is a difference in the reaction of mothers of young children from those of adolescent children, with the younger mothers being more ready to separate. How widespread is that tendency? Is that an artifact of a particular clinical population? Does the capability to be self-supporting play a determining role in this? These and other questions are among those that, if answered, could help guide the clinician.

This book has not focused on the population of women whose children are adult at the time of the disclosure of family sexual abuse. The disclosure may follow a period of emotional cutoff from the adult child or stimulate it. Although in my experience, many issues are similar between this group and those women still caring for their children at the time of disclosure, there are also crucial differences. In terms of similarities, the traumatic effects are often manifest in that the mother feels betrayed, stigmatized, and powerless. The disclosure typically instigates a psychological crisis for the nonoffending parent of adult children as well. Protective issues can be present, just as in the case of a nonoffending parent with younger children still at home, if there are *grandchildren* who are in contact with the alleged perpetrator. Although CPS, law enforcement, and the family or criminal justice system rarely mobilize, they can become involved if there is unsupervised contact between the alleged offender and children younger than 18.

If the nonoffending parent is still with the perpetrator, it sets into motion the same kind of crisis in the nonoffending parent's relationship with her partner as well as with her adult child. However, the crisis of parenting is not there in the same way that it is for a woman with children younger than 18 still in her care, and lack of legal involvement may militate against the alleged offender seeking treatment. The opportunity for family work may not present itself because adult children may be unavailable due to geographical separation or reluctance to participate in treatment with the nonoffending parent. The nonoffending parent has less control over access and use of therapy for her children than when she has children living with her. Differences may exist if the perpetrator is deceased. Although relieving the issue of protection of younger children in the family, it can heighten the lack of closure for the nonoffending parent as well as the adult child. This entire area would benefit from further study and explication.

Another area that warrants further research is the impact of a child's gender on both the nature of the trauma for the nonoffending parent and the implications for treatment. This book has emphasized the importance of gender in the treatment of the mother. A parallel emphasis is probably warranted in the treatment of the mother-child relationship. The relationship of a male child to a mother has different facets from that of a female child. This undoubtedly has implications not only for the nonoffending parent's perception of her role and the impact of the sexual abuse on the developing child but also for the child's experience.

The issue of outcome research is another area of need. How are treatment providers currently conceptualizing treatment, and what outcome measures are being used to illustrate effective or even adequate completion of treatment? Beyond the recent work of Cohen and Mannarino (1998), little is known. A major starting point, it seems, is the need to *describe* treatment interventions, as has been done by Deblinger and Heflin (1996) in their recent work. Beyond that, a great deal needs to be done in specifying and measuring outcomes.

In conclusion, it is hoped that this book has stimulated the reader to think critically about the treatment needs of the nonoffending parent in the incest family. Readers have been urged to consider the notion that the disclosure of family sexual abuse may have the impact of a traumatic life event. Consequently, the psychological repercussions can immobilize a woman, and this contributes to a stance heretofore attributed to denial and resistance. Their subsequent life choices (postdisclosure) are influenced not only by women's resolution of the trauma but also by their socialization experiences as women. Women of color struggle not only with gender discrimination but also with oppression due to race and ethnicity.

Whether readers agree with this position or not, it is hoped that they will be encouraged in further study of women's needs as they relate to parenting sexually abused children. For the majority of sexually abused children, living with the nonoffending parent will probably continue to be their future. Providing treatment that is sensitive to the mothers' needs, both at the crisis of disclosure and in subsequent months, can only serve to strengthen mothers' potential to provide and sustain healthier relationships with their children and to be more fulfilled in their own lives.

REFERENCES

Abbott, B. R. (1995). Some family considerations in assessment and case management of intrafilial child sexual abuse. In T. Ney (Ed.), *True and false allegations of child sexual abuse: Assessment and case management* (pp. 260-274). New York: Brunner/Mazel.

Abel, G. G., Becker, J. V., Cunningham-Rathner, J., Rouleau, J., Kaplan, M., & Reich, J. (1984). *The treatment of child molesters.* (Available from SBC-TM, 722 West 168th Street, Box 17, New York, NY 10032)

Abel, G. G., Becker, J. V., Murphy, W. D., & Flanagan, B. (1981). Identifying dangerous child molesters. In R. B. Stuart (Ed.), *Violent behavior.* New York: Brunner/Mazel.

Abel, G. G., Gore, D. K., Holland, C. L., Camp, N., Becker, J. V., & Rathner, J. (1989). The measurement of cognitive distortions in child molesters. *Annals of Sex Research, 2,* 135-153.

Abel, G. G., Mittelman, M. S., Becker, J. V., & Djenderedjian, A. (1978). Differentiating sexual aggressiveness with penile measures. *Criminal Justice and Behavior, 5,* 315-332.

Adams-Tucker, C. (1980). A socioclinical overview of 28 sex-abused children. *Child Abuse & Neglect, 5,* 361-367.

Adoption and Safe Families Act. (1997). PL (105-89) of 1997

Alpert, J. (1995). *Sexual abuse recalled.* Northvale, NJ: Jason Aronson.

American Psychiatric Association. (1994). *Diagnostic and statistical manual of mental disorders* (4th ed.). Washington, DC: Author.

Anderson, L. M., & Shafer, G. (1979). The character-disordered family: A community treatment model for family abuse. *American Journal of Orthopsychiatry, 49* (3), 436-445.

Apel, S. (1989). Custodial parents, child sexual abuse and the legal system: Beyond contempt. *American University Law Review, 38* (Spring), 491-529.

Armsworth, M. W., & Holaday, M. (1993). The effects of psychological trauma on children and adolescents. *Journal of Counseling and Development, 72,* 49-56.

Austin, W. (2000). Refugee experiences and Southeast Asain women's mental health. *Western Journal of Nursing Research, 22* (2), 164-166.

Awad, G. A., & McDonough, H. (1991). Therapeutic management of sexual abuse allegations in custody and visitation disputes. *American Journal of Psychotherapy, 45* (1), 113-123.

Barnard, C. P. (1983). Alcoholism and incest: Improving diagnostic comprehensiveness. *International Journal of Family Therapy, 5* (2), 136-144.

Barrett, M., Trepper, T. S., & Fish, L. S. (1990). Feminist-informed family therapy or the treatment of intrafamily child sexual abuse. *Journal of Family Psychology, 4* (2), 151-166.

Becker, J. (1990). Treating adolescent sex offenders. *Professional Psychological Research and Practice, 21,* 362-365.

Beitchman, J.H., Zucker, K.J., Hood, J.E., da Costa, G.A., & Akman, D. (1991). A review of short-term effects of child sexual abuse. *Child Abuse &Neglect, 15* (4), 537-556.

Benjamin, J. (1984). The convergence of psychoanalysis and feminism: Gender identity and autonomy. In C. M. Brody (Ed.), *Women therapists working with women* (pp. 37-45). New York: Springer.

Berliner, L., & Conte, J. R. (1990). The process of victimization: The victim's perspective. *Child Abuse & Neglect, 14* (1), 29-40.

Berliner, L., & Wheeler, J. R. (1987). Treating the effects of sexual abuse on children. *Journal of Interpersonal Violence, 2,* 415-434.

Berliner, L., & Wheeler, J. R. (1992). A review of the long-term effects of child sexual abuse. *Child Abuse & Neglect, 16* (1), 101-118.

Birns, B., & Meyer, S. K. (1993). Mothers' role in incest: Dysfunctional women or dysfunctional theories. *Journal of Child Sexual Abuse, 2* (3), 127-135.

Blake-White, J., & Kline, C. M. (1985). Treating the dissociative process in adult victims of childhood incest. *Social Casework, 66* (7) , 394-402.

Bloch, J. R. (1991). *Assessment and treatment of multiple personality and dissociative disorders.* Sarasota, FL: Professional Resource Press.

Blush, G. J., & Ross, K. L. (1987). Sexual allegations in divorce: The SAID syndrome. *Conciliation Courts Review, 25* (1), 1-11.

Boney-McCoy, S., & Finkelhor, D. (1996). Is youth victimization related to trauma symptoms and depression after controlling for prior symptoms and family relationships? *Journal of Consulting and Clinical Psychology, 64* (6), 1406- 1416.

Bowen, G. L., & Richman, J. M. (1991). The willingness of spouses to seek marriage and family counseling services. *Journal of Primary Prevention, 11* (4), 277-293.

Boyd-Franklin, N. (1989). *Black families in therapy.* New York: Guilford.

Bradshaw, C. K. (1994). Asian and Asian American women: Historical and political considerations in psychotherapy. In L. Comas-Diaz & B. Greene (Eds.), *Women of color: Integrating ethnic and gender identities in psychotherapy.* New York: Guilford.

Brandler, S., & Roman, C. P. (1991). *Group work: Skills and strategies for effective interventions.* New York: Haworth.

Breese, P., Stearns, G., & Bess, B. H. (1986). Allegations of child sexual abuse in child custody disputes. *American Journal of Orthopsychiatry, 56* (4), 560-569.

Brende, J. O. (1983). A psychodynamic view of character pathology in Vietnam combat veterans. *Bulletin of the Menninger Clinic, 47,* 193-216.

Brende, J. O., & McCann, I. L. (1984). Regressive experiences in Vietnam veterans: Their relationship to war, post-traumatic stress symptoms and recovery. *Journal of Contemporary Psychotherapy, 14,* 57-75.

Brende, J. O., & Parson, E. R. (1985). *Vietnam veterans: The road to recovery.* New York: Plenum.

Brickman, E. (1993). *Final report: Child sexual abuse public policy study.* New York: Victim Services.

Briere, J. (1987). Post sexual abuse trauma: Data and implications. *Journal of Interpersonal Violence, 2* (4), 367-379.

Briere, J. (1996). *Therapy for adults molested as children: 2nd Edition.* New York: Springer.

Briere, J. (1992). *Child abuse trauma.* Newbury Park, CA: Sage.

Briere, J. (1997a). *Psychological assessment of adult posttraumatic stress.* Washington, D.C.: American Psychological Association.

Briere, J. (1197b). Treating adults serverely abused as children: The self-trauma model. In D.A. Wolfe, B. McMahon, & R. D. Peters (Eds.). *Child abuse: New direction in treatment and prevention across the life span.* Newbury Park, CA: Sage.

Briere, J., & Runtz, M. (1986). Adolescent acting out and childhood history of sexual abuse. *Journal of Interpersonal Violence, 1* (3), 326-333.

Brodsky, A. M., & Hare-Mustin, R. (1980). Psychotherapy and women: Priorities for research. In A. M. Brodsky & R. Hare-Mustin (Eds.), *Women and psychotherapy* (pp. 385-410). New York: Guilford.

Brody, C. (1984). *Women therapists working with women*. New York: Springer.

Burgess, A. (1987). Child molesting: Assessing impact in multiple victims (Part I). *Archives of Psychiatric Nursing, 1*, 33-39.

Cammaert, L. P. (1988). Nonoffending mothers: A new conceptualization. In L. E. A. Walker (Ed.), *Handbook on sexual abuse of children: Assessment and treatment issues* (pp. 309-323). New York: Springer.

Campbell, R., Raja, S., & Grinig, P.L. (1999). Training mental health professionals on violence against women. *Journals of Interpersonal Violence, 14* (10), 1003-1013.

Caplan, P. J., & Hall-McCorquodale, I. H. (1985). Mother-blaming in major clinical journals. *American Journal of Orthopsychiatry, 55* (3), 345-353.

Carnes, P. (1983). *The sexual addiction*. Minneapolis, MN: CompCare.

Carter, B. (1993). Child sexual abuse: Impact on mothers. *Affilia: Journal of Women and Social Work, 8* (1), 72-90.

Casement, P. J. (1986). Countertransference and interpretation. *Contemporary Psychoanalysis, 22* (4), 548-559.

Chatters, L. M., Taylor, R. J., & Neighbors, H. W. (1989). Size of informal helper network mobilized during a serious personal problem among Black Americans. *Journal of Marriage and the Family, 51*, 667-676.

Child Abuse Prevention and Treatment Act. PL (93-247), 1974.

Chin, J. L. (1983). Diagnostic consideration in working with Asian Americans. *American Journal of Orthopsychiatry, 53* (1), 100-109.

Chodorow, N. (1978). *The reproduction of mothering*. Berkeley: University of California Press.

Ciottone, R. A., & Madonna, J. M. (1996). *Play therapy with sexually abused children: A synergistic clinical-developmental approach*. Northvale, NJ: Jason Aronson.

Clark, C. A., O'Neil, M. R., & Laws, D. R. (1981). A comparison of intrafamilial sexual and physical abuse. In M. Cook & K. Howells (Eds.), *Adult sexual interest in children* (pp. 3-39). New York: Academic Press.

Cohen, J. A., & Mannarino, A. P. (1998). Interventions for sexually abused children: Initial and outcome findings. *Child Maltreatment, 3* (1), 17-26.

Cole, W. (1992). Incest perpetrators: Their assessment and treatment. *Psychiatric Clinics of North America, 15* (3), 689-701.

Collings, S., & King, M. (1994). Ten-year follow-up of 50 patients with bulimia nervosa. *British Journal of Psychiatry, 164*, 80-87.

Comas-Diaz, L. (1989). Culturally relevant issues and treatment implications for Hispanics. In D. R. Koslow & E. Salett (Eds.), *Crossing cultures in mental health* (pp. 31-48). Washington, DC: Society for International Education Training and Research.

Comas-Diaz, L. (1994) (Eds.). Women of color. Integrating ethnic and gender identities in psychotherapy. New York: Guilford

Conte, J. (1984). Progress in treating the sexual abuse of children. *Social Work, 29*(3), 258-263.

Conte, J., & Berliner, L. (1981). Sexual abuse of children: Implications for practice. *Social Casework, 62* (10), 606-606.

Conte, J., & Schuerman, J. R. (1987). The effects of sexual abuse on children: A multidimensional view. *Journal of Interpersonal Violence, 2* (4), 380-390.

Coulson, K. W., Wallis, S., & Clark, H. (1994). The diversified team approach in the treatment of incest families. *Psychotherapy in Private Practice, 13* (2), 19-43.

Courtois, C. (1988). *Healing the incest wound: Adult survivors in therapy*. New York: Norton.

Courtois, C. (1992). The memory retrieval process in incest survivor therapy. *Journal of Child Sex Abuse, 1*(1), 15-31.

Dadds, M., Smith, M., & Webber, Y. (1991). An exploration of family and individual profiles following father-daughter incest. *Child Abuse & Neglect, 15*(4), 575-586.

Davies, J. (1998). *Safety planning with battered women.* Thousand Oaks, CA: Sage.

Deblinger, E., Hathaway, C. R., Lippmann, J., & Steer, R. (1993). Psychosocial characteristics and correlates of symptom distress in non-offending mothers of sexually abused children. *Journal of Interpersonal Violence, 8* (2), 155-168.

Deblinger, E., & Heflin, A. (1996). *Treating sexually abused children and their non-offending parents.* Rockville, MD: Launch.

Deblinger, E., Stauffer, L., & Landsberg, C. (1994). The impact of a history of child sexual abuse on maternal response to allegations of sexual abuse concerning her child. *Journal of Child Sexual Abuse, 3* (3), 67-75.

DeJong, A. (1988). Maternal responses to the sex of a child. *Pediatrics, 81,* 14-20.

DeJong, P., & Miller, S. D. (1995). How to interview for client strengths. *Social Work, 40* (6), 729-736.

DelPo, E., & Koontz, M. A. (1991). Group therapy with mothers of incest victims. *Archives of Psychiatric Nursing, 5* (2), 64-75.

Derogatis, L. R. (1983). *The SCL-90-R: Administration scoring and procedures manual-II.* Baltimore, MD: Clinical Psychometric Research.

DeYoung, M. (1994). Women as mothers and wives in paternally incestuous families: Coping with role conflict. *Child Abuse & Neglect, 18* (1), 73-83.

Dinnerstein, D. (1977). *The mermaid and the minotaur.* New York: Harper & Row.

Eist, H. I., & Mandel, A. U. (1968). Family treatment of ongoing incest behavior. *Family Process, 7,* 216-232.

Elbow, M., & Mayfield, J. (1991). Mothers of incest victims: villains, victims or protectors? *Families in Society, 72* (2), 78-86.

Elliott, D. M., & Briere, J. (1995). Posttraumatic stress associated with delayed recall of sexual abuse: A general population study. *Journal of Traumatic Stress. 8,* 629-642

Erikson, E. H. (1963). *Childhood and society* (2nd ed.). New York: Norton.

Erikson, E. H. (1968). *Identity, youth and crisis.* New York: Norton.

Ethical issues in the legal representation of children (special issue). (1996). *Fordham Law Review, 64*(4).

Everson, M. D., Hunter, W. M., Runyon, D. K., Edelsohn, G. A., & Coulter, M. L. (1989). Maternal support following disclosure of incest. *American Journal of Orthopsychiatry, 39* (2), 197-207.

Faller, K. C. (1988a). *Child sexual abuse: An interdisciplinary manual for diagnosis, case management, and treatment.* New York: Columbia University Press.

Faller, K. C. (1988b). The myth of the collusive mother: Variability in the functioning of mothers of victims of intrafamilial sexual abuse. *Journal of Interpersonal Violence, 3* (2), 190-196.

Faller, K. C. (1989). Why sexual abuse? An exploration of the intergenerational hypothesis. *Child Abuse & Neglect, 13,* 543-548.

Faller, K. C. (1991). Possible explanations for child sexual abuse allegations in divorce. *American Journal of Orthopsychiatry, 61* (1), 86-91.

Faller, K. C., Corwin, D. L., & Olafson, E. (1993). Literature review: Research on false allegations of sexual abuse in divorce. *The Advisor, 6* (3), 7-10.

Farber, N. B. (1989). The significance of aspirations among unmarried adolescent mothers. *Social Service Review, 63* (4), 518-532.

Fausto-Sterling, A. (1985). *Myths of gender.* New York: Basic Books.

Feinauer, L. L., Mitchell, J., Harper, J. M., & Dane, S. (1996). The impact of hardiness and severity of childhood sexual abuse on adult adjustment. *American Journal of Family Therapy, 24* (3), 206-214.

Finkelhor, D. (1979). *Sexually victimized children.* New York: Free Press.

Finkelhor, D. (1989). *Child sexual abuse: New theory and research.* New York: Free Press.

Finkelhor, D., & Browne, A. (1985). The traumatic impact of child sexual abuse: A conceptualization. *American Journal of Orthopsychiatry, 55* (4), 530-541.

Finkelhor, D., Gelles, R., Hotaling, G., & Straus, M. (1983). *The dark side of families.* Beverly Hills, CA: Sage.

Finkelhor, D., & Yllö, K. (1985). *The license to rape: Sexual abuse of wives.* New York: Free Press.

Fish, V., & Faynik, C. (1989). Treatment of incest families with the father temporarily removed: A structural approach. *Journal of Strategic and Systemic Therapies, 8* (4), 53-63.

Fredrickson, R. (1992). *Repressed memories: A journey to recovery from sexual abuse.* New York: Fireside.

Freeman-Longo, F., Bird, S., Stevenson, W., & Fiske, J. (1995). *Nationwide survey of treatment programs and models.* Branden, VT: Safer Society.

Friedrich, W. N. (1990). *Psychotherapy of sexually abused children and their families.* New York: Norton.

Friedrich, W. N. (1991). *Casebook of sexual abuse treatment.* New York: Norton.

Fullilove, M. T. (1993). Violence, trauma and posttraumatic stress disorder among women drug users. *Journal of Traumatic Stress, 6* (4), 533-543.

Gardner, R. A. (1987). *The parental alienation syndrome and the differentiation between fabricated and genuine child sexual abuse.* Creskill, NJ: Creative Therapeutics.

Gelinas, D. J. (1983). The persisting negative effects of incest. *Psychiatry, 46,* 312-332.

Gelinas, D. J. (1987). Family therapy: Characteristic family constellation and basic therapeutic stance. In S. Sgroi (Ed.), *Vulnerable populations: Evaluation and treatment of sexually abused children and adult survivors* (pp. 25-49). Lexington, MA: Lexington Books.

Gelles, R., & Straus, M. (1988). *Intimate violence: The causes and consequences of abuse in the American family.* New York: Touchstone.

Giarretto, H. (1992). *Integrated treatment of child abuse and neglect.* Palo Alto, CA: Science Behavioral Books.

Gil, E. (1991). *The healing power of play.* New York: Guilford.

Gil, E., & Johnson, T. L. (1993). *Sexualized children.* Rockville, MD: Launch.

Gil, E., & Johnson, T. L. (1996). *Treating abused adolescents.* New York: Guilford.

Gilgun, J. (1984, Fall). Does the mother know? Alternatives to blaming mothers for child sexual abuse. *Response,* pp. 2-4.

Gilligan, C. (1982). *In a different voice.* Cambridge, MA: Harvard University Press.

Gomes-Schwartz, B. (Ed.). (1990). *Child sexual abuse: The initial effects.* Newbury Park, CA: Sage.

Goodwin, J. (1988). Post-traumatic symptoms in abused children. *Journal of Traumatic Stress, 1* (4), 475-488.

Gordon, M. (1989). The family environment of sexual abuse: A comparison of natal and stepfather abuse. *Child Abuse & Neglect, 13* (1), 121-130.

Green, A. H., Coupe, P., Fernandez, R., & Stevens, B. (1995). Incest revisited: Delayed post-traumatic stress disorder in mothers following the sexual abuse of their children. *Child Abuse & Neglect, 19* (10), 1275-1282.

Groth, A. N. (1979). *Men who rape: The psychology of the offender.* New York: Plenum.

Gutheil, T. G., & Avery, N. C. (1977). Multiple overt incest as family defense against loss. *Family Process, 16,* 105-116.

Gutierrez, L. M. (1990). Working with women of color: An empowerment perspective. *Social Work, 35* (2), 149-153.

Hagood, M. M. (1991). Group art therapy with mothers of sexually abused children. *Arts in Psychotherapy, 18* (1), 17-27.

Halfon, N. (1990). Continuum of care models. Crack and other addictions: Old realities and new challenges for child welfare. In *Proceedings of a symposium and policy recommendations, March 12-13, 1989.* Washington, DC: Child Welfare League of America.

Harper, K. V., & Lantz, J. (1996). *Cross-cultural practice.* Chicago: Lyceum.

Hartmann, H. (1958). *Ego psychology and the problem of adaptation.* New York: International Universities Press.

Haskett, M. E., Nowlan, N. P., Hutchinson, J. S., & Whitworth, J. M. (1991). Factors associated with successful entry into therapy in childhood sexual abuse cases. *Child Abuse & Neglect, 15* (4), 467-476.

Helper, P. L., Quesda, G. M., & Chalfant, H. P. (1983). Class perceptions of disordered behavior and suggestions for therapy: A tri-cultural comparison. *Sociology of Health & Illness, 5* (2), 196-207.

Herman, J. L. (1981). *Father-daughter incest.* Cambridge, MA: Harvard University Press.

Herman, J. L. (1992). *Trauma and recovery.* New York: Basic Books.

Hewitt, S. K. (1991). Therapeutic management of preschool cases of alleged but unsubstantiated sexual abuse. *Child Welfare, 70* (1), 59-67.

Hewitt, S. K. (1999). *Assessing allegations of sexual abuse in preschool children.* Thousand Oaks, CA: Sage.

Hines, P. M. (1989). The family life cycle of poor Black families. In B. Carter & M. McGoldrick (Eds.), *The changing life cycle* (pp. 515-544). Boston: Allyn & Bacon.

Hooks, B. (1989). *Talking back, thinking feminist, thinking Black.* Boston: South End.

Horowitz, M. J. (1975). Intrusive and repetitive thoughts after experimental stress. *Archives of General Psychiatry, 32,* 1457-1468.

Horowitz, M. J. (1976). *Stress response syndromes.* New York: Jason Aronson.

Horowitz, M. J. (1979). Psychological response to serious life events. In V. Hamilton & D. M. Warburton (Eds.), *Human stress and cognition: An information processing approach* (pp. 235-263). New York: John Wiley.

Horton, A. L., Johnson, B. L., Roundy, L. M., & Williams, D. (Eds.). (1990). *The incest perpetrator.* Newbury Park, CA: Sage.

Humphreys, C. (1992). Disclosure of child sexual assault: Implications for mothers. *Australian Social Work, 45* (3), 27-35.

in re Gault. 387 US.1 (1967).

James, B. (1989). *Treating traumatized children.* Lexington, MA: Lexington Books.

Janoff-Bulman, R. (1986). The aftermath of victimization: Rebuilding shattered assumptions. In C. R. Figley (Ed.), *Trauma and its wake: The study and treatment of post-traumatic stress disorder* (pp. 15-36). New York: Brunner/Mazel.

Janoff-Bulman, R. (1992). *Shattered assumptions: Toward a new psychology of trauma.* New York: Free Press.

Jasinski, J. L., & Williams, L. M. (1998). *Partner violence: A comprehensive review of 20 years of research.* Thousand Oaks, CA: Sage.

Johnson, T. C. (1988). Child perpetrators: Children who molest other children. *Child Abuse & Neglect, 12* (2), 219-230.

Johnson, T. C. (1989). Female child perpetrators: Children who molest other children. *Child Abuse & Neglect, 13* (2), 571-586.

Jones, D. L. (1979). African-American clients: Clinical practice issues. *Social Work, 24* (2), 112-118.

Jones, D. P. H., & McGraw, J. M. (1987). Reliable and fictitious accounts of sexual abuse to childern. *Journal of Interpersonal Violence, 2,* 27-45.

Jordan, J. V. (1996). *Women's growth in diversity.* New York: Guilford.

Jordan, J. V., Kaplan, A., Miller, J. B., Stiver, I. P., & Surrey, J. L. (1991). *Women's growth in connection.* New York: Guilford.

Justice, B., & Justice, R. (1979). *The broken taboo: Sex in the family.* New York: Human Sciences.

Kaufman, L., Peck, A. L., & Taguri, C. K. (1954). The family constellations and overt incestuous relations between father and daughter. *American Journal of Orthopsychiatry, 24* (2), 266-277.

Kempe, C. H., Silverman, F., Steele, B., Droegemueller, W., & Silver, H. (1962). The battered child syndrome. *Journal of the American Medical Association, 181,* 17-24.

Kendall-Tackett, K. A., Williams, L. M., & Finkelhor, D. (1993). Impact of sexual abuse on children: A review and synthesis of recent empirical studies. *Psychological Bulletin, 113* (1), 164-180.

Kinard, E. M. (1996). Social support, competence, and depression in mothers of abused children. *American Journal of Orthopsychiatry, 66* (3), 449-462.

Kirkwood, C. (1993). *Leaving abusive partners.* Newbury Park, CA: Sage.

Kleinman, A. M., & Lin, T. Y. (1981). (Eds.), *Normal and deviant behavior in Chinese culture.* Dordrecht, the Netherlands: D. Reidel.

Kliman, J. (1994). The interweaving of gender, class and race in family therapy. In M. P. Mirkin (Ed.), *A guide to feminist family therapy* (pp. 164-189). New York: Guilford.

Knight, R. (1989). An assessment of the concurrent validity of a child molester typology. *Journal of Interpersonal Violence, 4* (2), 131-150.

Knight, R., Carter, D. L., & Prentky, R. A. (1989). A system for the classification of child molesters: Reliability and application. *Journal of Interpersonal Violence, 4* (1), 3-24.

Knopp, F. H. (1984). *Retraining adult sex offenders: Methods and models* (Rev. ed.). Syracuse, NY: Safer Society Programs of the New York State Society of Churches.

Kohut, H. (1977). *The restoration of the self.* New York: International Universities Press.

Kolko, D. J., Moser, J. T., & Weldy, S. R. (1988). Behavioral emotional indicators of sexual abuse in child psychiatric inpatients: A controlled comparison with physical abuse. *Child Abuse & Neglect, 12,* 519-541.

Koopman, C., Gore-Felton, C., & Spiegel, D. (1997). Acute stress disorder symptons among female sexual abuse survivors seeking treatment. *Journal of Child Sexual Abuse Volume, 6* (3), 65-86.

Krystal, H. (1978). Trauma and affects. *Psychoanalytic Study of the Child, 33,* 81-187.

Kulka, R. A., Veroff, J., & Douvan, E. (1979). Social class and the use of professional help for personal problems: 1957 and 1976. *Journal of Health & Social Behavior, 20* (1), 2-17.

Lang, R., Pugh, G., & Langevin, R. (1988). Treatment of incest and pedophile offenders: A pilot study. *Behavioral Sciences and the Law, 6,* 239-255.

Larson, N. R., & Maddock, J. W. (1986). Structural and functional variables in incest family systems: Implications for assessment and treatment. *Journal of Psychotherapy and the Family, 2* (2), 27-44.

Lauterbach, D., & Vrana, S. (1996). Three studies on the reliability and validity of a self-report measure of posttraumatic stress disorder. *Assessment, 3* (1), 17-25.

Lee, E. (1997). Overview: The assessment and treatment of Asian families. In E. Lee (Ed.). Working with Asian Families. New York; Guilford Press, pp. 3-36.

Leifer, M., Shapiro, J. P., & Kassem, L. (1993). The impact of maternal history and behavior upon foster placement and adjustment in sexually abused girls. *Child Abuse & Neglect, 17* (6), 755-766.

Levin, A. E. (1992). Group work with parents in the family foster care system: A powerful method of engagement. *Child Welfare, 71* (5), 457-473.

Leitenberg, H., Greenwald, E., & Cado, S. (1992). A retrospective study of long-term methods of coping with having been sexually abused during childhood. *Child Abuse & Neglect, 16,* 399-407.

Lindberg, H. W., & Distad, L. J. (1985). Post-traumatic stress disorder in women who experienced childhood incest. *Child Abuse & Neglect, 9,* 329-334.

Lipovsky, J. A., Saunders, B. E., & Murphy, S. M. (1989). Depression, anxiety, and behavior problems among victims of father-child sexual assault and nonabused siblings. *Journal of Interpersonal Violence, 4* (4), 452-468.

Loevinger, J., & Wessler, R. (1970). *Measuring ego development.* San Francisco: Jossey-Bass.

Lorenzo, M. K., & Adler, D. A. (1984). Mental health services for Chinese in a community mental health center. *Social Casework, 65* (10), 600-614.

MacFarlane, K. (Ed.). (1986). *Sexual abuse of young children.* New York: Guilford.

Machotka, P., Pittman, F., & Flomenhaft, S. (1967). Incest as a family affair. *Family Process, 6* (1), 98-116.

Marshall, H. (1991). The social construction of motherhood: An analysis of childcare and parenting manuals. In A. Phoenix, A. Woollett, & E. Lloyd (Eds.), *Motherhood: Meanings, practices and ideologies* (pp. 66-85). Newbury Park, CA: Sage.

Marshall, W., & Anderson, D. (1996). An evaluation of the benefits of relapse prevention programs with sex offenders. *Sexual Abuse: Journal of Research and Treatment, 8,* 209-221.

Marshall, W., & Barbaree, H. (1988). An outpatient treatment program for child molesters. *Annuals of the New York Academy of Science, 528,* 205-213.

Massat, C. R., & Lundy, M. (1998). "Reporting costs" to nonoffending parents in cases of intra-familial child sexual abuse. *Child Welfare, 78* (4), 371-388.

Mayer, A. (1988). *Sex offenders: Approaches to understanding and management.* Holmes Beach, FL: Learning Publications.

McCann, I. L., & Pearlman, L. A. (1990). *Psychological trauma and the adult survivor.* New York: Brunner/Mazel.

McKinley, V. (1987). Group therapy as a treatment modality of special value for Hispanic patients. *International Journal of Group Psychotherapy, 37* (2), 255-268.

McLeer, S. V., Deblinger, E., Atkins, M. S., Foa, E. B., & Ralphe, D. L. (1988). Post-traumatic stress disorders in sexually abused children: A prospective study. *Journal of the American Academy of Child and Adolescent Psychiatry, 138,* 119-125.

McLeer, S. V., Deblinger, E., Henry, D., & Orvaschel, H. (1992). Sexually abused children at high risk for PTSD. *Journal of the American Academy of Child and Adolescent Psychiatry, 31* (5), 875-879.

Meiselman, K. (1978). *Incest.* San Francisco: Jossey-Bass.

Menicucci, L. D., & Wermuth, L. (1989). Expanding the family systems approach: Cultural class, developmental and gender influences in drug abuse. *American Journal of Family Therapy, 17* (2), 129-142.

Miller, A. (1984). *Thou shalt not be aware: Society's betrayal of the child.* New York: Farrar, Straus, & Giroux.

Miller, J. B. (1983). *The construction of anger in women and men.* Wellesley, MA: Stone Center for Developmental Services & Studies, Wellesley College.

Mills, L. (1996). Empowering battered women transnationally: The case for postmodern interventions. *Social Work, 41* (3), 261-268.

Minuchin, P., Colapinta, J., & Minuchin, S. *Working with families of the poor.* New York: Guilford.

Minuchin, S. (1974). *Families and family therapy.* Boston: Harvard University Press.

Moore, K. A., Simms, M. C., & Betsey, C. I. (1986). *Choice and circumstance: Racial differences in adolescent sexuality and fertility.* New Brunswick, NJ: Transaction Books.

Morrison, N. C., & Clavenna-Valleroy, J. (1998). Perceptions of maternal support as related to self-concept and self report of depression in sexually abused female adolescents. *Journal of Child Sexual Abuse, 7* (1), 23-40.

Mowrer, C. (1987, Spring). The family worker and the incestuous family: Integrating Levels of understanding: Part 2. Implications for risk assessment and treatment. *Prevention Report,* pp. 1-3.

Mrazek, P., & Mrazek, D. (1981). *Sexually abused children and their families.* New York: Pergamon.

Myer, J. L. (1992). Legal issues in child abuse and neglect. Newbury Park, CA: Sage.

Myer, M. H. (1985). A new look at mothers of incest victims. *Journal of Social Work and Human Sexuality, 3* (2-3), 47-58.

Neighbors, H. W., & Jackson, J. S. (1984). The use of informal and formal help: Four patterns of illness behavior in the Black community. *American Journal of Community Psychiatry, 12,* 629-644.

Newberger, C. M., Gremy, I. M., Waternaux, C. M., & Newberger, E. H. (1993). Mothers of sexually abused children: Trauma and repair in longitudinal perspective. *American Journal of Orthopsychiatry, 63* (1), 92-102.

Nichols-Casebolt, A. M. (1988). Black families headed by single mothers: Growing numbers of increasing poverty. *Social Work, 33,* 306-313.

O'Connell, M. A. (1986). Reuniting incest offenders with their families. *Journal of Interpersonal Violence, 1* (3), 374-386.

Ofshe, R. (1994). *Making monsters.* New York: Scribner.

Palmer, R. (1997). Assessment and treatment of incest families. In B. K. Schwartz & H. R. Celline (Eds.), *The sex offender* (Vol. 2, pp. 18.1-18.12). Kingston, NJ: Civic Research Institute.

Palombo, J. (1983). Borderline conditions: A perspective from self-psychology. *Clinical Social Work Journal, 11* (4), 323-338.

Parson, E. R. (1988). Post-traumatic self disorders: Theoretical and practical considerations in psychotherapy of Vietnam war veterans. In J. P. Wilson, Z. Hareel, & B. Kahana (Eds.), *Human adaptation to extreme stress: From the Holocaust to Vietnam* (pp. 245-284). New York: Plenum.

Pellegrin, A., & Wagner, W. G. (1990). Child sexual abuse: Factors affecting victims' removal from home. *Child Abuse & Neglect, 14* (1), 53-60.

Pelton, L. H. (1985). *The social context of child abuse and neglect.* New York: Human Sciences.

Peterson, R. F., Basta, S. M., & Dykstra, T. A. (1993). Mothers of molested children: Some comparisons of personality characteristics. *Child Abuse & Neglect, 17* (3), 409-418.

Phoenix, A., & Woollett, A. (1991). Motherhood: Social construction, policies and psychology. In A. Phoenix, A. Woollett, & E. Lloyd (Eds.), *Motherhood: Meanings, practices and ideologies* (pp. 13-27). Newbury Park, CA: Sage.

Pierce, R., & Pierce, L. (1985). The sexually abused child: A comparison of male and female victims. *Child Abuse & Neglect, 9,* 191-199.

Pithers, W. (1988). *Relapse prevention in a practitioner's guide to treating the incarcerated male sexual offender* (pp. 123-140). Washington, DC: Government Printing Office.

Prentky, R., & Burgess, A. (1990). Rehabilitation of child molesters: A cost benefit analysis. *American Journal of Orthopsychiatry, 60,* 108-117.

Prochaska, J. D., Declementa, C. C., & Norcross, J. C. (1992). In search of how people change: Applications to addictive behaviors. *American Psychologist, 47* (9), 1102-1114.

Report of the President's Commission on Mental Health. (1978). Washington, DC: U. S. Government Printing Office

Rhodes, A. & Goering, P. (1998). Gender differences in the use of out patient mental health services. In B. L. Levin, A. K. Blanch (Eds) *Women's mental health services.* (pp. 19-33). Thousand Oaks, CA: Sage.

Ruderman, E. (1986). Gender-related themes of women psychotherapists in their treatment of women patients. *Clinical Social Work Journal, 14* (2), 103-126.

Russell, D. E. H. (1984). *Sexual exploitation: Rape, child sexual abuse and workplace harassment.* Beverly Hills, CA: Sage.

Russell, D. E. H. (1986). *The secret trauma: Incest in the lives of girls and women.* New York: Basic Books.

Russell, D. E. H. (1990). *Rape in marriage.* Indianapolis: Indiana University Press.

Saleebey, D. (1997). *The strengths perspective in social work practice.* New York: Longman.

Salter, A. C. (1988). *Treating child sex offenders and victims: A practical guide.* Newbury Park, CA: Sage.

Sato, M. (1980). Concept of shame and the mental health of Pacific Asian Americans. *Exploration in Ethnic Studies, 3* (1), 3-11.

Saunders, J. E., Arata, C. M., & Kilpatrick, D. G. (1990). Development of a crime-related post-traumatic stress disorder scale for women within the Symptom Checklist-90—Revised. *Journal of Traumatic Stress, 3* (3), 439-448.

Schwartz, B. K., & Cellini, H. R. (1995). *The sex offender* (Vol. 1). Kingston, NJ: Civic Research Institute.

Schwartz, B. K., & Cellini, H. R. (1997). *The sex offender* (Vol. 2). Kingston, NJ: Civic Research Institute.

Sgroi, S. (1984). *Handbook of clinical intervention in child sexual abuse.* Lexington, MA: Lexington Books.

Sgroi, S. (1988). *Vulnerable populations: Education and treatment of sexually abused children and adult survivors.* Lexington, MA: Lexington Books.

Sirles, E. A., & Franke, P. J. (1989). Factors influencing mothers' reactions to intrafamily sexual abuse. *Child Abuse & Neglect, 13* (1), 131-140.

Smith, T., & Wolfe, R. (1988). A treatment model for sexual aggression. *Journal of Social Work and Human Sexuality, 7,* 149-164.

Steen, C., & Monnette, B. (1989). *Treating adolescent sex offenders in the community.* Springfield, IL: Charles C Thomas.

Stern, S. B., & Azar, S. T. (1998). Integrating cognitive strategies into behavioral treatment for abusive parents and families with aggressive adolescents. *Clinical Child & Psychology and Psychiatry, 3* (3), 387-403.

Stiver, I. (1991). Beyond the Oedipus complex: Mothers and daughters. In J. V. Jordan, A. G. Kaplan, J. B. Miller, I. P. Stiver, & J. L. Surrey (Eds.), *Women's growth in connection* (pp.97-121). New York: Guilford.

Strand, V. (1990). Treatment of the mother in the incest family: The beginning phase. *Clinical Social Work Journal, 18* (4), 353-366.

Strand, V. (1991). Mid-phase treatment issues with the mother in the incest family. *Clinical Social Work Journal, 19* (4), 377-389.

Straus, M. A. (1989). The national family violence surveys. In M. A. Straus & R. J. Gelles (Eds.), *Physical violence in American families.* New Brunswick, NJ: Transaction Publishers.

Sue, S., & McKinney, H. (1975). Asian Americans in the community men-tal health care system. *American Journal of Orthopsychiatry, 45,* 111-118.

Sue, S., & Morishima, J. (1982). *The mental health of Asian Americans: Contemporary issues in identifying and treating mental problems.* San Francisco: Jossey-Bass.

Sue, D. W., & Sue, D. (1999). *Counseling the culturally different: Theory and Practice.* (3rd ed.) New York: John Wiley and sons.

Summit, R., & Kryso, J. (1978). Sexual abuse of children: A clinical spectrum. *American Journal of Orthopsychiatry, 48,* 237-251.

Surrey, J. C. (1991). The "self-in-relation": A theory of women's development. In J. V. Jordan, A. G. Kaplan, J. B. Miller, I. P. Stiver, & J. L. Surrey (Eds.), *Women growth in connection* (pp. 51-66). New York: Guilford.

Tamraz, D. N. (1996). Non-offending mothers of sexually abused children: Comparison of opinions and research. *Journal of Child Sexual Abuse, 5* (4), 75-104.

Tarasoff v. Regents of University of California. 529 P.2nd 553 (1974).

Taubman, S. (1984). Incest in context. *Social Work, 29* (1), 35-40.

Taylor, M. (1999). Changing what has gone before: The enhancement of an inadequate psychology through the use of an Afrocentric-feminist perspective with African American women in therapy, *Psychotherapy, 36* (2), 170-179.

Thoennes, N., & Tjaden, P. G. (1990). The extent, nature, and validity of sexual abuse allegations in custody/visitation disputes. *Child Abuse & Neglect, 14* (2), 151-163.

Timmons-Mitchell, J., Chandler-Holtz, D., & Semple, W. E. (1996). Post-traumatic stress symptoms in mothers following children's reports of sexual abuse: An exploratory study. *American Journal of Orthopsychiatry, 66* (3), 463-467.

Trepper, T., & Barrett, M. J. (1986). Treating incest: A multimodal systems perspective. *Journal of Psychotherapy and the Family, 2*(2), 5-12.

Trepper, T., & Barrett, M. J. (1989). *Systemic treatment of incest: A therapeutic handbook.* New York: Brunel/Mazel.

Tsui, A. M. (1985). Psychotherapeutic considerations in sexual counseling for Asian immigrants. *Psychotherapy: Theory, Research and Practice, 22,* 357-362.

Van Den Bergh, N. (1995). *Feminist practice in the 21st century.* Washington, DC: National Association of Social Workers Press.

Van der Kolk, B. A., McFarlane, A. C., & Weisaeth, L. (1996). (Eds.). *Traumatic stress: The effects of overwhelming experience on mind, body, and society.* New York: Guilford

Van der Kolk, B. A., & Fisler, R. E. (1994). Childhood abuse and neglect and loss of self-regulation. *Bulletin of the Menninger Clinic, 58* (2), 145-168.

Van der Veer, G. (1998). Counseling and therapy with refugees and victims of trauma. (3rd Ed.) New York: John Wiley and Sons.

Vander Mey, B. J., & Neff, R. L. (1986). *Incest as child abuse: Research and applications.* New York: Praeger.

Vander Mey, B. J., & Neff, R. L. (1988). The sexual victimization of male children: A review of previous research. *Child Abuse & Neglect, 12,* 61-72.

Vargas, L. A., & Willis, D. J. (1994). New directions in the treatment of ethnic minority children and adolescents. *Journal of Clinical Child Psychology, 23,* 2-4.

Wagner, W. G. (1991). Depression in mothers of sexually abused vs. mothers of non-abused children. *Child Abuse & Neglect, 15,* 99-104.

Walker, L. E. (1985). Feminist therapy with victims/survivors of interpersonal violence. In L. B. Rosewater & L. E. Walker (Eds.), *Handbook of feminist therapy* (pp. 201-214). New York: Springer.

Walker, L. E. (Ed.). (1988). *Handbook on sexual abuse of children: Assessment and treatment issues* (pp. 309-323). New York: Springer.

Walters, M., Carter, B., Papp, P., & Silverstein, O. (1988). *The invisible web.* New York: Guilford.

Wattenberg, E. (1985). In a different light: A feminist perspective on the role of the mother in father-daughter incest. *Child Welfare, 64,* 203-211.

Weinberg, S. K. (1955). *Incest behavior.* New York: Citadel.

Wells, L. (1981). Family pathology and father-daughter incest. *Journal of Clinical Psychiatry, 42,* 197-302.

Werner, E. E., & Smith, R. S. (1992). *Overcoming the odds: High risk children from birth to adulthood.* Ithaca, NY: Cornell University Press.

White, R. W. (1974). Strategies of adaptation: An attempt at systemic description. In G. Coelho, D. Hamburg, & J. Adams (Eds.), *Coping and adaptation* (pp. 47-68). New York: Basic Books.

Williams, O. J., & Becker, R. L. (1994). Domestic partner abuse treatment programs and cultural competence: The results of a national survey. *Violence and Victims, 9* (3), 287-296.

Wilson, M. K. (1995). A preliminary report on ego development in non-offending mothers of sexually abused children. *Child Abuse & Neglect, 19* (4), 511-518.

Woollett, A. (1991). Having children: Accounts of childless women and women with reproductive problems. In A. Phoenix, A. Woollett, & E. Lloyd (Eds.), *Motherhood: Meanings, practices and ideologies* (pp. 47-65). Newbury Park, CA: Sage.

Wyatt, G. E., & Mickey, M. R. (1987). Ameliorating the effects of child sexual abuse. *Journal of Interpersonal Violence, 2* (4), 403-414.

Wyatt, G. E., & Powell, G. J. (1988). *The lasting effects of child sexual abuse.* Newbury Park, CA: Sage.

Yalom, I. D. (1985). *The theory and practice of group psychotherapy.* New York: Basic Books.

Zuelzer, M. B., & Reposa, R. E. (1983). Mothers in incestuous families. *International Journal of Family Therapy, 5* (2), 98-110.

INDEX

Abbott, B. R., 157
Abel, G. G., 5
Abel, S., 5, 204
Adams-Tucker, C., 5
Adaptation, 70
Adler, D. A., 44
Admission in contemplation of dismissal (ACD), 192, 193, 196
Adoption and Safe Families Act, 2, 198
African Americans:
    as professional psychotherapists, 40
    child abuse/neglect reports and, 40
    See also African American women
African American women, 42-44
    informal helping networks, 42
    sexual history, 91
    trust and, 42
    view of mental health providers, 42, 44
    See also Case studies

Alcoholics Anonymous (AA), 59, 118
Alpert, Judith, 7
American Psychiatric Association, 64
Anderson, D., 7
Anderson, L. M., 4
Arata, C. M., 7
Armsworth, M. W., 15
Asian Americans:
    as professional psychotherapists, 40
    child abuse/neglect reports and, 40
    See also Asian American women
Asian American women:
    as caretakers, 42
    as nurturers, 42
    family position, 42
    outside help and, 42
    shame and, 42
    societal position, 42
Assessment. See Mother (nonoffending), evaluating
Atkins, M. S., 5

Avery, N. C., 4
Awad, G. A., 204, 207
Azar, S. T., 104

Barbaree, H., 5
Barnard, C. P., 157
Barrett, M. J., 158, 159, 161, 165, 167,
    173, 175
Basta, S. M., 87
Battered child syndrome, 183
Becker, J. V., 5, 7
Becker, R. L., 52
Benjamin, J., 11
Berliner, L., 5, 7
Bess, B. H., 207
"Best interests," 190
Betsey, C. I., 45
Betrayal, 17, 18, 55, 72, 93, 144
    assessing degree of, 72-76
    case study, 73-75
    dealing with in individual therapy,
        97-99
    See also Confidentiality
Bird, S., 7
Birns, B., 11
Blake-White, J., 5
Blaming mother, 4, 11, 32-33
Bloch, J. R., 16
Blush, G. J., 204, 205
Body language:
    in therapy, 103
Boney-McCoy, S., 7
Boundary issues, 127
Bowen, G. L., 46
Boyd-Franklin, N., 40, 41, 42
Bradshaw, C. K., 42
Brandler, S., 132

Breese, P., 207
Brende, J. O., 14
Brickman, E., 16, 17
Briere, J., 5, 7, 15
Brodsky, A. M., 28
Brody, C., 11
Browne, A., 17, 72, 93, 127
Burgess, A., 15
Buryers, A., 7

Cado, S., 7
Cammaert, L. P., 10
Caplan, P. J., 32
Carnes, P., 5
Carter, B., 16, 33, 162
Carter, D. L., 5
Case coordination, 179-182, 200-201
    case study, 179-181
    individuals involved, 180-182
    See also Case investigation phase;
        Case litigation phase; Case su-
        pervision phase
Case investigation phase, 181, 182-188
    Child Protective Services (CPS)
        role, 181, 182, 183-184
    law enforcement role, 181, 182,
        184-188
    possible outcomes, 183
Case litigation phase, 182, 188-197
    criminal court, 188, 194-197
    juvenile court, 188-193
    use of closed circuit TV, 188
Casement, P. J., 38
Case studies, 22-32, 34-37, 43-44, 46-49,
    51, 53-57, 60, 73-75, 77-79, 81-83,
    85-86, 94-95, 102, 104-106, 108-
    117, 119-121, 124-125, 133, 141-

142, 146, 147, 148-152, 179-181, 208-214

Case supervision phase, 182, 197-200
  criminal justice system, 198, 199-200
  juvenile court system, 197-199

Cellini, H. R., 7, 158, 173

Chalfant, H. P., 45

Chandler-Holtz, D., 16, 50

Chatters, L. M., 42

Child abuse, medicalization of, 2

Child Abuse Prevention and Treatment Act (1974), 183
  mandated reporting laws, 183

Child Protective Services (CPS), 8, 22, 26, 29, 30, 47, 51, 54, 65, 73, 75, 76, 77, 79, 82, 85, 95, 97, 99, 104, 105, 116, 134, 135, 136, 138, 159, 160, 163, 180, 181, 182, 186, 187, 189, 190, 191, 192, 203, 208, 209, 210, 213, 214, 216, 222, 224
  educating mother about, 184
  helping mother negotiate, 99
  purpose of, 183
  See also Case coordination; Case investigation phase

Child sexual abuse field developments, intervention/treatment conceptualization and, 10-18
  feminist theories, 10-14
  trauma theories, 14-18

Child sexual abuse field developments, nonoffending mother and, 4-10
  1980s, 4-7
  1950s, 4
  1990s, 7-10
  1970s, 4
  1960s, 4

See also Mother (nonoffending)

Child sexualized behavior, managing, 148-149
  case study, 148-149

Chin, J. L., 42

Chodorow, N., 11

Ciottone, R. A., 7

Clark, C. A., 5

Clark, H., 159

Class, 39, 45-48
  and attitude toward mastering environment, 45
  and attitude toward sexuality, 45-46, 48
  and attitude toward therapy, 45, 46, 48
  case study, 46-48

Clavenna-Valleroy, J., 9

Clients of color, mental health system and, 40. *See also specific racial and ethnic groups*; Women of color

Clinical Analysis Questionnaire-CAQ, 87

Cognitive distortions, 104
  case study, 104-105
  reducing, 104, 128

Cognitive theorists, 14-15

Cohen, J. A., 106, 224

Cole, W., 157

Collings, S., 46

Comas-Diaz, L., 41, 44

Communication, family:
  about incest, 161-164

Confidentiality, 97, 136-139, 140, 159-160

Conte, J. R., 5, 7

Conversion phenomena, 16

Coping, 70

abilities, 88
See also Coping capacities, strengthening
Coping capacities, strengthening, 100-107
  breathing/relaxation techniques, 100, 103
  careful use of time, 103
  case study, 102
  guided imagery, 101-102
  identifying mother's strengths, 103-104
  physical grounding strategies, 100, 103
  thought-stopping technique, 102-103
Corwin, D. L., 7, 33, 205
Coulson, K. W., 159
Coulter, M. L., 7, 14, 52, 89
Countertransference, 19, 28-29, 220
  induced, 19, 37
  personal, 19, 37
  positive aspects, 37-38
  reparative effects, 38
Coupe, P., 16
Courtois, C., 5, 7
Court system, helping mother negotiate, 99. *See also* Custody/visitation disputes, working with mothers in
Crime-Related Posstraumatic Stress Disorder (PTSD) Scale, 50
Crisis of parenting, 164-167
Crisis theory, 80
Cunningham-Rathner, J., 5
Custody proceedings, sexual abuse allegations and, 33
Custody/visitation disputes, therapeutic management in, 207-208, 214-217

case study of disclosure after separation, 212-214
case study of disclosure before divorce, 208-211
non-court-ordered cases, 208-214
Custody/visitation disputes, working with mothers in, 203-204
  problem with "blame-the-mother," 204-206
  treatment approaches, 206-208
  See also Custody/visitation disputes, therapeutic management in; Parental alienation syndrome; Sexual allegations in divorce (SAID) syndrome

Dadds, M., 8
Dane, S., 103
Davies, J., 52
Deblinger, E., 5, 8, 16, 17, 50, 87, 101, 104, 108, 148, 161, 167, 171, 224
Declementa, C. C., 59
DeJong, A., 6
DeJong, P., 70
DelPo, E., 7
Denial, defense of, 15
Denver Department of Social Services, 205
Depression, 142-143
  case study, 106
  reducing symptoms of, 105-107
Derogatis, L. R., 50
DeYoung, M., 88, 121, 160
Dinnerstein, D., 11, 25
Disclosure, incest, 16, 61
  as traumatic event, 64, 219, 225
  obtaining siblings' reactions to, 164
  to baby sitter, 34
  to daycare provider, 29

to mother, 46, 54, 56, 60, 74-75, 77, 81, 104, 106
to school counselor, 22, 119
to teacher, 26, 94
Dissociation, 16
Distad, L. J., 5
Djenderedjian, A., 5
Douvan, E., 45
Drive theorists, 14, 32
Droegemueller, W., 183
Dykstra, T. A., 87

Edelsohn, G. A., 7, 14, 52, 89
Effectance drive, 70
Ego psychologists, 32, 70
Eist, H. I., 4
Elbow, M., 8
Elliott, D. M., 7
Engagement, 66-69, 91
conveying empathy, 66
evaluating biases, 66-68
in group treatment, 140
See also Solution-focused interviewing; Strengths perspective
Epigenesis, 70
Erikson, E. H., 70
Evaluation. *See* Mother (nonoffending), evaluating
Everson, M. D., 7, 14, 52, 89

Faller, K. C., 5, 7, 16, 17, 33, 204, 205, 206, 209, 212
Family sexual abuse, definition of, 3. *See also* Incest
Family treatment. *See* Treatment, family
Farber, N. B., 43, 45
Fausto-Sterling, A., 2

Faynik, C., 159
Feinauer, L. L., 103
Feminist theories, 10-14, 18
Fernandez, R., 16
Finkelhor, D., 5, 7, 17, 34, 52, 53, 72, 93, 127, 157
Fish, L. S., 158
Fish, V., 159
Fiske, J., 7
Fisler, R. E., 15
Flanagan, B., 5
Flomenhaft, S., 4
Foa, E. B., 5
Franke, P. J., 6
Freeman-Longo, F., 7
Friedrich, W. N., 7, 156, 157, 159, 167
Fullilove, M. T., 58
Fullilove, R. E., 58

Gardner, R. A., 7, 204
Gelinas, D. J., 5, 159, 160, 161, 165, 167, 175
Gelles, R., 52
Giarretto, H., 5
Gil, E., 7, 155, 159, 161, 165, 167
Gilligan, C., 11
"Glass ceiling," 68
Gomes-Schwartz, B., 7, 8, 16, 17, 50, 51, 52
Goodwin, J., 5
Gordon, M., 157
Green, A. H., 16
Greene, B., 42
Greenwald, E., 7
Gremy, I. M., 16
Groth, A. N., 5, 158
Group treatment. *See* Treatment, group
Guardian ad litem, 181, 182, 189, 190

Gutheil, T. G., 4
Gutierrez, L. M., 40

Hagood, M. M., 7
Halfon, N., 59
Hall-McCorquodale, I. H., 32
Hardiness, 103
Hare-Mustin, R., 28
Harper, J. M., 103
Harper, K. V., 41
Hartmann, H., 70
Haskett, M. E., 42
Hathaway, C. R., 8, 87
Heflin, A., 101, 104, 108, 148, 161,
    167, 171, 224
Helper, P. L., 45
Herman, J. L., 7, 10, 15, 53, 71, 76,
    157
Hewitt, S. K., 207
Hines, P. M., 43, 171
Hispanics:
    as professional psychotherapists, 40
    child abuse/neglect reports and, 40
    disclosure and, 41-42
    preference for informal solutions,
        41
    See also Hispanic women
Hispanic women, 41-42, 147
    culturally proscribed role, 41

Jackson, J. S., 42
James, B., 5
Janoff-Bulman, R., 15, 53
Jasinski, J. L., 52
Johnson, B. L., 7, 158
Johnson, T. C., 5

sexual history, 91
shame and, 41
See also Case studies
Holaday, M., 15
hooks, b., 52
Horowitz, M. J., 14, 15
Horton, A. L., 7, 158
Hotaling, G., 52
Humphreys, C., 8
Hunter, W. M., 7, 14, 52, 89
Hutchinson, J. S., 42

Immigration status, women's, 44-45
Incest:
    definition, 3
    intent, 157-158
    See also Family sexual abuse; Incest
        families
Incest families:
    abusive family relationships in, 165
    boundary maintenance issues, 159
    common characteristics, 157
    power imbalances in, 165
    preconditions, 157
    types, 157
    See also Incest
"Incompetent," juvenile court defini-
    tion of, 190
In re Gault, 189

Johnson, T. L., 7, 155, 159, 165, 167
Jones, D. L., 41, 44
Jones, D.P.H., 205
Jordan, J. V., 13, 18
Justice, B., 4, 157
Justice, R., 4, 157

Kaplan, M., 5
Kassem, L., 8, 58
Kaufman, L., 4
Kempe, C. H., 183
Kendall-Tackett, K. A., 7
Kilpatrick, D. G., 7
Kinard, E. M., 89
King, M., 46
Kirkwood, C., 52
Kleinman, A. M., 42
Kliman, J., 40
Kline, C. M., 5
Knight, R., 5
Knopp, F. H., 5
Kohut, H., 14
Kolko, D. J., 5
Koontz, M. A., 7
Kryso, J., 5
Krystal, H., 14
Kulka, R. A., 45

Landsberg, C., 17, 50
Lang, R., 5
Langevin, R., 5
Lantz, J., 41
Larson, N. R., 157
Lauterbach, D., 50
Law enforcement. *See* Case investigation phase
Laws, D. R., 5
Learned helplessness, 15
Leifer, M., 8, 58
Leitenberg, H., 7
Levin, A. E., 128
Lin, K. M., 42
Lin, T. Y., 42
Lindberg, H. W., 5

Lipovsky, J. A., 5
Lippmann, J., 8, 87
Loevinger, J., 87
Lorenzo, M. K., 44
Lundy, M., 9, 24

MacFarlane, K., 5
Machotka, P., 4
Maddock, J. W., 157
Madonna, J. M., 7
Mandel, A. U., 4
Mannarino, A. P., 7, 106, 224
Marshall, H., 21
Marshall, W., 5, 7
Massat, C. R., 9, 24
Maternal substance abuse, 58-60, 61, 116-117, 118, 125
    case study, 60
    consequences for child, 58
    mother-child relationship and, 59-60
    recovery stage, 59
    unrecognized, 58
Mayer, A., 5
Mayfield, J., 8
McCann, I. L., 14
McDonough, H., 204, 207
McGraw, J. M., 205
McKinley, V., 41
McKinney, H., 42
McLeer, S. V., 5
Megan's law, 188
Meiselman, K., 4
Menicucci, L. D., 45
Meyer, S. K., 11
Mickey, M. R., 5, 13
Miller, A., 23, 34

Miller, J. B., 25, 41
Miller, S. D., 70
Mills, L., 55
Mitchell, J., 103
Mittelman, M. S., 5
Monnette, B., 5, 167, 174
Moore, K. A., 45
Morishima, J., 42
Morrison, N. C., 9
Moser, J. T., 5
Mother-child relationships, 148-153
    case studies, 150-151, 152
    substance abuse and, 59-60
    See also Mother (nonoffending)
Motherhood, social construction of,
    20-25
    case study, 22-25
Mother (nonoffending):
    ambivalence, 13, 99-100, 173
    as domestic violence victims, 9
    believing children, 6, 9, 79
    childhood sexual victimization his-
        tory, 16-17
    collusive, 4
    continuum of belief, 8
    psychopathology, 4, 5, 220
    reaction at disclosure, 50
    support at disclosure, 7, 13-14
    unprotective, 4
    See also Mother (nonoffending),
        contextual considerations in
        treating
Mother (nonoffending), contextual
    considerations in treating, 220
    class, 39, 45-48, 61, 220, 221
    family history, 39, 61
    history of childhood sexual abuse,
        49-52, 61
    history of partner violence, 52-56,
        61

race and ethnicity, 39-45, 61, 220,
    221
raising special needs children, 56-
    57, 61
substance abuse, 58-60, 61
work history, 48-49, 61
See also Maternal substance abuse;
    Mothers, battered; Mothers,
    sexually abused as children;
    Mothers of special needs chil-
    dren
Mother (nonoffending), evaluating,
    63, 64, 65, 91
    engagement, 66-69, 91
    for degree of betrayal, 72-76
    for degree of powerlessness, 76-79
    for degree of stigmatization, 80-83
    for degree of traumatic sexualiza-
        tion, 83-86
    for traumatic effects, 65, 70-72
    sexual history, 65, 90-91
    social roles, 65, 86-89
    See also Strengths perspective
Mother role, sexual abuse and, 116-119
    case study, 116-117
Mothers, battered, 52-56, 61
    case study, 53-55
    constriction symptoms, 53
    "damaged self," 53
    disclosure crisis and, 53
    intrusion symptoms, 53
    psychological effects, 52-53
Mothers of special needs children, 56-
    57, 61
    case study, 56-57
Mothers sexually abused as children,
    49-52, 61
    believing child's disclosure, 50, 51-
        52
    case study, 51

treatment, 50
Mowrer, C., 156
Mrazek, D., 17
Mrazek, P., 17
Murphy, S. M., 5
Murphy, W. D., 5
Myer, M. H., 6, 191

Narcotics Anonymous (NA), 59
Neff, R. L., 5
Neighbors, H. W., 42
Newberger, C. M., 16
Newberger, E. H., 16
Nichols-Casebolt, A. M., 43
No-contact order, 160. *See also* Order
    of protection
Norcross, J. C., 59
Nowlan, N. P., 42

Object relations theorists, 32
O'Connell, M. A., 156, 174
Offender:
    discussing effect on family, 164
    helping with relapse prevention,
      176
    removing from home, 157-158
    termination of parental rights, 199
    See also Case studies
Ofshe, R., 7
Olafson, E., 7, 33, 205
O'Neil, M. R., 5
Order of protection, 184, 186, 193

Palmer, R., 156, 173, 174
Palombo, J., 14
Papp, P., 162

Parental alienation syndrome, 204
Parentification, child victim, 176, 177
Parenting crisis with offender gone,
    164-167
    mother feeling ineffective, 166
    mother's lack of authority, 165-166
    victim's power over family, 166
    See also Treatment, family
Parson, E. R., 14
Partner role, sexual abuse and
    woman's, 119-124
    case study, 119-121
Pearlman, L. A., 14
Peck, A. L., 4
Pellegrin, A., 8
Pelton, L. H., 2, 40
Peterson, R. F., 87
Phoenix, A., 20
Pierce, L., 6
Pierce, R., 6
Pithers, W., 158, 174, 176
Pittman, F., 4
Porochaska, J. D., 59
Posttraumatic stress, 15, 17, 52
    treating symptoms of, 97
    See also Posttraumatic stress disor-
      der
Posttraumatic stress disorder, 71
    DSM criteria, 64
    See also Posttraumatic stress
Powell, G. J., 5
Powerlessness, 17, 18, 55, 72, 76, 93,
    127, 144
    assessing degree of, 76-79
    case studies, 77-79, 94-95
    dealing with in individual therapy,
      94-97
    facilitating feelings of competence,
      96
    facilitating feelings of success, 96

perceived, 76-77
reality-based, 76, 77
Prentky, R. A., 5, 7
President's Commission on Mental
　　Health Report (1978), 28
Problem-solving abilities, increasing,
　　128
Professional training, effects of, 20, 28-
　　32
　　case study, 29-32
Pugh, G., 5
Purdue Posttraumatic Stress Disorder-
　　Revised (PPTSD-R) Scale, 50

Quesda, G. M., 45

Race and ethnicity, 39-45. *See also spe-
　　cific racial and ethnic groups*; Immi-
　　gration status, women's; Women
　　of color
Ralphe, D. L., 5
Reich, J., 5
Relationship, definition of, 31
Reposa, R. E., 5
Repressed memories, 7
Repressed memory controversy, 7
Richman, J. M., 46
Reunification issues, 147, 198. *See also*
　　Case studies
Role conflict, 88, 91, 125, 160
Roman, C. P., 132
Ross, K. L., 204, 205
Rouleau, J., 5
Roundy, L. M., 7, 158
Ruderman, E., 28, 29, 38
Runtz, M., 5
Runyon, D. K., 7, 14, 52, 89

Russell, D.E.H., 5, 34, 49, 53

Saleebey, D., 69
Salter, A. C., 6, 10, 156, 158, 173, 174
Sato, M., 42
Saunders, B. E., 5
Saunders, J. E., 7
Schuerman, J. R., 5
Schwartz, B. K., 7, 158, 173
SCL-90-R, 50
Secondary victims, 64
　　examples, 64
Self-in-relation theory, 12-13, 31
Self-psychologists, 14, 32
Semple, W. E., 16, 50
Sexual allegations in divorce (SAID)
　　syndrome, 205
Sexual contact, definition of, 3
Sexual history, obtaining, 90-91
Sexual trauma, traumagenic dynamics
　　in, 17-18, 55, 72, 93, 144. *See also*
　　Betrayal; Powerlessness; Stigmati-
　　zation; Traumatic sexualization
Sgroi, S., 5, 6, 56
Shafer, G., 4
Shapiro, J. P., 8, 58
Silver, H., 183
Silverman, F., 183
Silverstein, O., 162
Simms, M. C., 45
Sirles, E. A., 6
Smith, M., 8, 58
Smith, R. S., 69
Smith, T., 5
Social roles, assessment of, 86-89
　　employment history, 86
　　family history, 86
　　financial history, 86-87

peer group involvement, 87
social supports, 87
See also Role conflict; Social support
Social support, 89, 91
lack of, 89
Solution-focused interviewing, 69, 70
Speak Out About Sexual Abuse (SASA) game, 170
Stage development theory, Erickson's, 12
Stauffer, L., 16, 17, 50
Stearns, G., 207
Steele, B., 183
Steen, C., 5, 167, 174
Steer, R., 8, 87
Stern, S. B., 104
Stevens, B., 16
Stevenson, W., 7
Stigmatization, 17, 60, 72, 76, 93, 128, 144
assessing degree of, 80-83
case study, 81-83
depression, 81
emotional manifestations of, 81

guilt, 81
isolation, 80
low self-worth, 81
self-blame, 80
shame, 80, 81, 83, 89
withdrawal, 81
Stiver, I., 25
Stone Center, Wellesley College, 12, 13
Strand, V., 7, 17, 163
Straus, M. A., 52
Strengths perspective, 69-70
resilience, 69
self-righting tendencies, 70, 129, 131
study supporting, 69-70
survivor's pride, 69
See also Solution-focused interviewing
Substance abuse. *See* Maternal substance abuse
Sue, S., 42
Summit, R., 5
Surrey, J. C., 31

Taguiri, C. K., 4
Tamraz, D. N., 9
Tarasoff v. Regents of University of California, 97
Taubman, S., 11
Taylor, R. J., 42
Therapist, childhood sexual victimization history of, 33-37
case study, 34-37
Therapy. *See* Treatment, family; Treatment, group; Treatment, individual
Thoennes, N., 7, 33, 205

Timmons-Mitchell, J., 16, 50
Tjaden, P. G., 7, 33, 205
Trauma encapsulation, 15
Trauma theories, 14-18
biological/behavioral, 14
cognitive, 14-15
gender-neutral, 14
psychoanalytic, 14
Traumatic dynamics model, 127
Traumatic effects, assessing for, 70-72
constriction-intrusion oscillation and, 71-72
Traumatic effects, surfacing, 107-115

case studies, 108-115, 141-142
discussing nature of sexual victim-
    ization, 108
in group treatment, 141-145
revisiting mother/perpetrator rela-
    tionship, 107-108, 115
Traumatic event:
    disclosure as, 64, 219, 225
    DSM definition, 64
    secondary victim of, 64
Traumatic sexualization, 17, 72, 76,
    93, 128, 144
    assessing degree of, 83-86
    case study, 85-86
    cognitive distortion, 84
    performance guilt, 84
Treatment. See Treatment, family;
    Treatment, group; Treatment, in-
    dividual; Treatment, topics for
    future research; Treatment ap-
    proach, proposed; Treatment re-
    ferral
Treatment, family, 155-157
    apology session, 173-175
    beginning phase issues, 158-167
    choice of therapist, 159
    confidentiality issue, 159-160
    co-therapists, 159
    developing new ways of relating,
        170
    discussing crisis of parenting, 164-
        167
    discussing effect of offender's be-
        havior on family, 164
    discussing what has occurred, 163
    educating family, 162
    evaluating family, 167
    family therapists versus victim
        advocates, 156

forum for mother-victim interac-
    tion, 166
fostering age-appropriate nurtur-
    ing, 169
gender-sensitive, 158
inventory of interactions, 162
major purpose, 155
major trends, 156-157
marital/partnership relationship
    consequences, 173-177
mid-phase issues to address, 158,
    167-177
mother-child relational conse-
    quences, 167-172
mother-child sessions, 158
obtaining children's reactions to
    disclosure, 164
play therapy, 170-171
pre-apology work, 173-175
referral route, 160
supporting children's peer relation-
    ships, 171
supporting healthy sibling relation-
    ships, 171-172
team approach, 159
therapist as crisis manager, 166
Treatment, group:
    altruism and, 129
    case studies, 133, 141-142, 146, 147,
        148-149
    co-leadership, 129-131
    confidentiality, 136-139, 140
    crisis intervention, 140
    effective modeling and, 145
    engagement, 140
    excluding prospective members,
        132
    feedback, 134

for increasing problem-solving abilities, 128
for reducing cognitive distortions, 128
goals, 127
group age, 132
group formation, 128, 132
identifying relational consequences, 145-152
incorporating new members, 134
leadership, 129-131
mandated versus volunteer members, 135
member sensitivity, 128
membership, 132-135
member tolerance, 134
new member introduction, 128
outside-group contact, 137-138
problem-solving in, 145
sexual traumatization and, 128
stigmatization issues and, 128
surfacing traumatic effects, 141-145
therapist sensitivity in, 127
traumatic effects intervention, 140-141
trust among members, 136
trust in therapist, 138-139
ventilation of feelings in, 145
See also Boundary issues; Treatment approach, proposed
Treatment, individual:
dealing with betrayal, 97-99
dealing with powerlessness, 94-97
encouraging ventilation of feelings, 103-104
identifying consequences of sexual abuse on mother role, 116-119

identifying consequences of sexual abuse on female partner role, 119-124
overcoming anxiety, 101-103
reducing cognitive distortions, 104-105
reducing depressive symptoms, 105-107
reframing ambivalence, 99-100
resolution, 124-125
surfacing traumatic incest-related issues, 107-115
working through, 124
See also Treatment approach, proposed
Treatment, topics for future research, 221-224
effective use of legal leverage, 222
gender of child victim, 224
harm reduction, 221
intimate partner violence, 221, 222
new child sexual abuse laws, 222
outcome research, 224
parents' rights versus protection of child, 223
special needs child victims, 221-222
substance abuse problems, 221
Treatment approach, proposed, 91, 219-220
group therapy, 139-152
intensive, 65
introduction to, 63-66
long-term, 65
phases, 63-64, 93
See also specific types of treatment; Mother (nonoffending), evaluating
Treatment referral, 65, 135, 160

Trepper, T., 158, 159, 161, 165, 167,
    173, 175
Tsui, A. M., 42

UNGAME, 170, 171

Van Den Bergh, N., 2
Van der Kolk, B. A., 15
Vander Mey, B. J., 5
Vargas, L. A., 40
Veroff, J., 45
Vrana, S., 50

Wagner, W. G., 8, 87
Walker, L. E., 5, 53
Wallis, S., 159
Walters, M., 162
Waternaux, C. M., 16
Wattenberg, E., 11
Webber, Y., 8
Weinberg, S. K., 4
Weldy, S. R., 5
Wells, L., 17
Wermuth, L., 45
Werner, E. E., 69
Wessler, R., 87
Wheeler, J. R., 5
White, R. W., 70
Whitworth, J. M., 42
Williams, D., 7, 158
Williams, L. M., 7, 52

Williams, O. J., 52
Willis, D. J., 40
Wilson, M. K., 87
Winkler, K., 58
Wolfe, R., 5
Women, ambivalent view of, 20, 25-28
    case study, 26-28
    women devalued, 25
    women idealized, 25
Women of color, 220
    as subordinate to White women,
        41
    considering immigration status, 44-
        45
    unique needs, 40
    See also African American women;
        Asian American women; His-
        panic women
Woollett, A., 20, 21
Work history, mother's, 48-49, 61
    case study, 48-49
    focusing on real-life concerns, 49
Working through/resolving incest is-
    sue, 124
    case study, 124-125
Wyatt, G. E., 5, 13

Yalom, I. D., 132
Yllö, K., 53

Zuelzer, M. B., 5

ABOUT THE AUTHOR

Virginia C. Strand, MSW., is Associate Professor at Fordham University Graduate School of Social Service, as well as the director of Children FIRST, a research and training institute that supports programs focused on enhancing intervention with children and their families. She continues to maintain a psychotherapy practice specializing in the assessment and treatment of sexually abused children and their family members and has worked directly for more than 20 years with nonoffending mothers. Prior to coming to Fordham University in 1988, she supervised specialized treatment programs for incest victims and their families at two different mental health clinics, one in New York and one in Minnesota. She currently lives in White Plains, New York.